SCANNER MASTER

Greater Philadelphia/ South Jersey
Pocket Guide

including Delaware, Lehigh Valley, Reading, Lancaster and Shore areas

CHUCK GYSI, N2DUP - EDITOR

Third Edition

"HAM" BUERGER, INC.
417 Davisville Road
WILLOW GROVE, PA 19090-2703
(215) 659-5900

Printed in USA
SCANNER MASTER CORPORATION
PO Box 428   Newton Highlands MA 02161
1995

Call for your free
SCANNER MASTER
communications catalog!
(800) 722-6701

**Additions, corrections and updates
are greatly appreciated for future editions.**
Please send them to the editor, Chuck Gysi,
via the Internet at SCAN911@aol.com, or to:

Scanner Master Corp.
PO Box 428
Newton Highlands MA 02161
Phone (800) 722-6701   Fax (508) 655-2350
1995

CONTENTS

This is the fifth Scanner Master guide I have edited for the Pennsylvania/New Jersey/Delaware area in the past 12 years and it required perhaps the most extensive changes ever to this series.

Never before have there been so many changes to the radio systems used by municipalities, counties and states, not to mention the private sector as well. In this edition, we present the new 506 MHz systems being used by Delaware, Camden and Gloucester counties and offer information on 800 MHz systems that other entities plan to start using. As you page through this guide, you also will note the extensive use being made of not only the 800 MHz band, but also the 900 MHz band, particularly by utilities.

While this book was limited to 192 pages, we could have easily filled many more pages. We know this pocket guide serves a practical use for those of you on the go, whether you are with the news media, the emergency services, technical support or you are like the many users of this guide and just like to be on the go with your scanner and related radio equipment.

While we use official sources for a lot of the information in this guide, we also rely heavily on others who have shared information with us in the preparation of this guide. Many of you have been so kind to share information with me and I am very grateful.

I'd like to personally thank many persons who helped in the preparation of this guide with their input. These people included Carter Ames, Jim Bonner, Edmond J. Angiolillo, Robert Scull, Russ Veale, Steve Bower Jr., Dan Miller, Ed O'Connell, Jim Campbell, Daniel Myers, Warren Silverman, John Wallach and Jack McCartan. I'd also like to thank those on the Scanner BBS, the Philadelphia Fire Films BBS, America Online and the Internet who have communicated with me electronically.

However, this guide could not have been possible without the help of my friend, Terry Pavlick, who always has the patience to spend some time with me on the phone and help trouble shoot some frequencies or CTCSS tones, get my computer humming or give me some power I didn't previously have on the computer that is valuable in the production of this guide in some way or another. I am deeply indebted to him for consistent help and appreciate the willingness of his wife, Patty, to let him spend time with me. I'd be terribly remiss if I did not dedicate this edition of the Scanner Master guide to Terry. I couldn't have done it without him.

Chuck Gysi, N2DUP, Editor
Internet: SCAN911@aol.com
Scanner Master Corp.
P.O. Box 428
Newton Highlands MA 02161

Before you start pouring through the pages of this edition of the Scanner Master Greater Philadelphia/South Jersey Pocket Guide's Third Edition, take a moment to read this page so as not to be confused by the way some listings are presented.

First of all, CTCSS tones are presented in this guide. We first offered this information in the second edition of this guide in 1992. We have not been able to include all CTCSS tones -- also known by trademarks such as Private Line, PL, Quiet Channel, etc. -- but only those we have monitored in use over the past few years. There is no data bank of CTCSS, or Continuous Tone Coded Squelch Systems, tones available anywhere. All the tones presented in this guide were monitored on the air by the editor or others. Tones are presented on the right-hand side of each page and are in Hertz. Those with CTCSS-capable scanners, such as the Uniden Bearcat series, can use this information to screen out other users on a frequency. The tone is subaudible.

When "CS" is listed instead of a tone, that means no tone is used -- carrier squelch. "DPL" means a digital tone is being used, however, the Uniden series of scanners cannot decode these tones. In a few instances, digital tones have been included and these tones are indicated by numbers beginning with a "D" such as D032 or D532. We welcome your input on CTCSS tones for future editions. It should be noted that most counties use a common CTCSS tone on most frequencies, as you will notice in this guide.

Where known, channelization plans for radio systems are indicated such as F1, F2, etc. This is equivalent to terms such as "Frequency 1," "Channel 1" or "Tac 1."

Letters after frequencies, such as 462.5625M, indicate the following uses: B - base; M - mobile; P - paging only; R - repeater; T - trunked; BM - base and mobile (where repeaters aren't used on UHF frequencies); H - handhelds only.

When the letter "T" appears after a given frequency, that indicates a trunked radio system. We present only the first frequency in each of a trunked system's five-channel groups. Each of the five frequencies used are 1 MHz apart. **For a listing of 861.1875T, you need to monitor 861.1875, 862.1875, 863.1875, 864.1875, 865.1875.** Trunked systems in the 866-869 MHz public safety and 935-940 MHz bands are indicated by showing each frequency in the trunked group with an "R" after each frequency and a notation indicating the frequencies are all within the same trunking group.

Toward the end of this guide are several general listings to help you get more out of your scanners. We welcome your input on this section and other sections of this guide, too.

CITY OF PHILADELPHIA

Police

453.050R	KGF587	N Band - North Band	203.5
		Districts 14, 35	
453.150R	KGF587	C Band - Central Band	203.5
		Districts 6, 9	
453.200R	KGF587	D Band - North-Central Band	203.5
		Districts 22, 23	
453.250R	KGF587	T Band - Traffic (citywide)	203.5
453.300R	KGF587	E Band - East Band	203.5
		Districts 24, 25, 26	
453.350R	KGF587	A Band - West Band	203.5
		Districts 16, 19, 90 (Fairmount Park)	
453.400R	KGF587	H Band - Detectives (citywide)	203.5
453.500R	KGF587	P Band - Southwest Band	203.5
		Districts 12, 18	
453.550R	KGF587	M Band - Emergency (citywide)	203.5
453.600R	KGF587	U Band - Command (citywide)	203.5
453.650R	KGF587	B Band - South Band	203.5
		Districts 1, 3, 4, 17	
453.750R	KGF587	J Band - Administration (citywide)	203.5
453.800R	KGF587	G Band - Northwest Band	203.5
		Districts 5, 39, 92 (Fairmount Park)	
453.950R	KGF587	F Band - Northeast Band	203.5
		Districts 2, 7, 8, 15	
453.450R	KNDN543	Phila. International Airport police	107.2

Miscellaneous law enforcement:

39.04	KQS520	Bank alarm units	
39.30	KQS520	Bank alarm units	
154.770M	KEX220	Surveillance	CS
154.890M	KEX220	Surveillance	CS
154.650M	KEX220	Surveillance	CS
155.250M	KEX220	Surveillance/Detectives	CS
155.625R	KEX220	Court Beat 1/Surveillance	CS
155.655R	KEX220	Court Beat 2/Surveillance	CS
155.070	KTR589	Transit police/subway	
453.900R	various	Transit police/X Band	
156.800M		Marine unit (VHF Channel 16)	CS
460.150R	KWM747	Sheriff's office	CS
460.250R	KWN748	Drug task force	94.8
460.350R	KWM749	District attorney	
500.4625R	KIA884	Housing Department police	97.4
159.210	WNRD678	Police	

453.100R	WNUM344	Police	
458.9875M	WPBT282	Low-power use	

Fire

154.235R	KGB476	F1 South Band	CS
		Dispatch south of Lehigh Avenue	
		and West Philadelphia	
153.950R	KGB476	F2 Emergency Band	CS
		Citywide fireground	
154.145R	KGB476	F3 North Band	CS
		Dispatch north of Lehigh Avenue	
153.830M	KF9481	F4 Fireground portables	CS
153.935M	various	F5 Fireground portables	CS
154.965R	various	F6 Underground/subway	CS
33.42	KF9481	Fire mobiles (not used)	
170.150R	KGB476	Rescue dispatch	CS
463.000R	KWX662	MED-1 Paramedics	
47.54P	WZM898	Hospital alerting	
857.7375R	WNKV367	Data printers	

City Operations

453.725R	KGF991	Public Property	CS
453.775R	KGF991	Streets Department	CS
453.925R	KGF991	Streets Department	CS
451.250R	KGC742	Water Department F1	
451.575R	KMG368	Water Department F2	
451.100R	WPED337	Utilities	
463.600R	KBV363	School District	114.8
461.1875R	WPEF270	School District	
460.450R	KQR594	Civic Center security	
500.4625R	KIA884	Housing Department PD	97.4
500.4375R	KNM390	Redevelopment Authority F1	
501.0625R	KNM390	Redevelopment Authority F2	
500.3875R	KGE583	Parking Authority F1	79.7
500.8875R	KGE583	Parking Authority F2	79.7
502.8375R	KGE583	Parking Authority F3	79.7
508.3875R	WIJ772	Parking Authority	
453.450R	KGC761	International Airport police F1	107.2
453.850R	KGC761	International Airport ops F2	107.2
155.040	WQH265	International Airport operations	
158.940	KLM719	Holmesburg Prison	
158.940	KCN979	House of Corrections	
47.46	KGG45	Civil Defense	

47.62	KGI44	Civil Defense	
464.500M		Convention Center security	
153.815M	KA2660	Library security	
153.875M	KN7980	Government operations	
453.025P	KNAB726	City Nursing Home	
154.600M	KM5220	Community College security	
154.540	KNCZ257	Olney High security	
154.515M	KA39670	Edison High security	
151.715M	KD21943	William Penn High security	
154.600M	KB70798	Northeast High security	
153.410	KGA371	Gas Works construction	
153.560	KNAL276	Gas Works construction	107.2
173.250	KGY413	PGW F1 South/Central	107.2
173.300	KGY413	PGW F2 North/Northeast	107.2
173.350	KGY413	PGW F3 North/Northwest	107.2
861.9875T		Philadelphia Gas Works trunked	
861.9375T		Philadelphia Gas Works trunked	
861.4125T		Philadelphia Gas Works trunked	
861.3875T		Philadelphia Gas Works trunked	
451.025R		PECO Energy Co. F1 trouble	
451.075R		PECO Energy Co. F2 alternate	
451.125R	WGH431	PECO Energy F3 construction	114.8
451.200R	KRC886	PECO Energy Co. F4 equipment	
451.525R	WGI300	PECO Energy Co. F5 collectors	
451.625P	WGH430	PECO Energy Co. F6 paging	
37.78	various	PECO Energy Co.	
464.400R	WQM798	Municipal Workers Union	
861.9875T		Crisis Intervention	
151.715		Simon Gratz High School security	
151.865	KNFV840	Geo. Washington High School security	
158.940	WZC517	St. Luke's jail ward	
464.800R	KNCW368	Police Athletic League - Fishtown	
451.5125R	KB61125	Philadelphia Gas Works	
158.775	WNMJ331	Water Department	
861.2125T		Water Department	
856.2125T	WNGE384	Public safety trunked	
508.2125R	WIK357	City units	
857.7375T	WNGE384	City units (857-860 MHz only)	
855.9125R	WNKV367	School District (trunked)	
855.7875R	WNKV367	School District (trunked)	
856.8375R	WNKV367	School District (trunked)	
857.7375R	WNKV367	School District (trunked)	
857.9125R	WNKV367	School District (trunked)	
858.8125R	WNKV367	School District (trunked)	

858.8375R	WNKV367	School District (trunked)
859.8125R	WNKV367	School District (trunked)
859.8375R	WNKV367	School District (trunked)
860.8125R	WNKV367	School District (trunked)
860.8375R	WNKV367	School District (trunked)
860.9125R	WNKV367	School District (trunked)
855.1125R	WNCE617	Transit
855.4375R	WNCE617	Transit
857.2375R	WNCE617	Transit
462.1375R	KD34100	Trash transfer station
462.7625M	WPDF532	Recycling
173.2625B	various	Utility data telemetry
1610 kHz	WPCA647	Travelers Information Station
1610 kHz	WPCD802	Travelers Information Station at Philadelphia International Airport

Trunked public safety
NOTE: The following frequencies have been licensed to the city of Philadelphia for a 30-channel trunked public safety radio system, however, there is no indication these frequencies will be used soon. The system call sign is WNXV204.
866.0875, 866.1625, 866.2875, 866.4125, 866.550, 866.575, 866.600, 866.6875, 866.825, 866.9625, 867.125, 867.375, 867.400, 867.4625, 867.600, 867.6375, 867.6875, 867.9375, 868.100, 868.250, 868.275, 868.3125, 868.4875, 868.625, 868.650, 868.700, 868.775, 868.875, 868.900, 868.925

NOTE: The following public safety mutual aid frequencies also have been licensed to the city for repeater use under call sign WNXV205.
866.0125, 866.5125, 867.0125, 867.5125, 868.0125

Volunteer ambulance squads

33.02	KNBT417	Kensington Volunteer Ambulance F1	
33.06	KGR375	50th Ward Ambulance Association	
33.08	KNBT417	Kensington Volunteer Ambulance F2	
37.94	KGR375	50th Ward Ambulance Association	
37.98	KFR729	Olney Community Ambulance	
45.92	KLW257	South Philadelphia Community Amb.	
47.58	KGC972	Burholme First Aid Corps	
151.955	KFR811	Olney Community Ambulance	
155.160	KGC972	Burholme First Aid Corps F3	
155.160	KFQ696	Northeast First Aid Corps	110.9
155.175	KUJ661	Wynnebrook Community Ambulance	
155.205	WST758	Wissinoming First Aid Corps	

155.220	KJW584	Wissahickon Community Ambulance	
155.220	KDZ481	49th Ward Community Ambulance	
155.235	KGC972	Burholme First Aid Corps F2	
155.235	KWI667	Rhawnhurst-Bustleton Ambulance	
155.265	KGC972	Burholme First Aid Corps F1	141.3
155.280	KDZ481	49th Ward Community Ambulance	
155.280	KKC625	Centennial Ambulance Association	
463.850R	KVZ281	Northeast First Aid Corps	
501.9875R	KNO827	Burholme First Aid Corps	

Medical helicopters

155.220	KNJP460	MedEvac - Hahnemann Hospital	136.5
463.725R	WNKH939	MedEvac - operations	
155.235	WPBQ697	SkyCare - Brandywine Hosp. F2	67.0
155.325	WPBQ697	SkyCare - Brandywine Hosp. F1	67.0
155.355	WNNI922	PennStar - Univ. of PA Tac 2	100.0
155.385	WNNI922	PennStar - Univ. of PA Tac 1	100.0
155.340	WNNI922	PennStar - Univ. of PA HEAR	

FACTOID:

The Philadelphia Parking Authority is responsible for the second largest number of parking spaces in any U.S. city. It is responsible for monitoring 15,500 parking meters -- as well as parking lots -- throughout the city. On an average day, city parking enforcement officers write 4,500 parking tickets and tow away 63 cars.

BERKS COUNTY

Police

155.070R	KKC815	F1 dispatch	91.5
155.010	KNDS855	F2 information	91.5
45.50R	KZR584	Constables	
155.595R	KNHD996	Police	91.5
154.725M	KB36904	Police mobiles	
155.250	WNWP519	Police	

Fire

33.94	KNBX247	F1 County dispatch	CS
33.90	KGG557	Western Berks Zone 3	CS
33.68	WNDL758	F2 Fire	CS
33.80	WNDL758	F3 Fire	CS
154.310	KGB549	F1 Western Berks Zone 4	
154.400	KGB549	F2 Western Berks Zone 4	
154.160	KGB549	F3 Western Berks Zone 4	
154.385M	KB61890	Fire police	
154.385R	WNPX591	Fire police operations	
153.950M	WNPX591	Fire police	
153.830M	KD29640	Fireground	
154.265R	KD29640	Fire operations	
154.265M	KD29640	Fireground	
453.0375M	KB36804	Fire handhelds	
460.5875R	KD38140	Fire	

Ambulance

155.295	KNGZ321	Dispatch	173.8
155.160	KNGZ321	Ambulance	
155.340	KNGZ321	Ambulance	
155.220	KNGZ321	Hospital to ambulance	173.8

County operations

153.740M	KA79057	County prison
154.100R	KZT517	County departments
37.98P	KYS917	Medical paging
151.235	WNSL690	Parks
151.220R	WNMU915	Emergency Management
159.330	KJB211	Hawk Mountain Sanctuary F1
159.225	KJB211	Hawk Mountain Sanctuary F2
861.3875T	WNCJ812	Public safety use
861.4125T	WNCJ812	Public safety use

861.6625T	WNCJ812	Public safety use
861.9375T	WNCJ812	Public safety use
861.9875T	WNCJ812	Public safety use
158.865M	WPCZ969	County units
153.740	WPCP892	County units
153.800M	WPCP892	County units
153.875M	WPCP892	County units
154.100M	WPCP892	County units
153.905M	WPCP892	County units

Municipalities

Albany Township

45.08	KXA313	Roads Department

Amity Township

155.880	WXK611	Police
33.70	KFF225	Fire (Montgomery County)

Bally Borough

156.000M	KD53827	Borough units
45.60	WNVG779	Borough units

Bern Township

155.940	KRB856	Police/township units

Bernville Borough

33.58M	KC8284	Fire local

Bethel Township

39.10	KZR615	Township units

Birdsboro Borough

155.880	KXB759	Police car to car
33.90M	KGE647	Fire F2 (Chester County)
155.175	WPCS723	American Legion Ambulance

Boyertown Borough

45.64	KGG433	Police dispatch	141.3
45.74M	KA3889	Police car to car	141.3
33.54M	KGD390	Fire F2 local	

Brecknock Township

156.135		Roads Department
45.08	KWX483	Township units

Caernarvon Township

155.625	WPDZ502	Police
156.105		Roads Department

Cumru Township

154.965R	WPDA275	Police
155.295	KDV990	Governor Mifflin Ambulance

Douglas Township

45.52	KDA629	Township units

Exeter Township

155.880R	KCJ934	Police dispatch
155.595	KIA813	Police
155.700	KIA813	Police
33.50M	KNFC586	Fire local
155.295	KAW476	Exeter Township Ambulance
155.025M	KR9846	Township units
155.145	WYR638	Township units

Fleetwood Borough

155.820	KXQ631	Police
155.355	WPCS719	Fire company ambulance
173.2625B	various	Utility data
154.45625B	WNYB716	Utility data

Hamburg Borough

155.130R	WPBA581	Police
155.205	WSW794	Hamburg Community Ambulance

Heidelberg Township

155.205M	KR4193	Fire Department ambulance
155.340M	KR4193	Fire Department ambulance
155.355M	KR4193	Fire Department ambulance
155.400M	KR4193	Fire Department ambulance
45.24	KNDX259	Township units
45.64	KAS425	Township units

Hereford Township

33.70M	KDV808	Seisholtville Fire Co.
453.450R	WNNE351	Roads Department

Jefferson Township

155.115	KNCJ420	Township units

Kenhorst Borough

453.350R	WQV864	Borough units
158.775	WNSW992	Borough units

Kutztown Borough

155.250	KGD481	Police F1 dispatch
155.655	WNPM350	Police F2 cars
159.150	WNPM350	Police
155.100	KWX400	Borough units

Laureldale Borough

155.280	WSW330	Muhlenberg Ambulance
153.755M	KD30132	Borough units

Leesport Borough

155.265	KNFH751	Schuylkill Valley Ambulance
155.715	WNLI688	Borough units

Longswamp Township

155.025	WYK371	Township units

Lower Alsace Township
155.880	WZM968	Police

Lower Heidelberg Township
154.115M	KT7491	Township units
155.715	WQH467	Township units

Lyons Borough
33.80M	KGE310	Fire local

Maiden Creek Township
156.240		Roads Department

Marion Township
33.62M	KGE664	Marion Center Fire Co.
33.82	KEM670	Marion Township Fire Co.

Mohnton Borough
155.760	WZU648	Borough units

Mount Penn Borough
155.880	KXA403	Police

Muhlenberg Borough
155.565R	WNUJ401	Police
155.040	KUQ628	Police

Oley Township
155.880	KYL680	Police
155.280M	KV2117	Fire Department ambulance
155.385M	KV2117	Fire Department ambulance

Perry Township
158.820	KNGE665	Township units

READING CITY
866.300R	WNXC912	Trunked public safety
866.6125R	WNXC912	Trunked public safety
866.9125R	WNXC912	Trunked public safety
867.225R	WNXC912	Trunked public safety
868.325R	WNXC912	Trunked public safety
868.5875R	WNXC912	Trunked public safety
866.0125R	WNXC912	Public safety mutual aid - calling 156.7
866.5125R	WNXC912	Public safety mutual aid - Tac 1 156.7

NOTE: Most city agencies now on the 800 MHz trunked system, except BART buses, airport units and a few city fire departments.

453.250R	KGA396	Police F1 dispatch (old)
453.400R	KGA396	Police F2 info (old)
453.550R	KGA396	Police F3 vice (old)
453.650R	KGA396	Police special (old)
154.725M	KGA396	Police vice
155.070	KGA396	Police - county
155.595	KGA396	Police car to car
154.430R	KGE407	Fire F1 dispatch

154.205	KGE407	Fire F2 (also ambulance)	
463.100B		Paramedics MED-5	
468.100M		Paramedics MED-5	
453.100R	KXI930	Housing Authority security	
453.325R	KKR590	Housing Authority	
156.165R	KNHX459	Roads Department	173.8
453.425R	WNDQ655	Municipal Airport Authority	
452.675R	KXK396	BART buses	
452.725R	KXK396	BART buses	
154.025	KYD972	City departments	
852.9875R	WNVL764	City units	
853.8625R	WNVL764	City units	
854.2625R	WNVL764	City units	
461.050R	WPAK225	Schools	

Richmond Township

158.820	WPBP468	Township units
159.195	WPBJ908	Roads Department

Rockland Township

33.82	KGF512	Fire local

Shillington Borough

155.415	WNMZ457	Police
154.235	WPCZ997	Keystone Fire Co. No. 1 operations
154.040	KBH897	Borough units
159.015M	WPDJ821	Roads Department

Shoemakersville Borough

33.62	KGD377	Fire local
155.835	KNGU692	Borough units
453.2125M	WNUR758	Borough units

Sinking Spring Borough

154.860M	KD49748	Borough units

South Heidelberg Township

155.985	WZT834	Township units

Spring Township

154.785M	KD27700	Police
154.815M	KD27700	Police
155.490M	KD27700	Police
159.315	WNRA682	Police dispatch
154.115	KEU966	Township units

Temple Borough

33.84M	KGD237	Fire local

Topton Borough

155.250	KAQ258	Police
33.84M	KGD384	Fire local
154.295	WNGZ713	Fire police

154.445	WNGZ713	Fire local
155.220	WNBE758	American Legion ambulance
155.280	WNBE758	American Legion ambulance
155.925	KNGJ812	Police/Roads Department

Union Township

45.20	KFP363	Township units

Wernersville Borough

158.745	KNBI441	Municipal Authority

West Lawn Borough

155.160	KRZ860	Western Berks Ambulance

West Reading Borough

155.055	KNIV541	Police

Windsor Township

453.850R	WNNK478	Township units

Womelsdorf Borough

155.310	WPBR243	Police

Wyomissing Borough

151.190R	KGI260	Police dispatch F1
154.040	KGI260	Police F2
154.310R	WNCB939	Fire dispatch F1
153.890M	WNCB939	Fire mobiles F4
154.160	WNCB939	Fire F3
154.400M	KY7984	Fire local F5
158.835		Borough units
153.995	WNDH679	Borough units

Wyomissing Hills Borough

158.835	KNHB812	Borough units

BUCKS COUNTY

Police

501.1875R	KJW567	Zone 1 F1 *Bristol Borough, Bristol Township,* *Tullytown*	192.8
501.4125R	KJW567	Zone 1 F2 *Same as Zone 1 F1*	192.8
501.2125R	KJW567	Zone 2 *Falls, Morrisville*	192.8
501.0375R	KJW567	Zone 3 *Hulmeville, Langhorne,* *Langhorne Manor, Middletown,* *Penndel*	192.8
501.2375R	KJW567	Zone 4 F1 *Lower Southampton,* *Northampton, Upper Southampton*	192.8
501.5875R	KJW567	Zone 4 F2 *Same as Zone 4 F1*	192.8
501.3875R	KJW567	Zone 5 *Lower Makefield, Newtown Borough,* *Newtown Township, Upper Makefield,* *Wrightstown, Yardley*	192.8
501.2875R	KJW567	Zone 6 *Chalfont, Doylestown Borough,* *Doylestown Township,* *New Britain Borough and Township*	192.8
501.3125R	KJW567	Zone 7 *Bedminster, Bridgeton, Durham,* *Haycock, Nockamixon, Riegelsville,* *Springfield, Tinicum*	192.8
501.2625R	KJW567	Zone 8 F1 *Bensalem*	192.8
501.6625R	KJW567	Zone 8 F2 *Bensalem*	192.8
501.7125R	KJW567	Zone 9 *Ivyland, Warminster,* *Warrington, Warwick*	192.8
501.3375R	KJW567	Zone 10 *Dublin, East Rockhill, Hilltown,* *Milford Township, Perkasie,* *Quakertown, Richland,* *Richlandtown, Sellersville, Silverdale,* *Telford, Trumbauersville, West Rockhill*	192.8
501.1625R	KJW567	Zone 11 *Buckingham, New Hope,* *Plumstead, Solebury*	192.8

501.5625R	KJW567	Countywide 1	192.8
501.5125R	KJW567	Countywide 2	192.8
501.7375R	KJW567	Data - South	192.8
501.7625R	KJW567	Data - Central	192.8
501.7875R	KJW567	Data - North	192.8
501.3625R	KJW567	Sheriff	192.8
501.3625M	KZ5089	Courthouse security	192.8
501.6375R		Use undetermined	192.8
154.680	KCI570	New Jersey SPEN 1 coordination	131.8

Fire

46.10B	KGF318	Dispatch/alerting	123.0
46.14	KGF318	Emergency band	123.0
46.06	KGF318	East band	123.0
46.20	KGF318	South band	123.0
46.46	KGF318	North band	123.0
46.12	KGF318	West band	123.0
46.30M	KA48350	Fireground command	123.0
46.34M	KA48350	Fire police	123.0
46.28M	KA48350	Fire	123.0
46.32M	KA48350	Fire	123.0

Ambulance

46.00	KWV593	Rescue band - north	123.0
45.32	KUG686	Rescue band - south	123.0
45.96	KWV593	Hospital band - north	123.0
45.92	KWV593	Hospital band - south	123.0
45.44	KUG686	Rescue	123.0
155.400	KWV593	Command - officers	
463.150B	KWV593	Paramedics MED-7	186.2
468.150M	KWV593	Paramedics MED-7	186.2
463.025B	KWV593	Paramedics MED-2	186.2
468.025M	KWV593	Paramedics MED-2	186.2
463.050B	KWV593	Paramedics MED-3	186.2
468.050M	KWV593	Paramedics MED-3	186.2
463.100B	KWV593	Paramedics MED-5	186.2
468.100M	KWV593	Paramedics MED-5	186.2
463.125B	KWV593	Paramedics MED-6	186.2
468.125M	KWV593	Paramedics MED-6	186.2

County operations

500.3625R	KGC471	Water and Sewer Authority	192.8
173.210B	various	Water and Sewer Authority data	
155.940	KUG686	Miscellaneous units	123.0

158.880M	KM9901	County prison	123.0
154.980	KNBG300	Bucks County Community College	
155.745	WZC640	County units	
160.200R	WPEE280	County units	
154.600M	WNUV401	Housing Authority	

Municipalities
Bedminster Township
158.745R	KRB532	Roads Department	127.3

Bensalem Township
46.12	KNAL543	Fire local	123.0
46.12	KNBY570	Nottingham Fire Co. local	123.0
46.44	KGD988	Union Fire Co. local	123.0
46.12	KVJ769	Newport Fire Co. local	123.0
46.12	KGH405	Newportville Fire Co. local	123.0
506.3875R	WIK891	Union Fire Co. 46 MHz link, ops	
464.525R	WPBX823	Bensalem Rescue Squad	
155.280	WXF732	InterCounty Rescue	
155.835	KAV602	Township units	
155.940	KAV602	Township units	

Bristol Borough
158.880	KBC883	Police	
45.96	KXB648	Bucks County Rescue Squad	123.0
46.56	KIK840	Borough units	

Bristol Township
46.12	KLM659	Bristol Fire Co. 1 coordination	123.0
46.24M	KGH408	3rd District Fire Co. local	123.0
46.26	KGH406	Edgely Fire Co. local	123.0
46.48	KGE739	Croydon Fire Co. local	123.0
460.625R	WNGF452	Goodwill ops	94.8
460.6625R	WNXP267	Fire operations	
155.715	WNPW550	Township units	

Buckingham Township
156.165	WNIN295	Roads Department	
155.940	KY0249	Township units	

Doylestown Borough
155.190M	KGF340	Police car to car	123.0
155.430	KGF340	Police operations	123.0
46.16		Fire local	123.0
150.775M	WNYS855	Central Bucks Rescue Unit portables	
155.940	KYO263	Borough units	

Doylestown Township
154.800	WSB808	Police F2	123.0
155.820	KSS201	Township units	123.0

155.940	KSS201	Township units	

Durham Township

151.055	WPBK720	Roads Department	

Falls Township

156.030	KLK579	Police - administrators	123.0
155.475M	KLK579	Police car to car	
46.12	KGH407	Levittown Fire Co. No. 2 local	123.0
46.28	KGF937	Falls Township Fire Co. local	123.0
46.28	KDX425	Fairless Hills Fire Co. local	123.0
46.28	KEV921	Levittown Fire Co. No. 1 local	123.0
45.28	KGG235	Township units	
158.985M	KA48376	Roads Department	

Haycock Township

155.085	KNHS871	Township units	

Hilltown Township

155.625	WNSR870	Police operations	

Hulmeville Borough

46.12	KGD494	William Penn Fire Co. local	123.0

Lower Makefield Township

155.700	KFF299	Police	123.0
154.085	KEM600	Township units	

Lower Southampton Township

45.24	KDV742	Township units	
151.115	KUO898	Roads Department	
155.940M	KA79509	Township units	
155.010	KGE363	Police	123.0
154.055	KFF359	Township units	

New Britain Township

154.995	WNPH821	Township units	

Newtown Borough

153.695	KUI444	Water company	

Newtown Township

155.940	KNCW631	Township units	
153.965	KNCW631	Township units	

Nockamixon Township

155.940	KNIW577	Township units	

Northampton Township

465.3625M	WPDE465	Police portables	
460.600R	WNSW626	Fire operations	
45.08	KYI964	Municipal Authority	
45.44	KYI964	Municipal Authority	

Perkasie Borough

154.995	KGJ644	Borough units	

Plumstead Township
155.835	KJE967	Township units	203.5

Quakertown Borough
155.025R	KDV740	Borough units

Richland Township
154.100	WNBK829	Township units

Riegelsville Borough
45.92	KSP246	Emergency Squad dispatch	123.0

Sellersville Borough
151.130	WNLF733	Roads Department

Solebury Township
155.940	KDV431	Township units	CS

Telford Borough
151.070	Roads Department

Tinicum Township
39.90	WRG390	Township units
155.760	WRG390	Township units

Tullytown Borough
46.24	KGE638	Fire local	123.0

Upper Southampton Township
159.195R	WNVD660	Roads Department	
155.940	KNJZ358	Township units	123.0

Warminster Township
46.08	KGD741	Fire local	123.0
45.20	KJZ892	Municipal Authority	
500.4875R	KNA335	Roads Department	100.0

Warrington Township
156.090	KA62416	Police car to car	123.0
155.030M		Police portables	123.0
45.92	KNJE413	Ambulance Corps	123.0
453.225R	WYV450	Municipal Authority	
453.625R	KNIQ896	Township units	
155.940	KBH566	Township units	

Warwick Township
156.090M	KB24146	Police (Warrington)	123.0

West Rockhill Township
151.130	WNJY534	Roads Department

Wrightstown Township
45.92	KXR868	Rescue squad	123.0
155.940	KRZ298	Township units	

Yardley Borough
155.700R	KXA258	Police	123.0
155.340M	KZ5071	Emergency Unit	
155.040	WYK445	Borough units	

CHESTER COUNTY

Police

154.740R	KTO396	F1 East	71.9
		Easttown, Tredyffrin, Malvern,	
		Willistown, East Whiteland	
154.785R	KTO396	F3 Central	71.9
		Phoenixville, West Pikeland,	
		East Pikeland, Schuylkill, Westtown,	
		West Chester, West Goshen,	
		Thornbury, Birmingham, Spring City,	
		West Chester University,	
		East Coventry, East Vincent,	
		West Vincent, North Coventry,	
		Uwchlan, East Bradford,	
		West Whiteland, West Bradford	
155.760R	KVN537	F2 West	71.9
		Modena, East Fallowfield, Valley,	
		South Coatesville, Caln, Coatesville,	
		VA Hospital, Downingtown,	
		East Brandywine, Kennett Square,	
		New Garden, Kennett, Pennsbury,	
		Pocopson, West Marlboro,	
		Londonderry, West Grove, Oxford,	
		Elk, West Nottingham, Avondale,	
		Lincoln University, Sadsbury,	
		Atglen-West Fallowfield, West Caln,	
		Parkesburg, Wallace, West Nantmeal,	
		West Brandywine, Elverson, Highland,	
		Honey Brook Borough, West Sadsbury,	
		Honey Brook Township	
156.150M	KTO396	F4 Car to car	71.9
155.475M	KA59029	Nationwide emerg.	
156.210M	KA59029	Surveillance	
158.850M	KA59029	Surveillance	
159.105		Northwestern net	
		Honey Brook Township, Wallace,	
		West Brandywine, West Nantmeal	
500.4375R	WII481	East-Central dispatch	186.2
		West Whiteland, Upper Uwchlan,	
		Schuylkill	
460.500R	WNRR251	Investigators	

Future 800 MHz trunked public safety system:
855.7375R, 855.9875R, 856.2375R, 858.2375R, 859.2375R,
859.2625R, 860.2375R, 860.2625R, 860.4375R, 860.4875R
ALSO: 866.2125R, 866.725R, 867.075R, 867.100R, 867.2125R

Fire
33.90	KJY884	F1 Dispatch	CS
33.86	KJY884	F2 North	CS
33.96	KJY884	F3 South	CS
33.98	KJY884	F4 Medical	CS
33.42M	KJY884	F5 Fire police	CS
33.80M	KJY884	F6 Fireground	CS
33.92M	KJY884	F7 Fireground	CS
33.88	KJY884	Main Line area	CS

County operations
500.8875R	KXS844	Prison farm
33.10	KTY935	Emergency Management
153.800R	KVN537	County units
155.220M	KTY935	Emergency Management
458.7875M	KD53008	County Airport Authority
500.3875R	WIH666	County units

Municipalities
Avondale Borough
33.78M	KGC789	Fire local	CS

Caln Township
158.820	KNAI206	Police
154.250	WPCH284	Thorndale Fire Co. local

Coatesville City
153.800	WNAB766	Police	
154.160	KDN480	Fire dispatch	79.7
153.830M	KB64167	Fire fireground	
502.2625R	WII398	Water Authority	
451.4375R	WNZR737	City authority	
155.040	KNHG438	City units	

Downingtown Borough
158.805	KNAW979	Police
154.310	KGA366	Fire dispatch
154.310	KDY422	Minquas Fire Co.
154.400	WNXN540	Minquas Fire Co. local

East Bradford Township
45.36	WPDP839	Township units

East Brandywine Township

158.895	WQX201	Police dispatch	
158.805	WQX201	Police (Downingtown)	

East Coventry Township

151.025	WNRI687	Roads Department	

East Fallowfield Township

155.820	WZT827	Township units	

East Goshen Township

155.490M	KD38398	Police car to car	
156.030M	KD38398	Police car to car	
158.985	WPAY356	Roads Department	
155.040	WNFG761	Township units	

East Nottingham Township

156.165	WNNK484	Roads Department	

Easttown Township

45.64	KLO355	Police	
45.84	KLO355	Police	

East Whiteland Township

45.48	KJF832	Police	
154.265	KGF753	Fire local	71.9

Elverson Borough

33.76	KGD553	Fire local	CS
33.94	KGD553	Fire local	CS
155.280M	KU8802	Ambulance	
155.385M	KU8802	Ambulance	

Franklin Township

33.94	KLP479	Fire local	CS

Honey Brook Township

45.80	KCE658	Roads Department	
159.105M	KS2585	Roads Department	

Kennett Township

155.955	WQS456	Township units	

Kennett Square Borough

158.835	KLM765	Police	
33.78	KNBR728	Kennett Fire Co. No. 1 local	CS

London Britain Township

151.025	WNHE637	Roads Department	

London Grove Township

500.9375R	WII526	Township units	

Malvern Borough

156.000M	KO4514	Borough units	
461.125R	WNXI344	Emergency Services 4WD	

New Garden Township

154.100R	KXQ709	Township units	

North Coventry Township
151.100   KVD613   Roads Department
Oxford Borough
153.980   WNQC699   Borough units
Parkesburg Borough
154.220M   WPBK503   Fire local
Pennsbury Township
153.995   WNYY763   Township units
Phoenixville Borough
155.715   KLK681   Police dispatch
45.56   KDN943   Police
33.70   KXL314   Fire (Montgomery County)   CS
Pocopson Township
151.085   WNPI593   Roads Department
Schuylkill Township
500.4375R   WIK820   Police dispatch   186.2
Spring City Borough
33.70   KXI913   Liberty Fire Co. (Montgomery Co.)   CS
Tredyffrin Township
155.130R   KNJX796   Police dispatch   71.9
45.60   WPDS748   Police
45.62   KGF305   Police
155.220   KNDU704   Emergency Service Division
856.2125R   WNXU722   Township units
Upper Oxford Township
151.070   WNKH490   Roads Department
Upper Uwchlan Township
500.4375R   WIK230   Police dispatch   186.2
Uwchlan Township
500.4375R   WNBQ308   Police dispatch   186.2
500.6625R   WIL333   Police operations
500.9625R   WIK389   Police operations
153.725R   WYC808   Municipal Authority
Valley Township
159.210   WNQM910   Police operations
Wallace Township
156.165   WNNK483   Roads Department
Warwick Township
151.055   WPAK260   Roads Department
West Bradford Township
154.175   WPAE327   West Bradford Fire Co. local
159.120   WNMB918   Roads Department
West Brandywine Township
156.240   WNQK902   Roads Department

West Caln Township

153.830M	WNRO798	Martins Corner Fire Co. local	
153.830M	WNRQ932	Wagontown Fire Co. local	
153.830R	WNRQ932	Wagontown Fire Co. mobile repeaters	
156.240	WNAV277	Roads Department	

West Chester Borough

500.4125R	KWQ485	Police F1 dispatch	97.4
500.5125R	KWQ485	Police F2	97.4
45.32	KBZ947	Fire dispatch	
46.56	KBZ947	Fire operations	
47.50	KGE275	Good Fellowship ambulance	
47.66	WNRW320	Good Fellowship ambulance	
48.40	WNMA859	Area Municipal Utility	

West Fallowfield Township

460.625R	WPCQ977	Cochranville Fire Co. operations

West Goshen Township

158.745	KRZ861	Police
46.52	KFM406	Township units

West Grove Borough

155.145	WNGZ285	Borough units

West Marlborough Township

155.820	KQL747	Township units

Westtown Township

158.985	WPAW960	Roads Department

West Whiteland Township

500.4375R	WIE854	Police dispatch	186.2

Willistown Township

158.820	KQO365	Police

DELAWARE COUNTY

Police

506.7625R	WIJ815	Sector 1	114.8
		Aston, Upper Chichester, Bethel,	
		Marcus Hook, Trainer,	
		Lower Chichester	
506.8375R	WIJ815	Sector 2	110.9
		Parkside, Upland, Brookhaven,	
		Chester Township, Upper Providence,	
		Newtown, Morton, Swarthmore,	
		Nether Providence	
506.8625R	WIJ815	Sector 3 - Chester	114.8
508.0875R	WIJ815	Sector 4	136.5
		Lansdowne, Aldan, Clifon,	
		East Lansdowne, Yeadon, Darby,	
		Colwyn, Sharon Hill, Folcroft,	
		Collingdale, Darby Township	
508.1125R	WIJ815	Sector 5	141.3
		Glenolden, Prospect Park, Norwood,	
		Tinicum, Ridley Park	
506.7875BM	WIJ815	Sector 6 - Media	167.9
508.1875R	WIJ815	M-1 mutual aid	146.2
508.0625R	WIJ815	M-2 mutual aid	141.3
508.2375R	WIJ815	M-3 mutual aid	173.8
506.6375R	WIJ815	M-4 mutual aid	162.2
506.6125R	WIJ815	M-5 mutual aid	100.0
506.4125R	WIJ815	M-6 mutual aid	131.8
506.5625R	WIJ815	Data 1	151.4
508.4375R	WIJ815	Data 2	151.4
506.3625R	WIJ815	Criminal Investigation Div. East	127.3
506.3625R	WIJ815	Criminal Investigation Div. West	127.3
508.0375R	WIJ815	County 1	192.8
508.2375R	WIJ815	County 2	131.8
507.8125R	WIJ815	County 3, Prison	186.2
506.7125R	WIJ815	County 4	103.5
506.7375R	WIJ815	County 5	107.2
506.7375M	WIJ815	County A car to car	114.8
507.8125M	WIJ815	County B car to car	136.5
506.7375M	WIJ815	County C car to car	110.9
507.8125M	WIJ815	County D car to car	192.8
508.2375M	WIJ815	County E car to car	110.9
506.7125M	WIJ815	County F car to car	151.4
508.3375R	WIJ815	Park police, courthouse security	103.5

| 453.6125R | WPCV315 | Courthouse security dispatch | 203.5 |
| 453.5875R | WPCV315 | Sheriff courthouse operations | 203.5 |

NOTE: These old police frequencies are being used for municipal purposes in some communities now.

39.82	KGA905	Tac 1 - West (secondary/info)	CS
39.90	KGA905	Tac 2 - West (primary)	CS
39.78	KGA905	Tac 3 - East (secondary/info)	CS
39.50	KGA905	Tac 4 - East (primary)	CS
39.60	KZI389	Tac 5 - Courthouse/park police	CS
45.54	KGA905	Tac 6 - Dispatch for: *Norwood, Prospect Park, Tinicum, Glenolden*	CS

Fire

| 506.8125R | WIJ815 | Fire 1 primary | 173.8 |

Darby, Colwyn, Collingdale, Folcroft, Norwood, Glenolden, Sharon Hill, Briarcliffe, Goodwill, Darby Township, Clifton Heights, Yeadon, Lansdowne, East Lansdowne, Garretford, Millbourne, Highland Park, Cardington, Upper Darby, Primos, Secane

| 506.5875R | WIJ815 | Fire 2 secondary | 156.7 |

Darby, Colwyn, Collingdale, Folcroft, Norwood, Glenolden, Sharon Hill, Briarcliffe, Goodwill, Darby Township, Clifton Heights, Yeadon, Lansdowne, East Lansdowne, Garretford, Millbourne, Highland Park, Cardington, Upper Darby, Primos, Secane

| 508.1625R | WIJ815 | Fire 3 primary | 146.2 |

Morton, Rutledge, Swarthmore, Media, South Media, Rose Tree, Brookhaven, Garden City, Parkside, Upland, Springfield

| 506.6625R | WIJ815 | Fire 4 secodary | 110.9 |

Morton, Rutledge, Swarthmore, Media, South Media, Rose Tree, Brookhaven, Garden City, Parkside, Upland, Springfield

508.1375R	WIJ815	Fire 5 primary	100.0
		Marcus Hook, Trainer, Linwood,	
		Boothwyn, Viscose, Feltonville,	
		Ogden, Friendship, Reliance,	
		Green Ridge, Lennox Park,	
		Middletown, Lenni Heights,	
		Edgmont, Bethel, Lima, Chester Hghts,	
		Aston-Beechwood, Concordville	
506.6875R	WIJ815	Fire 6 secondary	141.3
		Marcus Hook, Trainer, Linwood,	
		Boothwyn, Viscose, Feltonville,	
		Ogden, Friendship, Reliance,	
		Green Ridge, Lennox Park,	
		Middletown, Lenni Heights,	
		Edgmont, Bethel, Lima, Chester Hghts,	
		Aston-Beechwood, Concordville	
508.6625R	WIJ815	Fire 7 primary	156.7
		Franklin, Hanley, Felton, Chester,	
		Folsom, Holmes, Milmont, Vauclain,	
		Woodlyn, Leedom, Ridley Park,	
		Prospect Park, Eddystone,	
		Essington, Lester	
506.5125R	WIJ815	Fire 8 secondary	107.2
		Franklin, Hanley, Felton, Chester,	
		Folsom, Holmes, Milmont, Vauclain,	
		Woodlyn, Leedom, Ridley Park,	
		Prospect Park, Eddystone,	
		Essington, Lester	
507.9875R	WIJ815	Fire 9	100.0
		Bon Air, Brookline, Llanerch. Manoa,	
		Oakmont, ARCO, Broomall,	
		Newtown Square, Radnor	
508.0375R	WIJ815	Fire 10 COMMAND	192.8
		(also Police COUNTY 1)	
506.6875M	WIJ815	Fire 11 mobiles - fireground	110.9
		Darby, Colwyn, Collingdale, Folcroft,	
		Norwood, Glenolden, Sharon Hill,	
		Briarcliffe, Goodwill, Darby Township,	
		Clifton Heights, Yeadon, Lansdowne,	
		East Lansdowne, Garretford,	
		Millbourne, Highland Park,	
		Cardington, Upper Darby, Primos,	
		Secane, Bon Air, Brookline, Llanerch,	
		Manoa, Oakmont, ARCO, Broomall,	
		Newtown Square, Radnor	

507.9875M	WIJ815	Fire 12 mobiles - fireground	167.9
		Franklin, Hanley, Felton, Chester,	
		Folsom, Holmes, Milmont, Vauclain,	
		Woodlyn, Leedom, Ridley Park,	
		Prospect Park, Eddystone,	
		Essington, Lester	
506.5875M	WIJ815	Fire 13 mobiles - fireground	192.8
		Morton, Rutledge, Swarthmore,	
		Media, South Media, Rose Tree,	
		Brookhaven, Garden City, Parkside,	
		Upland, Springfield	
507.9875M	WIJ815	Fire 14 mobiles - fireground	173.8
		Marcus Hook, Trainer, Linwood,	
		Boothwyn, Viscose, Feltonville,	
		Ogden, Friendship, Reliance,	
		Green Ridge, Lennox Park,	
		Middletown, Lenni Heights,	
		Edgmont, Bethel, Lima,	
		Chester Heights, Aston-Beechwood,	
		Concordville	
463.175B	KQG341	Paramedics MED-8	
468.175M	KQG341	Paramedics MED-8	

NOTE: These old fire frequencies still are used on a local basis. All alerting still is done on 46.48, but is expected to be moved to UHF.

46.38	KDK667	F1 Dispatch	CS
46.42	KDK667	F2 Fireground	CS
46.36	WNHG581	F3 Zone A	CS
46.16	KDK667	F4 Ambulance	CS
46.48	KDK667	F5 Alerting	CS
46.40	WNHG581	Zone D	CS
46.44	KDK667	Central zone	CS
46.50	KDK667	North - Zone C	CS
46.08	KDK667	Fire	CS
46.18	WNHG581	Fire	CS
46.22	WNHG581	Zone	CS
46.24	WNHG581	Fire	CS

County operations

453.975R	KYK373	County departments	
462.575R	KAC4413	Constables	173.8
453.0375R		Communications Center	
460.0375M	KB65124	County prison, K9 units	
463.375M		RHM Sewer Authority	

453.3125R	WNVG264	County units	
453.6875M	KD43996	Regional Water Authority (data)	
453.0125R	KB65014	County units	
456.1125M	KD43996	Regional Water Quality Authority	
151.805	WNSY667	Solid Waste Authority (Boyertown)	
463.225R	WNHD991	Transportation Consortium	
461.250R	WNGE457	Community Transit of Delaware County	

Municipalities
Aston Township
154.085	WNJN900	Township units	
464.950M	WPDU857	Aston-Beachwood Fire Co. operations	
462.100M	WPDU857	Aston-Beachwood Fire Co. local	

Bethel Township
39.10	KZR615	Township units	

Chester City
154.725	KFA484	Police F1 dispatch (old)	CS
155.415	KFA484	Police F2	
154.205	KGB398	Fire F2	
154.430	KGB398	Fire F1 (County Zone E)	
46.28	WNST581	Fire	
154.055	KCQ368	City units	
453.575R	KLI226	City units	

Chester Township
460.6375R	WPCE698	Felton Hose & Chemical Co. local	

Concord Township
159.180		Roads Department	

Darby Township
46.24	WNFA247	Holmes Fire Co. local	

Eddystone Borough
506.3125R		Police dispatch (Ridley)	88.5
508.9625R		Police Tac-2 car to car (Ridley)	88.5
508.9625M		Police Tac-3 operations (Ridley)	
506.4875R	WIL646	Fire and police (phone patch)	146.2
460.625R	WNYB541	Fire operations	D025
453.700R	WPBZ787	Borough units/fire F4 (phone)	D025
460.5125R	WPDJ899	Fire operations	
460.5375R	WPCG691	Fire operations	
46.26	WNDT977	Fire local	

Haverford Township
453.275R	KQL751	Police F1	74.4
453.475R	KQL750	Police F2	74.4
46.22	KGC512	Fire dispatch	
46.42	KGC512	Fire fireground	

46.30M	WNZH213	Fire local	
452.350R	WNGX536	Emergency Service	

Lansdowne Borough

39.06M	KGA951	Police car to car	CS

Marple Township

39.98	KNAF260	Police	CS
453.225R	KRP852	Police	74.4
155.205	KJU239	Ambulance Corps	

Media Borough

462.975R	WNYV251	Media Emergency Services	114.8

Middletown Township

155.475M	WNWW251	Police nationwide mutual aid	
460.575R	WNQZ797	Lima Fire Co. operations	79.7
453.825R	KVF546	Township units/townwatch	79.7

Millbourne Borough

33.52	KZQ667	Fire local	

Nether Providence Township

46.30M	KGF810	Garden City Fire Co.	CS
46.30M	WNMX588	South Media Fire Co.	CS
46.340M	WNVK275	South Media Fire Co.	CS
465.5625M	WPBD227	South Media Fire Co. local	203.5
460.600R	WPCD815	South Media Fire Co. operations	
37.98	WPCC442	Roads Department	CS

Newtown Township

39.68	KQL783	Police dispatch	CS
45.08	KTP974	Township units	

Norwood Borough

45.22	KRA517	Police F2	
46.18	KRF375	Fire local	

Prospect Park Borough

45.90	WYR613	Police F2	
46.06	KGG370	Fire local	

Radnor Township

500.3375R	KYO878	Police	141.3
33.82	WSW331	Fire (Chester County)	CS
33.86	WSW331	Fire (Chester County)	CS
33.70		Fire (Montgomery County)	CS
33.84		Fire (Lower Merion)	CS
33.88		Fire (Main Line)	CS
33.90		Fire (Chester County)	CS
46.56	KYB967	Township units	

Ridley Township

506.3125R	WIK302	Police Tac-1 dispatch	88.5
508.9625R		Police Tac-2 car to car	88.5
508.9625M		Police Tac-3 operations	88.5

506.3125M	WIK302	Police car to car	88.5
507.2625R	WIK302	Police	88.5
46.24	KFT582	Fire local	
46.24	WZC481	Leedom Fire Co. local	
46.12M	WNVD554	Woodlyn Fire Co. local	

Ridley Park Borough

39.58	KQY873	Police	CS
45.74M		Police F2	

Sharon Hill Borough

45.54	KGB367	Police	

Springfield Township

500.6125R	WIJ786	Police F1 dispatch	D364
500.6125M	WIJ786	Police F2 car to car	D364
506.3125M		Police F3 (Ridley)	
39.74M	KNEN261	Police car to car	CS
45.56	KBW802	Township units	
45.76M	KA41660	Roads Department	
159.165	WNGB386	Roads Department	

Tinicum Township

45.22	KGE545	Police car to car (old)	
45.74M	KB92386	Police car to car F2 (old)	

Upper Chichester Township

155.475	WNMV719	Police	CS
151.625M	KD34891	Police (Channel "10-23")	
150.995	WNNC630	Police operations F1	156.7
150.995	WNNC630	Road Department F2	
156.475B	WQB630	VHF Marine Channel 69	CS
156.800B	WQB630	VHF Marine Channel 16 calling	CS

Upper Darby Township

159.090R	KGA853	Police dispatch	107.2
155.070	KNGX597	Police	
154.190	KGA346	Fire F1	107.2
154.325	KGA346	Fire F2	107.2
453.625R	KQO263	Highways/Sanitation	
453.375R	KGW597	Township units	

Yeadon Borough

460.025R	KGB242	Police	
46.20	KNCG443	Fire local	
46.30M	KNCG443	Fire fireground	
151.685M	WPDN851	Fire local	
151.805M	WPDN851	Fire local	

LANCASTER COUNTY

Police

155.430R	KNGX660	Channel A - Metro	71.9
155.685R	KSZ232	Channel B - Countywide	71.9
155.640R	KSZ233	Channel C - Northwest	71.9
154.860R	WZN243	Channel D - South	71.9
155.535R	KNFQ506	Channel E - Northeast	71.9
155.595R	KNDM546	Police	71.9
155.895	KEQ428	Car to car	71.9
155.475M	KP4689	Nationwide police mutual aid	

Fire

33.90	KGC755	F1 Dispatch	CS
33.82	KGC755	F2 Lancaster City	CS
33.64	KGC755	F3 Fireground	CS
33.60	KGC755	F4 Ambulances	CS
33.68	KGC755	F5 Manheim Township	CS
33.76	KGC755	Alternate fireground - Northwest	CS
33.72	KGC755	Southern zone	CS
33.56	KUG740	Northeast zone	CS
33.46M	KD38109	Fire	CS
33.50M	KD47971	Fire Police Association	CS
153.770M	KD25175	Zone 1 Firemen's Association	

Ambulance

155.340	KWJ350	Hospital net
463.125B	WRA469	Paramedics calling
468.125M	WRA469	Paramedics calling

County operations

156.030	WQF228	County prison	CS
159.225	KNCV395	Parks Department	
155.745	WRB577	Airport operations	
154.995	KXQ915	Lancaster Area Sewer Authority	
453.975R	KJJ964	Red Rose Transit buses	94.7
155.025	KNHS669	County units	
155.055R	KNEJ770	County units	
453.850R	KNBH711	County units	136.5

Municipalities

Akron Borough

45.64	KNIE525	Borough units

Bart Township

33.46M	KB63750	Fire - local	
155.955R	WQK333	Township units	

Christiana Borough

33.46M	KB77494	Fire local	

Clay Township

45.16	WXJ787	Township units	

Colerain Township

155.955R	WNWK593	Township units	71.9
155.955M	KNES984	Township units	71.9

Columbia Borough

155.130	KGA443	Police
151.835	WPAM945	Vigilant Fire Co. operations
458.0125M	WPCM837	Community Ambulance portables
155.025	KNEZ479	Borough units

Conestoga Township

154.025	WPAD566	Township units

Conoy Township

155.895	KNBL853	Township units

Drumore Township

155.895	KNAF989	Township units

Earl Township

33.50M	KB53566	Fire local
33.94M	KB35366	Fire (Chester County)
45.24	KNEZ873	Township units

East Cocalico Township

158.805	KYL664	Township units
155.145	KNGY916	Township units

East Donegal Township

453.875	KGL797	Township units
155.055	WNMQ767	Township units
155.805	WNMQ767	Township units

East Drumore Township

155.130	KGG533	Police
155.040	KSJ283	Township units

East Earl Township

45.70	KZQ578	Police
33.50		Fire local
155.100R	WNZX817	Township units
45.28	KZQ794	Township units
45.44	KZQ794	Township units

East Hempfield Township

33.44	KNIX217	Wheatland Fire Co. local
155.880	KWX521	Township units

East Lampeter Township

155.595	WNCY310	Police
33.92	WNKC982	Fire local
155.085	KFZ919	Township units
158.775	KFZ919	Township units

East Petersburg Borough

33.46M	KB79928	Fire local
33.48	WNJB312	Fire local

Eden Township

33.68	WQG807	Fire local
33.52	WQG807	Fire local
33.48	WQG807	Fire local

Elizabeth Township

155.025	KXQ738	Township units
155.775	WNCZ411	Township units

Elizabethtown Borough

155.520	WNEB858	Police
33.98	WNHK683	Fire local
153.980	KXJ232	Borough units

Ephrata Borough

45.70	KRZ947	Police - Channel A
45.54	KRZ947	Police - Channel B
45.28	KGC558	Police - Channel C
45.56	KGC558	Police car to car
155.430	KRZ947	Police
155.535R	KNFQ506	Police dispatch
154.845	KRZ947	Police
33.56	KUG740	Fire dispatch
33.84	WNCR672	Pioneer Fire Co. local
33.92	WNCR672	Pioneer Fire Co. local

Ephrata Township

45.40	WXK779	Police dispatch
45.28	WXK779	Police (borough)

Fulton Township

155.895	KNAH383	Township units

LANCASTER CITY

154.875R	KGA583	Police F1 dispatch	71.9
154.800R	KQY818	Police F2 info	71.9
33.90	KGH277	Fire F1 county	CS
33.82	KGH277	Fire F2 dispatch	CS
33.60	KGH277	Fire F3 ambulance	CS
33.64	KGH277	Fire F4 fireground	CS
155.160	KCD854	Lancaster Volunteer Ambulance	
173.350	KFV525	Water authority	
462.725	KAA8072	Recreation Department	

464.825M	WNVX613	Schools	
155.940	KBE835	City units	
153.815M	KD29067	City units	

Lancaster Township

155.145	KNAS413	Township units	

Leacock Township

153.920	KQR534	Township units	
154.085	KQR534	Township units	

Lititz Borough

33.80	WPAY355	Lititz Fire Co. No. 1 local	
33.96	WPAY355	Lititz Fire Co. No. 1 local	
854.2875R	WNYK379	Borough units	

Little Britain Township

155.895	KNAT823	Township units	

Manheim Borough

33.42M	WNRU362	Hope Fire Engine & Hose Co. local	
33.62M	WNRU362	Hope Fire Engine & Hose Co. local	
158.955	WNSB283	Borough units	

Manheim Township

154.965R	KDL906	Police	
155.655	WSL565	Police F4 tac	71.9
33.48	WNIJ362	Fire dispatch	
33.68	WQH322	Neffsvlle Fire Co. local	
33.68	WQG806	South Manheim Fire Co. local	
33.08	WNAS701	Ambulance	
33.08	WNAN829	Emergency Management	
45.64	WYY980	Township units	
153.860	WNJZ206	Township units	

Manor Township

33.44	KNIX216	West Lanaster Fire Co. local	
155.880	KVI435	Township units	

Marietta Borough

156.150M	WNVM943	Police car to car	

Martic Township

155.115	WQG312	Township units	

Millersville Borough

155.715	KKL546	Police F4 tac	71.9
33.46M	KB93508	Fire local	
33.04	WNPC811	West End Ambulance Association	

Mount Joy Borough

45.04	KTV671	Forest Fire Crew	
155.145	KWF838	Borough units	

Mount Joy Township

158.745	KFR638	Township units	

Mountville Borough
150.995	WNXP264	Roads Department

New Holland Borough
159.150	KNEV405	Police
45.70	KZO364	Police
33.46M	KGC753	Liberty Fire Co. local
33.56	KGC753	Liberty Fire Co. (Ephrata)
45.28	KYD814	Borough units
155.925	WNAV331	Borough units
45.52	KYD814	Borough units

Paradise Township
159.195	KNFK669	Roads Department
45.20	WRB480	Township units

Penn Township
156.015	WYG415	Township units

Quarryville Borough
33.46M	KB52601	Fire local
156.000M	KD21584	Borough units

Rapho Township
154.725	WNJL615	Police
155.085	KVI620	Township units

Sadsbury Township
155.955R	KNFL986	Township units	71.9

Salisbury Township
33.46M	KB52602	Gap Fire Co. local
155.100R	KVN640	Township units

Strasburg Borough
33.46M	KB53135	Fire local

Strasburg Township
155.865	KNID206	Township units

Terre Hill Borough
45.20	WNPH589	Borough units

Upper Leacock Township
155.115	KOL954	Township units

Warwick Township
155.925	KNGZ248	Police
31.04	WNSS816	Community Ambulance Association
155.775	KNBB766	Township units
45.28	KNBB766	Township units

West Cocalico Township
46.58	KNGG794	Township units

West Donegal Township
158.805	KCS306	Township units

West Earl Township
45.12	WNLA422	Township units

45.70	WNLA422	Township units

West Hempfield Township

33.44	WNLF431	Silver Spring Fire Co. local
33.48	WNLF431	Silver Spring Fire Co. local
155.160	WXK554	Ambulance
155.280M	WXK554	Ambulance
155.340M	WXK554	Ambulance
155.055	KNFW802	Township units
154.100	WNMY443	Township units

FACTOID:

In 1990, Lancaster County had the largest number of registered motorized pedacycles of any county in Pennsylvania: 1,133. The next largest number for any county is York County, which had only about half at 643. In numbers of motorcycle registrations, Lancaster County ranks second (behind Allegheny County) with 9,672.

LEHIGH COUNTY

Police

158.775R	KIS735	F3 dispatch	186.2
158.850R	KJF715	F4 dispatch	186.2
155.805	KIS735	F5 sheriff, probation	
154.875	WNNG972	Police	
155.970M	KV9903	Police	
156.090M	KV9903	Police	
156.150M	KV9903	Police	
460.225R	WPCY396	Allentown-Bethlehem-Easton Airport Police, Hanover Township	

Fire

33.98	KGE450	F1 Operations	CS
33.52	KGE450	F2 Fireground	CS
33.48	KGE450	F3 Fireground	CS
33.72	KGE450	Alerting	CS
154.175	WNCL847	Salisbury dispatch	CS
158.745M	WNSR871	County fire police	
154.830	WNMI759	Fire	

Ambulance

155.265	KQR807	A1 Med radio
155.340	KQR807	A2 Regional
155.835	KIS735	A5 Dispatch/MedEvac
155.235	KQR807	Ambulance
155.325	KQR807	Ambulance
155.220	KNJP460	Lehigh Vly Hosp MedEvac copter 136.5
463.725R		Lehigh Valley Hospital Center MedEvac operations, Salisbury Twp.

County operations

453.675R	KEM730	Bureau of Aging specialized transp.
453.800R	KJF902	Bureau of Aging
453.275R	KXQ987	LANTA buses 67.0
453.225R	WNPH820	LANTA Metro Plus buses (Palmeri)
453.625R	KRV211	Allentown-Bethlehem-Easton Airport Fire Department
453.925R	WNMM739	Allentown-Bethlehem-Easton Airport operations
460.225R	WPCY396	Allentown-Bethlehem-Easton Airport police

458.200M	KB30144	Courthouse security	
458.500M	WNVG269	County units	
155.775	KIS735	County units	
453.0375M	KB88191	County Authority	
453.9875M	WNUJ451	County units	
453.575R	WNMT456	Parks and Recreation	
453.975R	WNVA828	County prison	
153.965M	WNNL728	County units	
153.980	WNNL728	County units	

Municipalities
Alburtis Borough

155.865	WNGP637	Borough units

ALLENTOWN CITY

158.790R	KGB326	Police dispatch F1	
159.090R	KGB326	Police F2	
155.040	KJF909	Police F3/ambulance	
154.725R	WNSL213	Police detectives	
159.060M	WNXJ633	Police car to car	
154.515M	WPEF732	Police reserves	
500.5875R	WIH876	Police (not in use)	
500.6125R	WIH876	Police (not in use)	
501.0125R	WIH876	Police (not in use)	
500.5875M	WIH876	Police car to car (not in use)	
500.6125M	WIH876	Police car to car (not in use)	
501.0125M	WIH876	Police car to car (not in use)	
453.475R	KNHT865	Fire dispatch	192.8
453.475M	KNHT865	Fire fireground	192.8
453.825R	KNHT865	Fire operations	192.8
453.825M	KNHT865	Fire fireground	192.8
154.070M	WPCY919	Fire mobile repeaters	
151.355	KSZ517	Cetronia Ambulance Corps F1	
155.295	KSZ517	Cetronia Ambulance Corps F4	
155.280M	KSZ517	Cetronia Ambulance Corps F6 mobiles	
155.340M	KSZ517	Cetronia Ambulance Corps	
150.775M	WPAK378	Cetronia Ambulance Corps portables	
158.250	KGE426	Water Department	
453.3875R	KD34619	City units	
158.985M	WPDM706	Roads Department mobile repeaters	
154.570M	KD46466	Schools	

Catasaqua Borough

155.265	WNNB487	Ambulance corps
159.150		Roads Department

Coopersburg Borough

46.10M	KGE624	Fire (Bucks County)	123.0
45.92M	KJ2211	Ambulance	

Coplay Borough

153.950M	WPCE484	Fire local

Emmaus Borough

158.835R	KVG852	Police
159.450R	WNVN360	Police operations
33.96	KGE741	Fire dispatch
154.295	KGE741	Fire
159.135R	KLE872	Roads Department
153.995	KVG852	Borough units
155.775	KNHV209	Borough units

Fogelsville Borough

154.010M	KD28146	Fire local

Fountain Hill Borough

155.610	KGF571	Police
158.910M	KA59052	Police coordination
158.925	KFF489	Fire

Hanover Township

154.205	WNHW508	HanLeCo Fire Co. local
154.250	WNHW508	HanLeCo Fire Co. local
453.700BM	KSM599	Roads Department

Heidelberg Township

153.950M	WNWC288	Goodwill Fire Co. No. 1 local
45.24	KNDX259	Roads Department
45.64	KAS425	Township units

Lower Macungie Township

154.145R	WNXJ532	Wescosville Fire Co. operations
153.830M	KD37172	Wescosville Fire Co. local
156.000	WPCP896	Township units
46.58	KQP545	Roads Department

Lower Milford Township

154.325	WNMD782	Fire
453.925R	WNDM835	Township units

Lowhill Township

37.90M		Roads Department

Lynn Township

33.10	KJF320	Roads Department

Macungie Borough

155.955	KNEN912	Borough units
154.010M	WPCM836	Macungie Fire Co. No. 1 local

North Whitehall Township

33.44	WNWB612	Schnecksville Fire Co. local
154.010M	WPCY945	Neffs Fire Co. local

Salisbury Township

154.175	KOP999	Fire dispatch
153.950M	WNYT825	Western Salisbury Fire Co. local
154.445	WNYQ761	Eastern Salisbury Fire Amb & Rescue
155.175	KNBH859	Salisbury Area Ambulance
155.340	KNBH859	Salisbury Area Ambulance
155.385	KNBH859	Salisbury Area Ambulance
159.120	KFB866	Roads Department
155.100R	KVN640	Township units

Slatington Borough

33.58M	KN5768	Fire local
156.015M	KU3183	Borough units
155.940	WNMY999	Borough units

South Whitehall Township

156.210	KNEJ567	Police
33.92	KFO270	Fire F4 local
154.220R	KNAU361	Fire
154.220M	KA21203	Fire police
155.250	KGD361	Fire
153.770M	KFO270	Fire
153.890M	KFO270	Fire
153.890M	WNRU342	Tri-Clover Fire Co. local
465.575M	KFO270	Fire mobile repeaters
151.040	KNEV538	Roads Department
151.130R	KDG402	Roads Department
151.250R	WNNI354	Roads Department
155.895R	WNNI354	Township units

Upper Macungie Township

33.54	KD26320	Goodwill Fire Co. No. 1 local
154.010M	KD28146	Fogelsville Fire Co. local
154.070M	KD28146	Fogelsville Fire Co. local
46.58	KJU924	Roads Department

Upper Milford Township

33.50M	KB63741	Fire local
154.400	WNLF486	Citizens Fire Co. local

Upper Saucon Township

159.150	KRT686	Police
33.68	WNCA536	Fire local
151.265	WNRW205	Fire dispatch
155.295M	KA80273	Ambulance mobiles
159.105	WPCI751	Roads Department

Walnutport Borough

37.10	KNAT361	Borough Authority

Weisenberg Township

37.90		Roads Department

Whitehall Township

460.475R	KFB940	Police
154.130R	KFB881	Fire F1 dispatch
154.010M	KFB881	Fire F2 fireground
154.235M	WNWU650	Fire local
155.295	WZU301	Emergency squad
462.950R	WNMC995	Whitehall Coplay Ambulance
462.975R	WNNG574	Whitehall Coplay Ambulance
151.085R	KSQ808	Roads Department
453.7375M	KB81004	Township units
453.9375M	KB79157	Township units

FACTOID:
Allentown has two television stations: WFMZ-TV, Channel 69, an independent station, and WLVT, Channel 39, an affiliate of the Public Broadcasting System.

MONTGOMERY COUNTY

Police

— 45.46	KGA243	Dispatch - East *Bryn Athyn, Rockledge, Jenkintown,* *West Conshohocken, Conshohocken,* *Ambler, Whitpain, East Norriton,* *North Wales, Coroner, Sheriff*	136.5
— 45.26	KGA243	Dispatch - West *Upper Providence, Collegeville,* *Limerick, Royersford, Douglass,* *Lower Pottsgrove, Upper Pottsgrove,* *West Pottsgrove, New Hanover,* *Spring City*	136.5
45.38	KGA243	Dispatch - North (North Penn) *Lower Salford, Franconia, Souderton,* *Telford, Lower Frederick, Marlborough,* *Schwenksville*	136.5
45.34M	KGA243	Car to car	136.5
45.78	KGA243	Data (information)	136.5
45.14R	WNMT464	Sheriff dispatch	136.5
45.14M	WNMT464	Sheriff car to car	136.5
155.970M	KGA243	Vehicle repeaters (old)	
154.025R	WNSF974	County detectives	114.8
155.475M	KGA243	Nationwide police emergency	CS
453.0375M	KGA243	Police	
460.3125R	KGA243	Police mobile extenders	
465.3125M	KGA243	Police portables input to extenders	

Fire

33.70	KUE698	Dispatch F1	CS
33.66	KUE698	Fireground F2	CS
33.60	KUE698	Fire police F3	CS
33.84	KUE698	Lower Merion units	CS
33.58	WNLN505	Fireground - new	
154.130	KUE698	Eastern county F1 dispatch	136.5
154.280	KUE698	Eastern county F2 response	136.5
---.---		Eastern county F3 local	136.5
153.830M	KUE698	Eastern county F4 fireground	136.5
154.370	KUE698	Norristown units	136.5

Ambulance

46.04	KUU476	Dispatch F1	CS/136.5

45.92	KUU476	Alternate F2	CS/136.5
45.96	KUU476	Alternate F3	CS/136.5
463.050B	KUU476	Paramedics MED-3	
468.050M	KUU476	Paramedics MED-3	

County operations

154.025R	KFD540	Emergency Mgt., EMS staff	136.5
		Highway Department, elections	74.4
155.925	KNHF504	County prison farm	
462.650R		Emergency Management CBers	
453.5125R	KD30057	County units	
506.3875R	WII527	County units	
506.3875M	WII527	County units car to car	
851.3625R	WNNY750	County park rangers	136.5
853.3375R	WNNY749	County units	
855.2375R	WNSN233	County units	
855.9375R	WNNY750	County units	
856.7375R	WNSN233	County units	

Municipalities

Abington Township

460.025R	KNHC269	Police F1 dispatch	D023
460.025M	KNHC269	Police F2 mobiles	D023
460.175R	KNHC269	Police F3 (Cheltenham)	D023
460.175M	KNHC269	Police F4 (Cheltenham)	D023
460.3125M	KNHC269	Police portables	D023
465.4875M	KNHC269	Police portables	D023
154.070M	KUP289	Fire "red band" - local	
153.770M	WNXJ908	Roslyn Fire Co. fire police	
155.820	KJS805	Township units	203.5
39.18	KGA260	Dog control, townwatch	162.2
453.2375M	KD47349	Township units	

Ambler Borough

155.145	WNUD831	Police car to car	
154.355	KNBY373	Wissahickon Fire Co. local	
463.1875M	WNVD913	Community Ambulance portables	

Bridgeport Borough

33.64	KGE756	Fire local	CS
155.205	WNYA681	Goodwill Ambulance operations	
156.180	KNBQ249	Roads Department	
155.040R	WPBN518	Borough units	

Bryn Athyn Borough

| 154.280 | | Fire dispatch | |

Cheltenham Township

460.100R	KNHC270	Police F1 dispatch	D023
460.100M	KNHC270	Police F2 mobiles	D023
460.175R	KNHC270	Police F3 (Abington)	D023
460.175M	KNHC270	Police F4 (Abington)	D023
158.850	KGA404	Police F1 (old)	
158.970M	KGA404	Police F2 (old)	
154.445	KSO961	Fire dispatch	CS
45.92	KNCB992	EMS F2	136.5
45.96	KNCB992	EMS F3	136.5
46.04	KNCB992	EMS F1 dispatch	136.5
155.025	KRX559	Township units	
462.575		Township units	

Collegeville Borough

155.700R	WNBN244	Police	
153.920R	WNSN655	Police	
33.76M		Fire fireground F4	
173.2875B	WNYB713	Municipal Authority data	

Conshohocken Borough

45.66M	KB64340	Police car to car	136.5
33.76	KGC902	Conshohocken Fire Co. #2 local	CS
33.76	KCD760	Washington Fire Co. #1 local	CS
155.040	WNLY783	Borough units	

Douglass Township

33.94	KNEL270	Gilbertsville Fire Co. (Berks Co.)	CS
45.12	KWH441	Township units	

East Norriton Township

45.36	WYK376	Township units
45.56	WYK376	Township units

Franconia Township

45.12	WSL750	Township units

Hatboro Borough

500.9375R	WIJ500	Police	136.5
33.60M	KGC577	Fire police	CS
46.04	WNXM320	Enterprise Fire Co. ambulance disp.	
45.92	WNXM320	Enterprise Fire Co. ambulance ops	
45.96	WNXM320	Enterprise Fire Co. ambulance ops	
46.00	WNXM320	Enterprise Fire Co. amb. (Bucks Co.)	
453.700BM	WQL875	Water authority	
45.12	KSQ272	Sewer authority	
156.240	WNCU447	Roads Department	127.3

Hatfield Borough

156.105	WNVH524	Roads Department

Hatfield Township

154.115	KGK712	Police (day)

155.640R		Police (night - Lansdale)	107.2
155.310R	WXW435	Police dispatch	107.2
465.050M	KB20001	Police handhelds	

Horsham Township

506.3125R	WII716	Police dispatch	136.5
153.770M	KGF350	Fire police	
458.900M	KGF350	Fire company chief mobile repeater	
155.280	WSV966	Emergency Patrol Air Unit	
453.6375M	WPDH947	Water Authority	
45.24	KUS607	Township units	

Jenkintown Borough

39.14	KMJ867	Police local	162.2
39.18M	KMJ867	Police (Abington)	162.2
155.055	WNJH764	Borough units	

Lansdale Borough

155.640R	KGK647	Police dispatch	107.2
155.535	KGK647	Police secondary	107.2
154.175	KGE438	Fire F1 dispatch	
154.400M	KT9223	Fire F2 fireground	
153.500	KNAI669	Water Department	

Limerick Township

155.145R	KNID768	Police dispatch
153.875M	KNID768	Police car to car
153.920R	KNID768	Police - regional ops
33.76M		Fire fireground F4

Lower Frederick Township

37.10	WNAC227	Township units

Lower Gwynedd Township

155.865	KAO482	Police
156.180	WNUV981	Roads Department
155.895	KAO482	Township units

Lower Merion Township

460.525R	KTR732	Police F1 dispatch	131.8
460.275R	KTR732	Police F2 tac (special ops, info, surveillance)	131.8
465.525M	KTR732	Police F3 mobiles	131.8
158.730	KGB325	Police teleprinter	
155.475M	KGB325	Nationwide police emergency	CS
33.84	KGC984	Fire dispatch F2	CS
33.86	KLX932	Gladwyne Fire Co. local	CS
33.76	KGC984	Fire F4 (Conshohocken)	CS
33.42	KGC984	Fire F3	CS
151.025R	KGG242	Roads/townwatch	
458.1625M	KB63719	Township units	
458.3375M	KB63719	Township units	

Lower Moreland Township

460.500R	WNPU375	Police dispatch	D023
154.280	KGC271	Fire dispatch	
155.955	KJG999	Township units	

Lower Pottsgrove Township

33.90M	KC8880	Sanatoga Fire Co. (Chester Co.)	CS
45.68	WNXC700	Roads Department	

Lower Providence Township

155.700R	WNBN243	Police dispatch	146.2
154.650M		Police car to car	
153.920R	KNGU560	Police F3	
151.775	WPCK229	Fire local	
463.625R	WNPO488	Ambulance	
46.58	KTS537	Sewer Authority	

Lower Salford Township

155.100	WXQ936	Township units

Marlborough Township

158.745R	WNKK736	Township units

Montgomery Township

155.610R	WNDP682	Police dispatch	123.0
154.995R	KSL431	Police info	123.0
852.4625R	WNMA731	Colmar Fire Co. operations	
154.295M	KK2496	Colmar Fire Co. local	

Narberth Borough

33.84	WRU754	Fire (Lower Merion)	CS
151.115	WNCP949	Highway Department	

New Hanover Township

33.94	KNHE665	Sassamanville Fire Co. (Berks)	CS
33.94M	KV2825	New Hanover Fire Co. (Berks)	CS
150.995R	WNBK764	Roads Department	

Norristown Borough

501.0625R	KGA484	Police F1	
501.1125R	KGA484	Police F2	
500.9875R	KZV272	Police detectives	
154.370R	KGE336	Fire dispatch	136.5
154.325M	KGE336	Fire fireground	
155.280M	KB61832	Fire Diving Unit	
45.92	KNIB801	Montgomery Hospital Ambulance	136.5
45.96	KNIB801	Montgomery Hospital Ambulance	136.5
155.115R	KDR392	Borough units	
158.835R	WNNY608	Borough units	

North Wales Borough

155.640R		Police dispatch (Lansdale)	107.2
155.535		Police secondary	107.2
156.105	KNCL541	Roads Department	

153.500	KDW508	Water Authority	
158.205	KDW508	Water Authority	
854.9625R	WNRU747	Water Authority	
155.100	WYF922	Borough Units	

Pennsburg Borough

33.94M	KGC549	Fire (Berks County)	CS

Perkiomen Township

155.700R	WNBN325	Police	
153.920R	KNID769	Police	
33.76M		Fire fireground F4	

Plymouth Township

453.875R	WNHG262	Police dispatch	156.7
458.4875M	WNHG262	Police handhelds	156.7
33.76	WNVG973	Fire F3 local	CS
153.830M	KB71125	Fire police	
33.50	KGB857	Harmonville Fire Co. local	CS
45.72	KVF518	Roads Department	
462.725R	KAE0490	Plymouth Community Ambulance	

Pottstown Borough

155.835R	KSQ734	Police dispatch	156.7
155.895	KSQ734	Police	156.7
155.475M	KD31199	Nationwide police emergency	CS
45.94	KGJ600	Police	
45.82M	KGJ699	Police car to car	
33.70	KGF392	Fire dispatch	CS
33.44	KGF392	Fire local	CS
154.385	WPDZ584	Philadelphia Steam Fire Engine Co.	
47.62	KRG827	Goodwill Ambulance	
153.590	KGF491	Water Department	
501.1375R	KNM355	Borough units	

Red Hill Borough

45.92	KYX245	Civil Defense	

Rockledge Borough

154.070M	KGC529	Fire (Abington red band)	
158.805M	KP4139	Roads Department	

Royersford Borough

33.76M		Fire fireground F4	
152.0075P	KMK214	Friendship Ambulance paging	
158.820	KXL419	Borough units	

Salford Township

158.835	KNFK286	Township units	

Schwenksville Borough

153.920R	WNHW725	Police/Borough Authority	

Skippack Township

153.920R	KNBJ907	Police	

45.96M	KNEU476	Ambulance local	136.5
39.58	KNBJ907	Township units	

Souderton Borough

45.96M	KBK651	Ambulance (Bucks County)	123.0
46.00M	KBK651	Ambulance (Bucks County)	123.0
151.010	WNQZ423	Roads Department	

Springfield Township

154.845R	KQM627	Police F1 dispatch	131.8
158.790M	KQM627	Police F2 mobiles	131.8
153.830M	KGC233	Flourtown Fire Co. local	
153.830M	KNET728	Wyndmoor Fire Co. local	
154.205	KGB993	Oreland Fire Co. local	
45.92M	KW3753	Ambulance local	136.5
155.325M	KA78501	Ambulance local	
46.52	KNGG791	Township units	

Telford Borough

151.835	WPDH933	Telford Diving Unit	
151.070		Roads Department	

Towamencin Township

154.965	WYK345	Police local	
155.640R		Police dispatch (Lansdale)	107.2
156.240	WNUM831	Roads Department	

Trappe Borough

33.76M		Fire fireground F4	
33.88M		Fire (Chester County)	
33.98M		Ambulance (Chester County)	
154.370M		Fire (Norristown)	136.5
173.2875B	WNYB713	Municipal Authority data	

Upper Dublin Township

460.550R	WNGL406	Police dispatch	D023
460.550M	WNGL406	Police car to car	D023
460.3625M	KD35382	Police handhelds	D023
154.055	KNFG715	Township units	123.0

Upper Frederick Township

153.920R	WPCZ975	Police/township units	

Upper Gwynedd Township

155.640R		Police dispatch (Lansdale)	107.2
154.980	KRA485	Police	
154.740	KRA485	Police	
155.535	KRA485	Police secondary	107.2
155.475M	KUG809	Nationwide police emergency	CS
33.64	KGJ778	West Point Fire Co. local	CS
33.52	KGJ778	West Point Fire Co. local	CS

Upper Hanover Township

158.745R	KBF471	Police	

Upper Merion Township

154.815R	KFT233	Police dispatch F1	131.8
154.815M	KFT233	Police car to car F2	131.8
153.860M	KCT209	Police/township units F3	123.0
154.680M		Police portables F4	131.8
155.475M		Nationwide police emergency F5	CS
155.595M		Police car to car F6	131.8
33.54	KN87274	Fire local	CS
33.56M	KA78673	Swedesburg Fire Co. local	CS
33.56M		King of Prussia Fire Co. local	CS
154.995	KFE336	Valley Forge Sewer Authority	
153.860	KCT209	Township units	123.0
852.0375R	WNNP372	Township units	

Upper Moreland Township

460.050R	KNIE338	Police dispatch	D023
154.130R	KGC578	Willow Grove Fire Co. repeater	136.5
153.740M	KA82868	Willow Grove Fire Co. F2 firegrnd	CS
153.770M	KGC578	Willow Grove fire police F3	CS
45.96	KLL750	Second Alarmers Rescue F1	136.5
45.92	KLL750	Second Alarmers Rescue F2	136.5
154.130	KBS490	Second Alarmers Rescue fire	CS
155.775	KNGQ669	Township units	127.3
45.12	KSQ272	Sewer Authority	

Upper Pottsgrove Township

45.24	KNJM337	Township units

Upper Providence Township

155.700R	WNBR357	Police	167.9
33.88M	KIL290	Montclare Fire Co. local	CS
46.56	KJI412	Township units	

Upper Salford Township

153.920R	WNBM891	Police
155.955		Township units

West Conshohocken Borough

33.76	WNMB942	George Clay Fire Co. (Consho.)	CS
33.84M	WNMB942	George Clay Fire Co. (L. Merion)	CS

West Norriton Township

45.66M	KA62441	Police local	136.5
153.965R	WNUN582	Police dispatch	107.2
154.055	WNRW759	Township units	

West Pottsgrove Township

154.085	KNEH272	Township units

Whitemarsh Township

45.62	KNDJ422	Police F2	136.5
45.40R	KSK484	Police F1 dispatch	136.5
158.805	KRC621	Township units	

Whitpain Township

45.54	KA60664	Police car to car (old)	136.5
453.675R	WNCW536	Police dispatch	156.7
453.675M	WNCW536	Police car to car	156.7

Worcester Township

153.920R	WNGN242	Police

FACTOID:

Montgomery County actually is the home of one television station, WCAU-TV, Channel 10, which has studios on City Avenue in Lower Merion Township, and hosts the transmitters of two of Philadelphia's four 50-kilowatt powerhouse AM broadcast stations: KYW and WZZD.

NORTHAMPTON COUNTY

Police

154.860R	KVP486	F1 Blue Mountain Control disp.	186.2
154.055R	KFB870	F2 Blue Mountain Control (fire)	186.2
158.730	KGA737	Sheriff's office	
460.500M	KA21075	Surveillance	

Fire

154.340	KNGQ560	F1 Dispatch	136.5
154.385	KNGQ560	F2 Fireground	136.5
154.370	KGG511	Fire	136.5
154.055R	KFB870	Blue Mountain Control fire F2	186.2
155.865M	KB53133	Fire police	

Ambulance

155.235	KXL362	F3 Ambulance to hospital	173.8
155.340	KXL362	F4 Regional hospital net	
155.160	WPAK290	Northeast Search and Rescue	

County operations

155.865M	KB53133	Emergency Management Agency	
453.275R	KXQ987	LANTA buses	67.0
453.225R	WNPH820	LANTA Metro Plus buses (Palmeri)	
155.055R	KFR507	County departments	186.2
155.055P	KFR507	County paging	CS
154.025R	WQI254	Blue Mountain Control roads F3	186.2
155.145M	KA49739	County units	
154.085R	WNFB578	County units	186.2

Municipalities

Allen Township

462.975R	WNCV586	Ambulance corps
154.965	WNAS201	Township units

Bangor Borough

154.010M	WNYU721	Liberty Hose Co. No. 1 local

BETHLEHEM CITY

866.1875R	WNWQ636	Public safety trunked (police, city)
866.875R	WNWQ636	Public safety trunked (police, city)
867.4375R	WNWQ636	Public safety trunked (police, city)
867.900R	WNWQ636	Public safety trunked (police, city)
868.425R	WNWQ636	Public safety trunked (police, city)
868.9125R	WNWQ636	Public safety trunked (police, city)

866.0125R	WNWQ636	Public safety mutual aid - calling	156.7
866.5125R	WNWQ636	Public safety mutual aid - Tac 1	156.7
867.0125R	WNWQ636	Public safety mutual aid - Tac 2	156.7
867.5125R	WNWQ636	Public safety mutual aid - Tac 3	156.7
868.0125R	WNWQ636	Public safety mutual aid - Tac 4	156.7
460.425R	KUG819	Police F1 "Base 1" (old)	
460.325R	KUG819	Police F2 "Info" (old)	
155.610R	KGB386	Police "Base 2" (still on air)	
854.5125R	WNQY657	Police mobile data terminals	
460.625R	KAG519	Fire dispatch	192.8
154.190	KGC619	Fire operations	
155.385	WNRG714	EMS ambulance	
463.175B		EMS hospital to paramedics	
468.175M		EMS paramedics to hospital	
159.795	WNCH469	Valley Transport Ambulance VHF-1	
452.325R	WPPA852	Valley Transport Ambulance UHF-1	
463.775R	WPPA852	Valley Transport Ambulance UHF-2	
464.825R	WPEA525	Schools	
463.375R	WNJU339	Schools	
155.085	KFI523	City units	
155.925	KDN552	City units	
158.760	KDN552	City units	
458.050M	KD35352	City units	

Bethlehem Township

158.805	KYQ582	Police F2
154.085	KQT892	Fire F2
460.5875M	WNUX674	Fire portables
155.280	KSI928	Ambulance
155.340	KSI928	Ambulance
462.950M	KSI928	Ambulance
462.975M	KSI928	Ambulance

Bushkill Township

154.160	WPAR281	Fire local

East Allen Township

153.905M	KA48264	Township units
155.115	KNFU694	Township units

EASTON CITY

460.350R	KTX792	Police F1
460.450R	KTX792	Police F2
460.1375R	KD43736	Police
460.1625R	KD43736	Police
460.1875R	KD43736	Police
460.2125R	KD43736	Police
460.2625R	KD43736	Police
460.2875R	KD43736	Police

158.820R	KGH769	Fire dispatch	127.3
45.92	KGH772	Emergency Squad dispatch	
155.295	KGH772	Emergency Squad	
453.400R	WNJA946	City units	
453.775R	WNQC362	City units	
155.685R	WPDC736	City units	

Forks Township

155.295	KNGT238	Emergency Squad
155.340	KVJ777	Emergency Squad
159.165	WNUB924	Roads Department

Fountain Hill Borough

155.610R	KGF571	Police
158.925	KFF489	Fire

Freemansburg Borough

156.150M	KA61497	Police
155.610R	KA49791	Police (Bethlehem)

Hanover Township

154.310	KLI937	Fire local
150.995	WZX570	Roads Department

Hellertown Borough

155.610R	KGR250	Police	
154.785	KNCX321	Police	
155.745	WSB919	Police	107.2
45.84		Police	
33.98	KGF298	Fire (Lehigh County)	

Lehigh Township

155.490R	KNHY400	Police (Northampton Borough)
154.800R	KNHY400	Police (Lehighton)
460.5375M	WNVT561	Emergency squad portables
153.740M	KB44230	Township units

Lower Nazareth Township

155.160	WNUN593	Hecktown Ambulance

Lower Saucon Township

154.710	KUQ784	Police	107.2
155.745	KUV571	Police (Hellertown)	107.2
465.600M	KD50633	SeWyCo Fire Co. local	
33.98	KUQ786	Fire (Lehigh County)	CS

Moore Township

154.415	WNDV379	Rangers Fire Co. local
155.925	KEP851	Township units

Nazareth Borough

155.340M	KZ6296	Ambulance

North Catasaqua Borough

155.070M	WPDX547	Police car to car
155.475M	WPDX547	Police nationwide mutual aid

Northampton Borough

155.490R	KGA948	Police	136.5
155.715	KJI471	Fire, ambulance dispatch	
155.340M	KZ5067	American Legion Ambulance	
48.36	KAZ274	Borough Utility	
155.040	KJI471	Borough units	

Palmer Township

154.980	KDG244	Police	114.8
465.250M	KD37922	Police mobiles	
154.235M	WNYD855	Fire local	
153.320	WNKA557	Suburban Rescue Squad F2	
		NOTE: Dispatch on 154.340	
155.385	WNKA557	Suburban Rescue Squad F1	

Walnutport Borough

37.10	KNAT361	Sewer Authority
156.000M	KB24573	Borough units

Williams Township

154.115	KNAA932	Township units

Wilson Borough

155.100R	KEY920	Police, fire, ambulance dispatch
156.150M	KB48008	Police

Wind Gap Borough

154.385	WNJB855	Fire local
154.190	WPDJ205	Fire local
453.0875M	KB78422	Borough units
453.1375M	KB78422	Borough units
851.6125R	WNQK993	Borough units

COMMONWEALTH OF PENNSYLVANIA

Law enforcement
Pennsylvania State Police

154.755M		F1 Car to car	186.2
155.580B	154.950M	F2 Channel A/gold	186.2
155.670B	155.910M	F3 Channel B/red	186.2
155.505B	155.850M	F4 Channel C/black	186.2
154.665B	158.910M	F5 Channel D/blue	186.2
154.695B	156.150M	F6 Channel E/green	186.2
154.920B	154.830M	F7 Channel F/white	186.2
155.790B	159.030M	F8 Channel G/brown	186.2
155.475M		F9 Nationwide police emergency	CS
159.210H	154.755M	F10 Mobile repeater	186.2
159.210H	154.755M	F11 Mobile to handheld	123.0
155.460M		F12 Tac 1 radar/surveillance	186.2
151.490M		F13 Tac 2 radar/surveillance	186.2
154.950M		F14 Monitor Channel A	186.2
155.910M		F15 Monitor Channel B	186.2
155.850M		F16 Monitor Channel C	186.2
158.910M		F17 Monitor Channel D	186.2
156.150M		F18 Monitor Channel E	186.2
154.830M		F19 Monitor Channel F	186.2
159.030M		F20 Monitor Channel G	186.2
--troop option--		F21	
155.490B	155.490M	F22 PA regional police/CLEAN	
--troop option--		F23	
--troop option--		F24	
151.295R	159.360M	F25 PA Dept. of Env. Resources	
151.385R	159.420M	F26 PA Dept. of Env. Resources	
151.175R	159.255M	F27 PA Dept. of Env. Resources	
155.370B	155.370M	F28 NY police statewide	
--troop option--		F29	
158.835M	158.835M	F30 PA Emergency Mgt. Agency	CS
162.4/.475/.55		F31 Local NOAA weather	CS
155.580B	155.790M	F32 Old Channel A	186.2

NOTE: This channel plan may vary between troops. Local option channels may include turnpike or county dispatch VHF channels.

Pennsylvania State Police barracks and channel assignments
Troop J - Embreeville (Old A), Avondale (B), Ephrata (B),
               Lancaster (A)
Troop K - Belmont-Philadelphia (B), Limerick (B), Media (C)
Troop L - Hamburg (C), Reading (E), Schuylkill Haven (C)

Troop M - Trevose (A), Dublin (C), Bethlehem (A), Stockertown,
        Fogelsville (B)
Troop N - Lehighton (C), Swiftwater (B)
Troop T - Bowmansville (159.045R), Plymouth Meeting (159.075R)
Executive protection (155.445)

Future 800 MHz system
*NOTE: The following 800 MHz channels have been licensed to the
commonwealth for future use.*

866.4375R	WNYR438	Gulph Mills, Parkesburg
867.625R	WNYR438	Gulph Mills, Parkesburg
866.4375R	WNYR437	Bethlehem, Doylestown, Bensalem
867.625R	WNYR437	Bethlehem, Doylestown, Bensalem

Department of Justice

45.16		Prisons - statewide	
153.905M		Corrections Bureau	
154.950M	KN6259	Drug Control	
155.415R	WYK571	Crime Commission, Philadelphia	
155.445M	KN6259	Drug Control	
155.445	KGW468	Drug Control, Reading	
155.445	KIT934	Drug Control, Salisbury Township	
155.475M	KB28800	Attorney General	
155.490M	KN6259	Drug Control	
156.150M	KP7038	Crime Commission	
158.925M		Corrections Bureau	
453.325	KXM750	Graterford Prison	
453.625	WNPA546	Graterford Prison	
453.375R	WNGY632	Bureau of Narcotics Investigation,127.3 Philadelphia	
460.200R	WNAP578	Dept. of Justice, Allentown	179.9
460.200R	KNFQ458	Dept. of Justice, Center Valley	179.9
460.200R	WNAL710	Dept. of Justice, Reading	179.9
460.200	WPDM644	Dept. of Justice, Reading	179.9
460.475R	KNAD714	Dept. of Justice, Philadelphia	179.9
460.475R	KNAD714	Dept. of Justice, Haverford	179.9
460.475R	KNAD742	Dept. of Justice, Gulph Mills	179.9
460.475R	KNAD742	Dept. of Justice, Philadelphia	179.9
460.475R	WNBX473	Dept. of Justice, Philadelphia	179.9
460.475R	WNRL506	Dept. of Justice, Concordville	179.9
460.475R	WNYI923	Dept. of Justice, Bensalem	179.9
460.475R	WNYL743	Dept. of Justice, Lancaster	179.9
460.475R	WNXP568	Dept. of Justice, Elm (Lancaster)	179.9

*NOTE: Primary user of 460 MHz Department of Justice channels is
the Bureau of Narcotics Investigation.*

Miscellaneous law enforcement

45.30M	KC4344	Liquor Control Board handhelds
153.785M	various	Department of Treasury investigators
153.785M		Horse Racing Commission (Phila. Park)
158.760R	WYF425	Liquor Control Board, Philadelphia
158.760R	WYF426	Liquor Control, Graterford/Malvern
158.760R	WYF428	Liquor Control Board, Bethlehem
158.760R	KVT778	Cigarette and Beverage Taxes, Phila.
453.1375M	KB32403	Liquor Control Board handhelds

Department of Environmental Resources

Fish Commission

45.04		F1	136.5
44.96		F2	
44.84		F3	

Game Commission

44.64		F1
44.84		F2
44.88		F3
151.370R		Statewide

Forest Bureau

151.175R		F1
151.295R		F2
151.385R		F3 (Philadelphia area)
151.400R		F4

State Parks

151.385		F1	103.5
151.445		F2 primary	103.5
155.370R	WNBK762	Washington Crossing State Park	123.0
153.935	KZH933	Washington Crossing State Park	
453.725	KOM417	Strasburg Historic Site	

Miscellaneous

31.54B	KGA621	Temporary bases
31.66B	KGA621	Temporary bases

State agencies

Department of Health

33.94	KJR232	Wernersville State Hospital fire dept.
35.64P	WZY497	Embreeville State Hospital, W. Chester
37.90P	KFX789	Haverford State Hospital
45.14	KGD352	Pennhurst State School, Spring City
46.54	KAQ708	Embreeville State Hospital
46.54	KAN858	Haverford State Hospital
46.54	KAX200	Eastern State School, Cornwells Hghts

46.54	KDX463	Wernersvlle State Hospital	
153.845	KDA631	Youth Development Center, Phila.	
154.055	KRB479	SPIASU, Cornwells Heights	
155.250	KGA810	Philadelphia State Hospital police	
155.700R	KGF405	Allentown State Hospital	
155.730	KNER810	Norristown State Hospital	
157.450P	KYF372	Philadelphia State Hospital paging	
157.450P	KYS896	Norristown State Hospital paging	
157.450P	KNFR838	Woodhaven Center, Phila., paging	
158.835R	KGF405	Allentown State Hospital	
453.300R	KNDD600	Embreeville State Hospital	
453.375	KDX331	Wernersvlle State Hospital	
453.875	KKD503	Pennhurst State School	

Emergency Management Agency

45.16	KFF342	Graterford	
45.16	KLK601	Nockamixon	
453.525R	various	Statewide system	
158.835M		statewide mobiles	CS

Department of Transportation (PennDOT)

47.04B	KGB673	Center Valley	
	KGB679	Reading	
	KGB676	Easton	
47.30B		F1 Base to mobile	136.5
	KGB578	Buckingham	
	KGB580	Coatesville	
	KGB675	Eagleville	
	KGB576	Media	
	KGB577	Philadelphia	
	KSO955	Trevose	
	KGB673	Center Valley	146.2
	KGB676	Easton	
	KGB572	Lancaster	
	KGB679	Reading	
	KGC835	Rosemont	
47.38M	KA2163	F1 mobile to base	136.5
47.28B		F2 - Same stations as F1	136.5
47.28M	KA2163	Mobile to mobile	
151.010M	KL6207	Statewide	136.5
151.100M	KM8424	Supervisors	136.5
159.195M	KM8424	Statewide	136.5
453.4125R	KD34785	Statewide	
453.4625R	WNVY939	Bucks County usage	
453.7125R	WNVY943	Delaware County usage	

458.2125M	WPCR929	Lancaster County usage
458.5625M	WNYR682	Statewide
1610 kHz	WPDX549	Travelers Information Station broadcasts, portable operation
530 kHz	WPDX548	Travelers Information Station broadcasts, portable operation

Pennsylvania Turnpike Commission

159.075R		East-West, E of Morgantown	CS
159.045R		NE Extension; W of Morgantown	CS
159.000M		Mobile to mobile	CS

NOTE: CTCSS tone 179.9 is being used on the repeater inputs for 159.075R and 159.045R at present and you may find some use of 179.9 on 159.000 simplex. However, the repeater outputs remain carrier squelch.

154.755M		State police radar patrols F1	186.2
151.490M		State police radar patrols Tac 2	186.2
453.150R		Tunnels	CS
453.300R		Tunnels	CS
75.74	WNUZ538	Link, Lionville	
75.76	WNUZ538	Link, Emmaus	
75.50	WNUZ538	Link, Bowmanstown	
75.94	WNWX249	Link, Willow Grove	
75.74	WNWX249	Link, Morgantown	
75.74	WNWX249	Link, Cornwall	
530 kHz	WNRW290	Travelers Information Station broadcasts, Washington Twp., Lehigh County (NE Extension)	

Miscellaneous state

154.100	WNIK811	State units, Philadelphia
169.500B	WPBA587	State remote links, Lancaster County
453.1125M	WPBN888	State units, Montgomery County
453.2125R	WNZS327	State units, statewide
453.375R	WNGY632	State units, Philadelphia
453.8375R	WNZS327	State units, statewide
464.500M	WPCT577	PA Higher Education Assistance Agy.
464.550M	WPCT577	PA Higher Education Assistance Agy.
469.500M	WPCT577	PA Higher Education Assistance Agy.
506.4375R	WIJ504	State units, Trevose

ATLANTIC COUNTY

Police

155.730	KXD237	Dispatch	
155.685R	KGN564	District 10 dispatch	118.8
156.210	KXD237	Intersystem	
156.090	KXD237	F1 Sheriff's office	118.8
155.070	KGN564	F2 Sheriff's office	118.8
155.415R	KXD237	Detectives, medical examiner	
154.755	WNRL509	Police	
155.610R	WNMV668	Corrections transportation, jail	

Fire

154.310	KQO207	F1 Dispatch	118.8
154.355	KQO207	F2 Fireground	118.8
154.265	KQO207	F3 South Jersey mutual aid	
155.925		F4 Municipal F4	
153.785M	KB28016	F5 SPEN 4 - mutual aid	131.8

Ambulance

155.175		F1 Dispatch	118.8
155.340		F2 Ambulance to hospital/HEAR	
154.310		F3 Fire coordination	CS
155.925		F4 Municipal	
463.050B		Paramedics primary	
468.050M		Paramedics primary	
463.150B		Paramedics secondary	
468.150M		Paramedics secondary	

County operations

155.040R	KSN233	Mosquito control/Utilities	
158.775R	WZZ239	Emergency Management/buses	118.8
151.040R	KCU266	Roads Department - operations	
156.060M	KCU266	Roads Department	
154.980R	WNNG471	County units	
155.040R	KSW233	Utilities Authority	
153.860M	KSW233	Utilities Authority	
453.800R	WPAN844	Utilities Authority	

District 10

Mid-Atlantic District 10 includes Egg Harbor City, Galloway Township, Absecon, Mullica Township and Port Republic City (fire)

155.685R	KGN564	F1 Police dispatch	118.8

155.310		F2 Police lookup	118.8
156.210		F3 County intersystem	
155.010		F4 Police car to car	118.8
155.925		Municipal	
155.175		Ambulance/rescue	118.8

Municipalities

Absecon City

154.740R	KNIM202	Police dispatch F1/Fire	
155.310		Police lookups F2	
156.210	KEE206	Police intersystem F3	
155.010M	KNIM202	Police car to car F4	
155.730	KEE206	Police - county	
155.685R	KNIM202	Police (Egg Harbor City)	
155.595	KEE206	Police - old dispatch	
154.755M	KNIM202	Police car to car	
156.090M	KNIM202	Police car to car	
154.310	KNCT731	Fire dispatch F1	
154.355	WRG644	Bayview Fire Co. local	
154.355	KNCT731	Fire fireground F2	
154.010M	KNCT731	Fire (Egg Harbor Township)	
154.175M	KNCT731	Fire (Pleasantville)	
154.025R		Fire (Atlantic City)	114.8
154.370R	KNCT731	Fire local F3	
153.785M	KNEH425	Fire F4 (SPEN 4)	
155.280	KNIF290	Ambulance	
155.925	KNEH425	Municipal F4	
156.015M	KNEH425	Emergency Management	
155.760	KNEH425	City units	
155.865M	KNEH425	City units	

ATLANTIC CITY

155.130R	KEB384	Police dispatch F1	118.8
155.010	KGW335	Police secondary F2	
155.190R	KGW341	Police info F3	
155.310R	KGW344	Police county F4	CS
156.210	KGW335	Police mutual aid F5	
155.730	KEB384	Police county F6	
155.415	KEB384	Police detectives	
159.090P	KEB384	Police paging	
453.350R	KEB384	Police Tac 1	
453.600R	KEB384	Police Tac 2	
460.150R	KEB384	Police Tactical 1	156.7
460.200R	KNCE996	Police Tac 4	156.7
460.325R	KNCE996	Police Tac 3 detectives	156.7

460.425R	KEB384	Police Tactical 2	156.7
460.525R	KEB384	Police data units	156.7
154.025R	KJW576	Fire dispatch F1	114.8
154.310	KDJ444	Fire F3 county	CS
154.415R	KDJ444	Fire F4	114.8
154.415M	KDJ444	Fire F6	114.8
153.770M	KDJ444	Fire F2 car to car	114.8
158.955M	KJW576	Fire F5 car to car	114.8
155.220	KFT605	Ambulance F1 dispatch	
155.175	KIU489	Ambulance F2 aid	118.8
155.340	KIU489	Ambulance HEAR	
453.350R	KIU815	Beach patrol	
453.600R	WNLN712	City units	
453.675R	WNKM636	City units	
453.100R	WNNN676	Housing Authority	
453.875R	WNNN676	Housing Authority	
154.055	KIL205	Traffic	118.8
154.100R	KFO847	Public works	118.8
158.865	KZV396	City tow trucks	
157.470	KUU819	City tow trucks	
39.34	KEB384	Beach Patrol	
153.725	KRO593	Water Department	
158.265	KRO265	Water Department	
151.655M	KD37435	Schools	

Brigantine City

156.210	KEB287	Police mutual aid F2	
460.025R	KEB287	Police dispatch	156.7
458.975M	KDC317	Police F2 car to car	156.7
453.975R	KDC317	Fire fireground	156.7
154.250	WNCR668	Fire/Rescue dispatch	123.0
155.820	KDC317	Fire F2	

Buena Borough

155.250	KEG737	Police dispatch	
155.730	KEG737	Police countywide	
156.210	KEG737	Police mutual aid	
155.805	KRI783	Borough units	

Buena Vista Township

155.040	KGK544	Township units	

Corbin City

155.160	KZG277	Ambulance local	

Egg Harbor City

155.715	WNSU454	City units	

Egg Harbor Township

155.655R	KDP285	Police dispatch F1	118.8
155.250	KDP285	Police info F2	

156.210	KDP285	Police mutual aid	
154.770M	KDP285	Police	
155.925	KFZ750	Municipal	
154.010	KDP284	Fire dispatch F1	
156.015M	WNAW653	Township units	

Folsom Borough
| 155.730 | KAF990 | Police dispatch | |
| 155.925 | KAN399 | Municipal | |

Galloway Township
155.550R	WNNU834	Police	
154.145	WNPV418	Fire local	
155.955R	WNNY998	Township units	

Hamilton Township
154.815R	WNJN646	Police dispatch	118.8
155.250	KFM400	Police	
155.550	KFM400	Police	
156.210	KFM400	Police mutual aid	

Hammonton Town
155.250	KEE202	Police	
155.550	KEE202	Police	
155.685	KEE202	Police (District 10)	118.8
155.730	KEE202	Police countywide	
156.210	KEE202	Police mutual aid	
158.760	KJG966	Roads Department	

Linwood City
155.625	KEA288	Police dispatch	118.8
155.730	KEA288	Police countywide	
156.210	KEA288	Police mutual aid	
155.925	KNBL467	Municipal	

Longport Borough
155.535	KEA308	Police dispatch	118.8
155.730	KEA308	Police countywide	
156.210	KEA308	Police mutual aid	
155.925	KFX394	Municipal	

Margate City
155.535	KEB407	Police dispatch F1	118.8
156.210	KEB407	Police mutual aid F2	
154.400	KNAB750	Fire dispatch	D152
155.925	KZV325	Municipal	

Mullica Township
| 155.925 | KTZ363 | Municipal | |

Northfield City
155.625	KEA300	Police dispatch F1	118.8
156.210	KEA300	Police mutual aid F2	
465.6125M	WNVC745	Fire portables	

155.925	KUA751	Municipal	

Pleasantville City

155.595	KNIV563	Police dispatch	118.8
155.730M	KNIV563	Police countywide	
154.175	KEF328	Fire dispatch	
155.865	KRB437	City units	

Port Republic City

151.865	WPAP359	Fire local	

Somers Point City

155.625	KEB428	Police dispatch	118.8
156.210	KEB428	Police mutual aid	
154.250	WNPH234	Fire dispatch	
154.070M	KNJF454	Fire local	
154.205	KNJF454	Fire local	
155.295	KYJ298	Rescue Squad local	
155.925	KFK683	Municipal	
155.880	KFK683	City units	

Ventnor City

155.535	KEA315	Police dispatch F1	118.8
155.925	KTK638	Police local F2	
154.710M	KEA315	Police mobiles F3	
155.730	KEA315	Police county F4	
156.210	KEA315	Police mutual aid F5	
460.075R	WNWH826	Police operations	D732
45.32	KTH638	Beach Patrol F6	
155.280M	WZU379	Ambulance local	
453.050R	WNBB937	City units	

BURLINGTON COUNTY

Police

500.7875R	P1	127.3
	Florence, Willingboro,	
	Burlington City, Burlington Township	
500.6875R	P2	127.3
	Delanco, Beverly, Delran,	
	Riverside, Riverton, Cinnaminson,	
	Moorestown, Maple Shade, Palmyra,	
	Edgewater Park	
500.7375R	P3	127.3
	Westhampton, Easthampton,	
	Mount Holly, Lumberton, Hainesport	
500.6625R	P4	127.3
	New Hanover, Fieldsboro,	
	Bordentown City, Bordentown Twp.,	
	Mansfield, Springfield, North Hanover,	
	Wrightstown, Chesterfield	
500.5125R	P5 - Countywide information/tac	127.3
500.4875R	P6 - Prosecutor, sheriff, corrections	127.3
500.9625R	P7	127.3
	Pemberton Twp., Pemberton Borough	
500.8625R	P8	127.3
	Mount Laurel, Evesham,	
	Medford, Medford Lakes	
500.5375R	P9	127.3
	Willingboro	
500.7125R	P10 - Prosecutor's office	127.3
500.8625R	Tacony-Palmyra,	127.3
	Burlington-Bristol toll bridge police	

NOTE: Various call signs are used in this UHF system.

Fire

154.220	KMA584	F1 Fire dispatch	127.3
154.190M	KLY718	F2 North fireground	127.3
154.205M	KF5746	F2 South fireground	127.3
154.400M	KF5746	F3 North fireground	127.3
154.250M	KF5746	F3 South fireground	127.3
154.205M	KF5746	F4 North drills	127.3
154.190M	KLY718	F4 South drills	127.3
---- ----		F5 Local municipal frequency	
154.265M	KMA584	F6 South Jersey mutual aid	127.3

154.250R	KMA587	North repeater	127.3
154.400R	KMA584	South repeater	127.3
154.130	KEI933	District 18 (Pemberton)	127.3
159.300	KQF872	Forest fire coordination	
159.375	KQF872	Forest fire coordination	

Ambulance

155.295	KMA728	E1 Dispatch	127.3
155.340	WYE416	E2 Hospital to ambulance/HEAR	127.3
155.280	KMA728	E3 State mutual aid	
155.325		E4 Ambulance to hospital	
155.355		E5 Ambulance to hospital	
		(or local municipal frequency)	
154.265	KMA584	E6 South Jersey fire mutual aid	
154.250R	KMA587	E7 North fire	127.3
154.400R	KMA584	E8 South fire	127.3
463.025B		Paramedics MED-2 primary	
468.025M		Paramedics MED-2 primary	
463.050B		Paramedics secondary	162.2
468.050M		Paramedics secondary	162.2
462.975R		MedComm MICUs MED-10	

County operations

155.805P	KQL692	County paging	127.3
155.805	KQL692	Emergency Mgt., jail, courthouse	127.3
45.80	KEB475	Roads, mosquito control	136.5
151.010	KDE220	Toll bridge maintenance	127.3
39.12	WNVK860	County units	
453.4625M	WNUD284	County units	

Municipalities

Bordentown City

155.685	KEB370	Police F2	
155.490	KEB370	Police	131.8
155.925	KNAB517	City units/police F3	
508.0375R	WII868	Sewerage Authority	

Bordentown Township

500.6125R	KNR666	Police dispatch	127.3
151.070	WNRR561	Roads Department	
155.925	WQN911	Township units	

Burlington City

500.3375R	KNM939	Police	127.3
501.0625R	WIK805	Police operations	127.3
154.085	WYG493	City units	

155.805	WYG493	Emergency Management	

Burlington Township

154.130	KDN522	Fire (Pemberton)	127.3
155.805	WZM637	Emergency Management	
155.820	KQS602	Township units	

Chesterfield Township

155.880	WSL882	Township units	

Cinnaminson Township

500.4125R	KNM937	Police	127.3
154.280M	KA76280	Fire local F5	127.3
151.205	KNGV995	Sewerage Authority	
153.800	WQS399	Township units	

Delanco Township

155.745	KIB890	Township units	

Delran Township

155.490	WNZY631	Police	
155.940	KRC678	Township units/police/EMS	

Easthampton Township

155.715	WNBU845	Township units	

Edgewater Park Township

155.745	KNGQ657	Township units	

Evesham Township

154.980	KLE777	Fire local F5	
500.4375R	KDB215	Township units	
508.9875R	WIK710	Township units	

Florence Township

154.800	KEA396	Police	
155.715	WRU808	Police dispatch	127.3

Hainesport Township

506.4875R	WIJ652	Police	127.3

Lumberton Township

154.995	KVF581	Township units	

Maple Shade Township

501.0125R	KNM941	Police dispatch	127.3
155.760	WXQ924	Township units/EMS	

Medford Township

500.6375R	KNM938	Police/EMS dispatch	127.3
501.3375R	KNM938	Police	127.3
506.3125R	WIK615	Township units	
154.995	KRZ965	Township units	CS

Medford Lakes Borough

500.6125R	KNM929	Police	127.3
155.880	KNDT273	Borough units	

Moorestown Township

500.4125R	KNQ505	Police dispatch	127.3

| 154.130 | KNCG434 | Fire (Pemberton) | 127.3 |
| 153.860 | KCW694 | Township units | |

Mount Holly Township

| 154.040 | KDV359 | Township units | |

Mount Laurel Township

500.5875R	KNM978	Police	127.3
453.825R	WNAH635	Municipal Utilities Authority	
155.760	KIZ263	Public Works	
154.980	KIZ263	Township units	

New Hanover Township

| 501.1375R | KNQ866 | Police | 127.3 |
| 155.880 | WZU266 | Township units | |

North Hanover Township

| 155.880 | WYV343 | Township units | |

Palmyra Borough

| 508.6875R | WIJ961 | Borough units | |
| 156.000 | KUX306 | Borough units | |

Pemberton Township

| 154.130 | KBS700 | Magnolia Road Fire Co. F5 | 127.3 |
| 153.800 | KJQ981 | Township units | |

Riverside Township

| 155.835 | KUE645 | Police | |

Shamong Township

| 154.115 | WNKJ384 | Township units | |

Southampton Township

| 155.025 | WYC822 | Township units | |

Tabernacle Township

| 153.815 | KNHM322 | Township units | |
| 154.115 | KNHM322 | Township units | |

Willingboro Township

500.5375R	KNM942	Police	127.3
460.0875R	WPBP837	Police portables	
460.2875R	WPBP837	Police portables	
154.115	KNHM971	Utility Authority F1	
153.980M	KNHM971	Utility Authority F2	
153.980	KBZ424	Township units	

Woodland Township

| 155.025 | WXY203 | Township units | |

CAMDEN COUNTY

Police

507.1125R	WIK700	Zone 1 - North	192.8
		Gloucester City, Haddonfield,	
		Tavistock, Audubon, Audubon Park,	
		Haddon Township, Oaklyn,	
		Collingswood	
507.5125R	WIK701	Zone 2 - East Central	192.8
		Magnolia, Runnemede, Barrington,	
		Lawnside, Haddon Heights, Bellmawr,	
		Mount Ephraim, Brooklawn	
507.1625R	WIK699	Zone 3 - South	192.8
		Lindenwold, Laurel Springs, Stratford,	
		Somerdale, Gibbsboro, Pine Hill,	
		Pine Valley, Clementon	
507.5625R	WII555	Zone 4 - East	192.8
		Waterford, Berlin Borough,	
		Berlin Township, Chesilhurst	
508.7875R	WII555	New Zone 5 - Northwest	192.8
		Gloucester City, Haddon Heights,	
		Bellmawr, Mount Ephraim	
508.0125R	WII555	Zone 1 & 2 switchover	192.8
507.9125R	WIK697	Zone 3 & 4 switchover	192.8
508.8875R	WIK280	Berlin police switchover	192.8
507.6625R	WII555	Data F5	192.8
507.7875R	WII555	Park police/sheriff	192.8
508.7125R	KNBB284	Sheriff	192.8
508.7375R	KNBB284	Sheriff	192.8
507.9375R	WIK698	Prosecutor's office	192.8
507.2125R	WII555	Police - future use	
507.6125R	WII555	Police - future use	
507.7125R	WII555	Police - future use	
507.7625R	WII555	Police - future use	
507.8375R	WII555	Police - future use	
508.7625R	WIK280	Police - future use	
508.8125R	WIK280	Police - future use	
508.8375R	WIK280	Police - future use	
508.8625R	WIK280	Police - future use	
508.8875R	WIK280	Police - future use	

Other:

155.370R	KXQ955	North dispatch - old	192.8
155.565R	KXQ955	South dispatch - old	192.8
156.210	KXQ955	Central dispatch/park police - old	192.8

154.740R	KNBB284	Sheriff's office - old	167.9
500.5625R	KWO598	Prosecutor's office	
501.1375R	WIE946	Prosecutor's office	
155.100	KCI689	Park Police F2 - old	
39.12	WNVG781	Statewide	

Fire

154.430	KVP480	F1 Dispatch	192.8
154.385	KVP480	F2 Fireground - south	192.8
154.160	KVP480	F3 Fireground - north	192.8
155.085	KVJ770	F4 Fire coordinator	192.8
153.770	KVP480	F5 Camden City dispatch	192.8
154.265	KVP480	F6 South Jersey mutual aid	
159.375		F7 Forest fire	

Ambulance

155.235	WQN900	E1 Dispatch	192.8
155.340	WQN900	E2 HEAR - ambulance to hospital	192.8
155.280	WQN900	E3 Statewide mutual aid	
153.785M		E4 SPEN-4 mutual aid	131.8
155.400	WNLC496	E5 Camden UMDNJ ambulance disp.	
463.125B		Paramedics primary	
468.125M		Paramedics primary	
463.150B		Paramedics secondary	
468.150M		Paramedics secondary	

County operations

155.100	KCI689	Park Commission	
151.430R	WNKG809	Parks	
500.3125R	KUZ647	Roads Department F1	114.8
500.3125M	KUZ647	Roads Department F2 mobiles	114.8
500.3625R	KUZ647	Roads Department F3	114.8
500.3625M	KUZ647	Roads Department F4 mobiles	114.8
151.055	KCR261	Roads	
457.325M	WNFX518	County Municipal Water	
856.8875T	WNCE573	Public safety use	
462.700	KAE2685	County units	

Municipalities

Audubon Borough

155.025	WNFX974	Police F2	

Barrington Borough

155.715	KNGH287	Police F2	192.8

Bellmawr Borough

155.715	KLR291	Police F2	

Berlin Borough

155.820	KEJ394	Police F2	

Berlin Township

155.820	KNAW772	Police F2	

Brooklawn Borough

153.980	KNFZ621	Police F2	

CAMDEN CITY

460.075R	KEB210	Police foot F1	151.4
460.125R	KEB210	Police dispatch F2	151.4
460.225R	KEB210	Police data F3	151.4
460.300R	KEB210	Police detectives, traffic, info F4	151.4
460.550R	KEB210	Police F5 not used	
153.770	KEG405	Fire dispatch F1	192.8
154.160	KEG405	Fire fireground mutual aid F2	192.8
153.905	KGJ621	Fire fireground - city	
155.400	WNLC496	EMS	
861.1875T	KB37688	Mayor's car phone	
501.3125R	WIJ485	City units	
856.9875T	WNWG655	Trunked public safety units	
463.2875M	WPDU669	Waterfront Management Corp.	
463.5875R	WPDU669	Waterfront Management Corp.	
464.2125M	WPDU669	Waterfront Management Corp.	
464.4625M	WPDU669	Waterfront Management Corp.	
469.2875M	WPDU669	Waterfront Management Corp.	

Cherry Hill Township

155.520R	KEA395	Police dispatch F1	136.5
155.310R	KEA395	Police mobiles F2	
155.010M	KEA395	Police detectives F3	
154.445	KDO312	Fire local	192.8
156.105	KJF706	Roads Department	
158.835	KNCW929	Township units	

Chesilhurst Borough

159.150	KNDV707	Police	
155.145	KUX515	Police F2	
155.370	WNHR830	Police	

Clementon Borough

155.880	KLK573	Police F2	

Collingswood Borough

155.040	KNFD336	Police F2 & Fire	

Gloucester City

155.775	KKC612	Police F2	
154.175	KNFQ671	Fire local	

155.925	WNND855	City units	
Gloucester Township			
506.9375R	WIK941	Police dispatch F1	100.0
506.8875R	WIL505	Police operations F2	100.0
155.595R	KED859	Police	
155.565	WNPE568	Police	
460.0375R	KD51349	Police	
72.74	WGI525	Police transmitter link	
158.175	various	Utilities Authority	
155.040	KTK729	Township units	
Haddon Township			
155.490	WNBE591	Police	
151.085	KQL915	Roads Department	
151.115	KQL915	Roads Department	
Haddon Heights Borough			
155.535	KEB374	Police	
155.100	KNBT919	Borough units	
Haddonfield Borough			
155.430	KEB467	Police	
155.040	KBN496	Borough units	
Lawnside Borough			
155.925	KQG327	Police F2 & Roads	
Lindenwold Borough			
155.535	KNCK896	Police F2	
153.995	KSS271	Roads Department	
Magnolia Borough			
155.145	KVJ671	Police F2	
Merchantville Borough			
460.200R	KTR803	Police (DVP used)	203.5
507.4125R	KTR803	Police	
48.44	KTL335	Water Department	
Mount Ephraim Borough			
155.865	WNMR931	Police F2	
155.370	WNMR931	Police	
Oaklyn Borough			
154.740		Police F2	
155.955	WZE747	Borough units	
Pennsauken Township			
460.200R	KTB350	Police F1 (DVP used)	203.5
460.325R	KTB350	Police F2 (DVP used)	203.5
155.610	KEB345	Police old system	
154.205	WNQF665	Fire local	
48.44	KTL335	Water Department	
453.325R	KNFS536	Zoning office	
158.745M	WNDJ355	Township units	

453.425R	WNDJ355	Township units	192.8
458.8875M	WNDJ355	Township units	

Pine Hill Borough

155.805	KVM279	Police F2	

Pine Valley Borough

155.715R	WPBG915	Borough units	

Runnemede Borough

155.805	KRW442	Police F2/borough units	

Somerdale Borough

155.145	KLP904	Police F2	

Stratford Borough

155.535	KEJ399	Police	

Voorhees Township

155.745R	KDZ363	Police	203.5
154.845M	KA48424	Police car to car	192.8
154.800	KNIC328	Police	192.8
45.68	KYQ226	Roads Department	
861.1875T	WNAY813	Public safety use	

Waterford Township

155.145	WNRB811	Fire local	

Westville Borough

507.3375R	WIK982	Police operations	

Winslow Township

508.9125R	WIK314	Police	192.8
508.9375R	WIK314	Police	192.8
154.800R	KDP992	Police F2	192.8
460.1375R	WNZC283	Police	
460.2875R	WNZC283	Police	
154.310	KJL493	Fire (Atlantic County)	
154.355M	KJL493	Fire (Atlantic County)	
453.900M	KJL493	Fire vehicle repeater	
155.175M	KA89522	Ambulance (Atlantic County)	118.8
155.145	KDT253	Township units	

CAPE MAY COUNTY

Police
155.070R	KGC775	F1 County north	118.8
155.190R	WNQF854	F2 Access information	118.8
156.210	KXX490	F3 Countywide net	
155.010R	KXX490	F4 Car to car	118.8
155.415R	KXX490	F5 South/prosecutor	118.8
159.090M	KP7071	Prosecutor's office	118.8
154.785R	KNIG205	Police	
154.725M	WPCP813	Police car to car	
460.225R	WNLR454	County detectives	

Fire
154.130		F1 Dispatch	118.8
154.190		F2 Fireground	118.8
154.265		F3 South Jersey mutual aid	118.8
154.250	WPCI504	Fire	

Ambulance
155.295		F1 Dispatch	118.8
155.340		F2 HEAR ambulance to hospital	118.8
155.280	WPCI999	Statewide mutual aid	
463.000B		Paramedics primary	
468.000M		Paramedics primary	
463.100B		Paramedics secondary	
468.100M		Paramedics secondary	

County operations
154.085	KWQ673	Emergency Management
155.745	WRB369	Public Works/Roads
158.820R	KVJ722	Public works
453.150R	KNDQ868	County units
153.995	WNJD914	County units (Erma)
453.9125R	KD31202	County units
151.010R	WNXQ587	Roads Department
453.850R	WNXJ935	Municipal Utilities Authority
453.925R	WPDY652	County units
453.775R	WPDY652	County units

Municipalities
Avalon Borough
155.670	KEC695	Police old F1

156.210	KEC695	Police old mutual aid F2	
460.125R	WNCW582	Police dispatch	173.8
154.310	KCX941	Fire local	118.8
155.235	KMA204	Ambulance local	
155.955	KNIV613	Borough units	
453.750R	WNCG543	Borough units F1	
453.750M	WNCG543	Borough units F2	
453.9875R	WNCG543	Borough units	

Cape May City

155.700	KEB419	Police dispatch F1	118.8
156.210	KEB419	Police mutual aid F2	
155.265	WNJL468	Ambulance	
153.860	KJY311	Public Works	
153.965	KNBE993	City units	
453.550R	WNSX269	City units	

Cape May Point Borough

155.085	WYC538	Borough units

Dennis Township

154.980	WRB523	Township units

Lower Township

155.700	KBH341	Police dispatch F1	118.8
156.210	KBH341	Police mutual aid F2	
154.370	WPAV855	Fire local	
154.400R	WPBX462	Fire operations	
155.820	KTL700	Public works	
451.125M	WPBY990	Utilities	
151.100R	WPBH208	Roads Department	
154.055R	WPAD534	Township units	

Middle Township

155.700	KEO252	Police dispatch F1	118.8
156.210	KEO252	Police mutual aid F2	
154.875R	KEO252	Police	118.8
156.180R	WNPK435	Road Department	
155.115	KRM348	Township units	
155.055R	WPCP900	Township units	

North Wildwood City

155.640	KEB401	Police dispatch F1	118.8
156.210	KEB401	Police mutual aid F2	
155.010M	KEB401	Police mobiles F3	118.8
155.190M	KEB401	Police info F4	
166.250M	WPDM642	Fire local	
155.220	KCS346	Rescue dispatch	118.8
155.340M	KCS346	Rescue HEAR system	
158.760	WYK347	Emergency Management	
155.160	WNLU635	Beach patrol	118.8

Ocean City

460.350R	KEA639	Police dispatch	173.8
156.210	WYX303	Police intersystem	
154.445R	KEE540	Fire dispatch F1	141.3
154.310	KEE540	Fire F2	
155.295	KWT654	Rescue dispatch F1	118.8
155.280	KWT654	Rescue mutual aid F2	
155.340	KWT654	Rescue HEAR F3	
155.175	KWT654	Rescue (Atlantic County)	118.8
155.145	KRS208	Beach Patrol (old)	
453.950R	KDS600	Beach Patrol/tag inspectors	173.8
153.845	KDS600	Public Works	141.3
462.125R	WYM728	Housing Authority	
453.700R	WNNQ561	City units	
453.375R	WPCI513	City units	
453.250R	WNXJ934	City units	

Sea Isle City

155.565R	WNBZ382	Police dispatch	118.8
155.670	KBQ631	Police F1	
156.210	KBQ631	Police mutual aid F2	
154.040	KDG829	City units	
155.805	WPCD647	City units	

Stone Harbor Borough

155.670	KEJ845	Police dispatch F1
156.210	KEJ845	Police mutual aid F2
153.830M	WPAP551	Fire local
154.385R	WPAP551	Fire operations
155.235	WNST853	Rescue
451.200M	WPDW826	Utilities
155.955	KNDT917	Borough units
155.145	WPED881	Borough units

Upper Township

154.220	KTL511	Seaville Fire Co. local
154.980	KZQ774	Township units
158.940R	KZQ774	Township units
154.995	WNVQ918	Township units
155.025	WNYU764	Township units

West Cape May Borough

155.040	WXY303	Borough units

West Wildwood Borough

155.640	WNGA786	Police dispatch F1
156.210	WNGA786	Police mutual aid F2
154.250	WNVS331	Fire local

Wildwood City

154.965R	WNAB302	Police F1 dispatch	118.8

154.965M	WNAB302	Police F2 car to car	118.8
155.640	KEA846	Police intersystem F1	118.8
155.190	KEA846	Police info F2	
155.010	KEA846	Police mobiles F3	118.8
156.210	KEA846	Police mutual aid F4	
155.745	KTR724	Public Works	118.8
155.745	WNVK259	Beach patrol	203.5
39.82	KNAU363	City units	
39.92	KNAU363	City units	

Wildwood Crest Borough

155.640	KEA750	Police dispatch F1	118.8
156.210	KEA750	Police mutual aid F2	
158.865	WXB812	Public works/Beach patrol	118.8

Woodbine Borough

155.670	KUU349	Police dispatch F1	
156.210	KUU349	Police mutual aid F2	
154.040	KCN357	Borough units	

FACTOID:
It may be hard to believe, but some of the largest cities in New Jersey can be found on the Jersey Shore -- that is if you count bodies during the summer. Ocean City, which normally is home to 18,000 yearround residents, bulges to 150,000 people in the summer. Likewise, the Wildwoods (Wildwood, North Wildwood and Wildwood Crest) normally have 13,500 residents, but the number bumps to 216,000 summer folks.

CUMBERLAND COUNTY

Police

155.865	KXK420	F1 Sheriff's office dispatch	
156.210	KUJ524	F2 Intersystem/mutual aid	
155.085	KXK420	F3 Sheriff's office	
458.8875M	KXK420	Jail paging, operations	

Channelization
F1 - Town dispatch channel
F2 - 156.210 alarms/special events
F3 - Town car-to-car channel
F4 - 155.730R Vineland info center

Fire

154.430	KNAA943	F1 Dispatch	179.9
154.325	KNAA943	F2 Fireground	179.9
154.265	KNAA943	F3 South Jersey mutual aid	
33.74	KNAA943	F4 Vineland dispatch	
154.400R	WPDJ988	Fire operations	
154.175	WPDJ987	Fire	
159.375		Forest Fire coordination	

Ambulance

155.220	WSU218	F1 Dispatch 1	179.9
155.280	WSU218	F2 On scene	179.9
155.340	WSU218	F3 Hospital to ambulance/HEAR	
463.025B		Paramedics primary	
468.025M		Paramedics primary	
463.125B		Paramedics secondary	
468.125M		Paramedics secondary	

County operations

154.085	KXK420	Emergency Management	
45.84	KAZ605	Roads Department	179.9
154.515	WNMB346	Solid waste landfill	
501.9375R	WEB548	Cumberland Senior Bus	

Municipalities

Bridgeton City

155.550R	KEA702	Police dispatch F1
156.210	KEA702	Police intersystem F2
155.685	KEA702	Police secondary (car to car) F3

155.730R	KEA702	Police information center F4	
154.950M		Police private channel	
159.165		Roads Department	
462.125R	WXM933	Housing Authority	
153.755	KTS603	City units	

Commercial Township

155.025	WZY343	Township units

Deerfield Township

155.550	KUP290	Police dispatch F1	179.9
156.210	KUP290	Police intersystem F2	
155.550R	KUP290	Police (Bridgeton) F3	
155.730R	KUP290	Police information center F4	

Downe Township

154.115	WXB732	Township units

Fairfield Township

155.580	KRW258	Police dispatch F1
156.210	KRW258	Police intersystem F2
154.830M	KRW258	Police (Millville) F3
155.730R	KRW258	Police information center F4
154.785R	KRW258	Police
154.055	WNED914	Township units

Lawrence Township

155.580	KSS863	Police dispatch F1
156.210	KSS863	Police intersystem F2
154.830M	KSS863	Police (Millville) F3
155.730R	KSS863	Police information center F4

Maurice River Township

155.295	KZC343	Bellplain ambulance F1
155.340M	KZC343	Hospital to Bellplain amb./HEAR F2
155.775	KNES297	Township units

Millville City

155.580R	KEB678	Police dispatch F1	179.9
156.210	KEB678	Police intersystem F2	
154.830R	KEB678	Police secondary F3	
155.730R	KEB678	Police information center F4	
154.890M	KEB678	Police car to car F5	
155.205	WNVD823	Rescue squad dispatch F1	
155.220	KNHZ599	Rescue squad county dispatch F2	
155.340M	KNHZ599	Rescue squad to hospital F3	
156.105	KYG765	Roads Department	
154.965R	KNBD957	City units	
158.820	WZN225	City units	

Upper Deerfield Township

155.550	KGR386	Police dispatch F1	179.9
156.210	KGR386	Police intersystem F2	

155.550R	KG2386	Police (Bridgeton) F3	
155.730R	KGR386	Police information center F4	
155.955	KNFW513	Township units	

Vineland City

155.520R	KZC543	Police dispatch F1	179.9
156.210	KZC543	Police intersystem F2	
154.710M	KZC543	Police car to car F3	
155.730R	KZC543	Police information center F4	179.9
155.910M	KZC543	Police car to car F5	
33.74	KEF828	Fire dispatch F1	
33.52	KEF828	Fire fireground F2	
155.160	KNFA688	Rescue squad dispatch EMS-1	
155.220	WNSN423	Rescue squad EMS-2	
155.340M		Rescue squad to hospital EMS-3	
33.10	KLU335	Emergency Management rescue	
856.4625T	WNXZ709	Trunked public safety (future use)	
151.040	KFV827	Roads Department	
45.40	KBP760	Water Department	
47.74	KEB677	Utility Department	
453.500R	WPCS753	Housing Authority F1 operations	
453.500M	WPCS753	Housing Authority F2 car to car	
154.040	KFV827	City units	
453.275R	WNAE436	City units	
453.600M	WNAE436	City units	
39.18	WNKY264	City units	

GLOUCESTER COUNTY

Police

507.0375R	WII365	F20 Prosecutor's office	167.9
507.0375M	WII365	F21 Prosecutor's office	167.9
507.6875R	WII365	F22 Countywide (158.970)	167.9
507.4875R	WII365	F23 Zone 1 dispatch	167.9
		Woodbury, Wenonah, Westville,	
		West Deptford, Deptford, National Park	
507.4875M	WII365	F24 Zone 1 car to car	167.9
		Woodbury, Wenonah, Westville,	
		West Deptford, Deptford, National Park	
508.5125R	WII365	F25 Zone 2 dispatch	167.9
		Mantua, Harrison, South Harrison,	
		East Greenwich, Woolwich,	
		Woodbury Heights	
508.5125M	WII365	F26 Zone 2 car to car	167.9
		Mantua, Harrison, South Harrison,	
		East Greenwich, Woolwich,	
		Woodbury Heights	
508.5625R	WII365	F27 Sheriff's Department	167.9
508.5875R	WII365	F28 Future use	167.9
507.4375R	WII365	F29 Zone 4 dispatch	167.9
		Clayton, Elk, Newfield, Franklin	
507.4375M	WII365	F30 Zone 4 car to car	167.9
		Clayton, Elk, Newfield, Franklin	
508.5375R	WII365	F31 Zone 5 dispatch	167.9
		Pitman, Glassboro, Monroe,	
		Washington	
508.5375M	WII365	F32 Zone 5 car to car	167.9
		Pitman, Glassboro, Monroe,	
		Washington	
----.----R		F33 Zone 6 dispatch - future	
----.----M		F34 Zone 6 car to car - future	
507.6375R	WII365	"Star One"	167.9

NOTE: Zone 3 includes Paulsboro, Logan, Swedesboro, Greenwich

158.970	KBC661	F1 Dispatch (old system)	167.9
158.730R	KBC661	Prosecutor's office (old)	167.9
158.790		SWAT team (Mantua - old)	167.9

Fire

507.7375B	WII365	F01 alerting	167.9
507.0625R	WII365	F02 Status/message data	167.9

507.0875R	WII365	F03 north response	167.9
507.0875M	WII365	F04 north response mobile	167.9
507.1375R	WII365	F05 south response	167.9
507.1375M	WII365	F06 south response mobile	167.9
507.2875R	WII365	F11 (Tac 1) fireground	167.9
507.2875M	WII365	F12 (Tac 1) fireground mobile	167.9
507.5875R	WII365	F13 (Tac 2) fireground	167.9
507.5875M	WII365	F14 (Tac 2) fireground mobile	167.9
507.5375R	WII365	F15 (Tac 3) fireground	167.9
507.5375M	WII365	F16 (Tac 3) fireground mobile	167.9
510.7375M	WII365	F17 (Tac 4) drills	
154.130	KNAW774	F1 Dispatch (old)	167.9
154.355	KNAW774	F2 Response (old)	167.9
154.265	KNAW774	F3 South Jersey mutual aid (old)	
153.785M	KNAN655	F4 SPEN 4 mutual aid	131.8
155.085	KNAN655	F5 Fireground (old)	167.9
159.375	KNAK406	Forest fire coordination	

Ambulance

507.2375R	WII365	F07 EMS-1 response	167.9
507.2375M	WII365	F08 EMS-1 mobiles	167.9
507.1875R	WII365	F09 EMS-2 telephone patch	167.9
507.1875M	WII365	F10 EMS-2 operations	167.9
507.2875R	WII365	F11 (Tac 1) fireground	167.9
507.2875M	WII365	F12 (Tac 1) fireground mobiles	167.9
507.5875R	WII365	F13 (Tac 2) fireground	167.9
507.5875M	WII365	F14 (Tac 2) fireground mobiles	167.9
507.5375R	WII365	F15 (Tac 3) fireground	167.9
507.5375M	WII365	F16 (Tac 3) fireground mobiles	167.9
510.7375M	WII365	F17 (Tac 4) drills	167.9
155.265	KNAT231	EMS-1 Dispatch (old)	
155.340	KNAT231	EMS-2 Ambulance to hospital/HEAR	
155.280	KNAT231	EMS-3 Mutual aid (old)	
153.785M	KNAN655	EMS-4 SPEN 4	131.8

County operations

507.0125R	WII365	F19 Animal control, buses	167.9
506.9125R	WII365	F18 County base	167.9
852.6125R	WNWL633	County units	
855.9625R	WNWL633	County units	
155.955	WNLL761	Gloucester County College security F1	
154.995	WNLL761	Gloucester County College security F2	

| 159.120R | KNFY410 | Roads Department | |
| 154.995 | WNLL761 | County | |

Municipalities
Clayton Borough
506.3875R	WIL566	Police dispatch	167.9
159.060		Police F2	
158.820	KVA534	Borough units/police F3	

Deptford Township
159.150R	KEJ871	Police dispatch F3	167.9
153.920	KCJ623	Township units/police F4	
37.72	KJZ813	Municipal Utility Authority	

East Greenwich Township
| 155.775 | WNMH303 | Police F4 | |

Franklin Township
508.0375R	WIK640	Police dispatch	167.9
159.165	WXQ926	Roads Department/police F3	
158.820	KCI753	Township units/police F2	

Gibbsboro Borough
| 155.565 | WNLB719 | Police dispatch | |
| 156.150M | WNLB719 | Police car to car | |

Glassboro Borough
508.6125R	WIJ868	Police dispatch	167.9
507.3125R	WNAB301	Police/borough units	167.9
158.895	KNHH817	Borough units/police F2	
151.685	WST979	Housing Authority	
158.775	WNAB301	Borough units/police F4	
151.370		Police F3 tac	

Greenwich Township
| 158.820 | WNGT261 | Township units/police F2 | |
| 154.085 | KLO370 | Township units/police F3 | |

Harrison Township
| 159.135 | WNFF887 | Roads Department | |

Logan Township
| 154.085 | KNJA517 | Township units/police/school buses | |

Mantua Township
506.5375R	WIJ784	Police dispatch	167.9
158.790R	KLK628	Police F3	
159.105	KZV350	Roads/police F4	

Monroe Township
508.4625R	WIJ743	Police F1 dispatch	167.9
508.4875R	WIJ743	Police F2	167.9
500.4375R	KNQ504	Police F3	167.9
158.865	KNIX218	Township units/police	

46.52	WXQ903	Police	
500.4375R	KNQ504	Township units	127.3

National Park Borough

158.760		Police (Woodbury)	
154.980	KAO362	Borough units/police F3	
155.715	KQW990	Police	

Paulsboro Borough

507.3875R	WIL621	Police dispatch	167.9
158.820	KMA552	Borough units/police F2	

Pitman Borough

506.4375R	WIL430	Police dispatch	167.9
155.685	KEB344	Police	
158.745	WNXU391	Borough units/police	

Washington Township

508.2875R	WIJ668	Police F1	167.9
508.3625R	WIJ668	Police F2	167.9
158.805R	KFT636	Township units/police F3	167.9
153.845	KVV746	Township units/police F2	
155.115	KNFH926	Township units/police F4	

Wenonah Borough

508.6375R	WIJ895	Police dispatch	167.9
153.980	KMK455	Borough units/police	

West Deptford Township

506.4875R	WIL620	Police dispatch	167.9
158.835	KDQ362	Township units/police F2	

Westville Borough

507.3375R	WIK982	Police dispatch	167.9
155.370	KEE405	Police F3	
155.145	KDR284	Borough units/police F2	

Woodbury City

508.9875R	WIK674	Police dispatch	167.9
158.970		Police	123.0
158.760	KNBW232	City units/police	123.0

Woodbury Heights Borough

508.4125R	WIJ715	Police dispatch	167.9

HUNTERDON COUNTY

Police

154.965R	KYI830	F1 Tactical/prosecutor	192.8
154.785R	KYI829	F2 North county	192.8
		Clinton Town, Clinton Township,	
		Readington, Lebanon Borough,	
		Lebanon Township, High Bridge,	
		Tewksbury, Califon, Hampton	
154.815R	KYI829	F3 South county	192.8
		Flemington, Raritan Township,	
		Delaware Township, West Amwell,	
		Lambertville, Frenchtown, Milford,	
		Franklin Township, Holland Township,	
		Alexandria, Bloomsbury	
154.965M	KV5069	F4 Car to car	192.8
155.730	WNMK960	Sheriff's tactical/special events	192.8
45.98	KGJ671	Sheriff's office	CS

Fire

33.74	KYO430	Dispatch F1	192.8
33.68	KYO430	Fireground F2	192.8
33.58M	KYO430	Fireground	192.8
33.62M	KYO430	Fireground	192.8

Ambulance

154.965R	KYI830	F1 Tactical	192.8
155.205	KYQ553	F2 Dispatch	192.8
155.340	KYO220	F3 HEAR/ambulance to hospital	192.8
154.965M	KV5069	F4 Car to car	192.8
33.04P	KYQ553	Alerting only	CS
155.235	KEM739	Somerset Medical Center MICU	156.7
155.220	KNJP460	Lehigh Valley MedEvac copter	136.5
463.175B		EMS1 to HMC primary	192.8
468.175M		EMS1 to HMC primary	192.8
463.050B		EMS1 to HMC secondary	192.8
468.050M		EMS1 to HMC secondary	192.8
458.175M		EMS1 telemetry packset	192.8

County operations

153.755M	WNMD643	County jail	192.8
151.070R	KAB292	Roads and Bridges	192.8
158.985M	KAB292	Roads and Bridges mobiles	192.8

151.235R	WRE529	Parks System	192.8
453.900R	KNCM823	Schools	
		Hunterdon Central High buses	131.8
		Delaware Township buses	146.2
		Flemington-Raritan District maint.	162.2
462.575R	KAD5590	Emergency Management F1	192.8
462.575M	KAD5590	Emergency Management F2	192.8
462.575R	KAD5590	Health Department F1	186.2
453.900R	KNCM823	Health Department F2	186.2
462.675R	KAE0571	Health Department F3 primary	186.2
462.675R	KAE0571	The Link public transit buses	94.8

Municipalities

Clinton Town

462.575R		Police security patrols	
45.64	KGV348	Town units	
154.025	KGV348	Town units	
154.040	WNHN793	Town units	

Clinton Township

159.150	WMHP784	Police local	192.8
462.575R	KAE1440	Police patrols	
460.1875M	WNHP784	Police special events	
460.3875M	WNHP784	Police special events	
465.1875M	WNHP784	Police special events	
465.3875M	WNHP784	Police special events	
158.835	WNWQ345	Sewerage Authority	
45.64	KGW681	Township units	

Delaware Township

45.48	KRT770	Township units	CS

East Amwell Township

45.76	KUG657	Roads Department	131.8

Flemington Borough

155.220	KSS243	Flem-Raritan Rescue Sq. local	192.8
151.685	WNZM410	Flem-Raritan Rescue Squad ops	
462.575R	KAD7813	Emergency Management F1	100.0
462.575M	KAD7813	Emergency Management F2	100.0
462.700BM	KAD7813	Emergency Management F3	100.0
467.700M	KAD7813	Emergency Management F4	100.0
453.600BM	WNAG901	Emergency Management F5	100.0

Franklin Township

45.64	KSM250	Township units	CS

Frenchtown Borough

155.040	WNNB456	Borough units	

High Bridge Borough

453.975R	WNXS525	Borough units	

Holland Township

154.445	KNCS287	Fire police/fireground	
154.070M	KNCS287	Fire police/fireground mobiles	
155.865	KJK695	Township units	
155.235	WNRV894	Emergency Management	

Kingwood Township

155.175	WNAU973	Rescue Squad local	192.8
45.52	KFK574	Roads Department	94.8

Lambertville City

33.04	KEL395	Lamb.-New Hope Rescue local	CS
153.005M	WNUH819	Water Company	
45.12	KDQ263	City units	
155.880R	KDQ263	City units	

Lebanon Township

45.64	KTX702	Township units	CS

Milford Borough

155.295M	KA78257	Milford-Holland Rescue local	192.8
47.66	KFR619	Garden State Underwater Recovery	

Raritan Township

151.205	KNET694	Building Department	123.0
154.040	KBW788	Township units	
453.300R	WNSN434	Township units	

Readington Township

45.64	KMA888	Township units	CS

Tewksbury Township

45.64M	KA36851	Township units	

MERCER COUNTY

Police

453.225R		Police mutual aid	103.5
453.225R		County strike force	179.9
453.575R	KSL375	Sheriff, prosecutor, corrections, parks	103.5
39.12	WNWD554	Statewide	
460.300R	WNZY953	Police	

Fire

154.430	KSO869	Fire 1 - Dispatch	103.5
154.295	KSO869	Fire 2 - Fireground/mutual aid	103.5
----.----		Fire 3 - Local use	
154.265	WXR315	Fire 4 - South Jersey mutual aid	
154.175		Tac 1 - East/Northeast tactical (Suburban chiefs) *East Windsor, Hightstown, West Windsor, Washington Twp.*	103.5
154.340		Tac 2 - West/Northwest tactical (Tri-township chiefs) *Ewing Twp., Lawrence Twp., Hopewell, Pennington, Princeton*	103.5
154.355		Tac 3 - Southeast tactical (Hamilton chiefs fireground) *Hamilton Township*	103.5
154.055	WRG829	Fire police	77.0

Ambulance

155.265	KNEG500	Ambulances/Lifemobile JEMS 1	
463.100B	KYO348	Lifemobiles primary	151.4
468.100M	KYO348	Lifemobiles primary	151.4
463.125B	KYO348	Lifemobiles secondary	151.4
468.125M	KYO348	Lifemobiles secondary	151.4
462.950R		Lifemobile dispatch	151.4

County operations

155.280	KTX589	Emergency Management	
453.575R	KSL375	Emergency Management	
155.115	KJF934	Mercer County Airport	71.9
453.625R	KVA558	Mercer-Metro/NJ Transit buses	110.9
151.040R	KEE552	Roads Department	151.4
453.900R	KNFC508	Stony Brook Sewer Authority	

453.275R	WNSB346	County units	
453.925M	WPCT502	County jail	

Municipalities
East Windsor
460.350R	WPDA304	Police F1 dispatch (base "36")	
460.150R	WPDA304	Police F2 (base "36")	
154.025R	KJW326	Police (old): detectives/ first aid squads dispatch	71.9
154.175	WNMM293	Fire	71.9
155.265	KNAW756	Rescue 1 operations	71.9
155.280M	KNAW756	Rescue 1 statewide mutual aid	
155.340M	KNAW756	Rescue 1 amb. to hospital/HEAR	
155.265	WRG553	Rescue 2 operations	71.9
155.280M	WRG553	Rescue 2 statewide mutual aid	
155.340M	WRG553	Rescue 2 amb. to hospital/HEAR	
154.085	KUB912	Municipal Utility Authority	
156.120	KDO212	Roads Department	

Ewing Township
453.975R	WPBX252	Police	103.5
154.340	KRE296	Prospect Hghts Fire Co. local F3	103.5
46.06	KNEV590	West Trenton Fire Co. (Bucks)	123.0
46.14	KNEV590	West Trenton Fire Co. (Bucks)	123.0
46.20	KNEV590	West Trenton Fire Co. (Bucks)	123.0
46.28	KNEV590	West Trenton Fire Co. (Bucks)	123.0
155.295	KVP792	Ambulance	103.5
154.055	WPBX252	Township units	103.5
155.055	WPBX252	Township units	

Hamilton Township
453.525R	KLW340	Police F1	103.5
460.075R	KNCS282	Police - future use	
460.450R	KNCS282	Police - future use	
154.220	various	Fire local/Burlington Co. mutual aid	
154.355	various	Fire local F3	103.5
155.160	KVF819	Yardville First Aid Squad	
155.385	WPED913	Rescue	
33.06	KCS522	Roads Department	
159.120	KGL630	Roads Department	
45.24	KCS522	Township units/animal control	
154.055	KNDZ214	Township units	

Hightstown Borough
453.700R	KVV724	Police dispatch (Cranbury, too)	156.7
453.750M	KP8052	Police car to car	
39.46	KBX612	Police (Monmouth County)	151.4

154.430		Fire dispatch	156.7
154.415	KEC839	Fire local	
154.175	KEC839	Fire local	
155.265	KXC976	First Aid Squad operations	156.7
155.340M	KZ6369	Engine 1 First Aid amb to hosp/HEAR	
155.340M	KB21956	Ambulance to hospital/HEAR	
158.745	KNDL392	Borough units	

Hopewell Township

155.520R	KYW959	Police	110.9
155.085	KGP793	Police F4	103.5
154.130	KGL510	Fire dispatch	103.5
154.340B	KGL510	Fire F3	103.5
155.220	WNGL355	Rescue dispatch	103.5
155.265	WNGL355	Rescue	103.5
155.280M	WPBX228	Union Fire Co. Rescue mutual aid	
150.790M	WPBX228	Union Fire Co. Rescue mobile rptrs	
155.205M	WPBX228	Union Fire Rescue (Hunterdon)	192.8

Lawrence Township

453.825R	KLW339	Police/EMS	103.5
154.340	KNBU368	Fire local	
154.055	WNUR545	Fire/fire marshal	
460.6125R	KD24443	Fire marshal phone patch	
154.995	KOB856	Public works	

Pennington Borough

154.130	KNBF383	Fire dispatch	103.5
154.340	KNBF383	Fire local F3	103.5
155.220	KRX532	First Aid Squad dispatch	CS
153.965	KON332	Roads Department	123.0

Princeton Borough

159.090	KTX677	Police	151.4
158.805R	KEI901	Fire/Rescue F1	162.2

Princeton Township

453.675R	KED993	Police dispatch F1	103.5
453.675M	KED993	Police mobiles F2	103.5
155.640	KED993	Police	
155.655	KED993	Police	
158.805	KEI900	Fire	162.2

TRENTON CITY

453.225R	KLR504	Police F2	103.5
453.225R	KLR504	Police vice units F3	179.9
453.375R	KLR504	Police F1 dispatch	103.5
453.425R	KLR504	Police vice units F4	103.5
460.575R	KED796	Fire dispatch F1	103.5
460.600R	KED796	Fire fireground F2	103.5
460.575M	KED796	Fire fireground F3	103.5

460.600M	KED796	Fire fireground F4	103.5
46.38B	KVD867	Fire	
155.265	KIU268	Ambulance dispatch	
155.280	KIO268	Ambulance mutual aid	
155.340	KIO268	Ambulance to hospital/HEAR	
155.160	KJE251	Trenton Emergency & Rescue Squad	
155.265	KJE251	Trenton Emergency & Rescue Squad	
155.280	KJE251	Trenton Emergency & Rescue Squad	
155.220	KQR441	Liberty Rescue Squad	
155.265	KQM746	11th Zone Emergency Unit	
155.280M	KQM746	11th Zone Emergency Unit	
155.340M	KQM746	11th Zone Emergency Unit	
150.995	KEG943	Roads Department	
853.9375R	WYH514	Water Division F1	103.5
854.2625R	WYH514	Water Division F2	103.5
451.6375R	WPCH650	Water Works	
153.965	WYV448	City units	
506.4875R	WIK563	City units - future use	
506.5375R	WIK563	City units - future use	
506.9125R	WIK563	City units - future use	
507.3125R	WIK563	City units - future use	
507.3375R	WIK563	City units - future use	
507.3625R	WIK563	City units - future use	
507.3875R	WIK563	City units - future use	
507.4125R	WIK563	City units - future use	
507.4625R	WIK563	City units - future use	
508.2125R	WIK563	City units - future use	
508.2875R	WIK563	City units - future use	
508.3625R	WIK563	City units - future use	
508.4125R	WIK563	City units - future use	
508.4625R	WIK563	City units - future use	
508.4875R	WIK563	City units - future use	
508.6125R	WIK563	City units - future use	
508.6375R	WIK563	City units - future use	
461.125M	WNXZ380	Trenton Downtown Association	
461.200M	WNXZ380	Trenton Downtown Association	

Washington Township

460.125R	WNPA545	Police	
154.175	KJY798	Fire dispatch	
151.145	WNWW905	Roads Department	
155.025	WQI575	Township units	

West Windsor Township

154.115R	KZK275	Police/rescue	
453.325R	KZB237	Police	103.5
154.175	WNGP575	Fire	

| 154.980 | KBC652 | Senior citizens transportation/ fire dispatch/first aid squad/ township units/Roads Department | 103.5 |

OCEAN COUNTY

Police

37.18	KEB431	F1 Dispatch	156.7
37.24	KEB431	F2 Information	156.7
37.40	KEB431	F3 Prosecutor's office, rangers	156.7
37.12	KEB431	F4 Sheriff	156.7
155.910	KEB431	Car to car	
460.0375R	KB74848	Police	
460.0625R	KB74848	Police	
460.0875R	KB74848	Police	
460.1125R	KB74848	Police	
460.1375R	KB74848	Police	
460.1625R	KB74848	Police	

Fire

33.78	KNEL935	F1 Dispatch	CS
33.64	KNEL935	F2 Fire mutual aid	CS
33.44	KEJ451	F3 Mutual aid	CS
33.98	KEJ451	F4 Zone 1 - Central	CS
33.58	KNEL935	F5 Zone 2 - South	CS
33.02	KEJ451	F6 Zone 3 - North	CS
33.04	KEJ451	F7 Zone 4 - West	CS
33.72	KNEL935	Dover Township dispatch	CS
33.80	KNEL935	Jackson Township dispatch	CS
154.265	WRZ563	South Jersey mutual aid	
159.375		Forest fire net	
465.5875M	KEJ451	Fireground	

Ambulance

155.205	KMK200	F1 Dispatch	186.2
155.280	KMK200	F2 Mutual aid	
155.340	KMK200	F3 Ambulance to hospital/HEAR	91.5
462.950R	KNFA354	MedComm medics	
463.175B		Paramedics primary	
468.175M		Paramedics primary	
463.100B		Paramedics secondary	
468.100M		Paramedics secondary	

County operations

155.085	KVJ762	Emergency Management
154.965R	KYL775	Public Works/Roads/Emerg. Mgt. F1
154.965M	KYL775	Emergency Management F2

155.880	WPBR242	Emergency Management F3	
153.785M		Emergency Mgt. F4 - SPEN 4	131.8
155.205		Emergency Mgt. F5 - Ambulance	186.2
155.340		Emergency Mgt. F6 - HEAR	91.5
155.280		Emergency Mgt. F7 - Amb. mutual aid	
153.785M		Emergency Mgt. F8 - SPEN 4	131.8
155.235		Emergency Mgt. F9	
155.175		Emergency Mgt. F10	
151.310R	KNFP297	Mosquito control	
37.90	KEH658	Roads Department F1	127.3
37.92	WNWC626	Roads Department F2	127.3
45.48	WNGA667	Utility Authority	
153.800M	WNGA667	Utility Authority	
453.0875M	WNGA667	Utility Authority	
45.64	KAW320	County units	
37.10	KNHQ301	Buildings and grounds	127.3
37.96	WNWC626	Transportation, vehicle maint.	127.3
453.500R	WNVT262	County units	
453.0625R	KD40754	County units	
453.1375R	KD40754	County units	
453.3875R	KD40754	County units	
31.04	WNSC260	Ocean County Landfill	
853.5625R	WNVN642	County units	
506.6375R	WIL552	County units (Toms River)	
506.7375R	WIL552	County units (New Egypt, Barnegat, Toms River)	
506.8375R	WIL552	County units (Toms River)	
508.0875R	WIL552	County units (New Egypt, Tuckerton, Barnegat, Toms River)	
508.1875R	WIL552	County units (Toms River)	
508.4375R	WIL552	County units (New Egypt, Barnegat, Toms River)	

Municipalities

Barnegat Township

460.450R	WNDD487	Police	123.0
155.220	KNHV690	Rescue local	
155.955	KNBL883	Township units	

Barnegat Light Borough

155.160	KTK629	First Aid Squad
155.055	KYU491	Borough units
159.105	WNUP731	Roads Department

Beach Haven Borough

460.500R		Police dispatch

460.375R	WPBI446	Police	
37.22	KEB512	Police local F2 (old)	156.7
155.235	KNEN728	First Aid Squad dispatch	
155.160M	KB86878	Beach patrol	

Beachwood Borough

37.06	WQV863	Police local	156.7
155.025	WNHR618	Borough units	
153.965M	WNHR618	Borough units	

Berkeley Township

852.2625R		Police F1	
852.2875R	KEJ877	Police F2	
37.06	KEJ877	Police	156.7
852.2875BM	WXE798	Fire	
807.3125M	WXE798	Fire fireground	
33.72	KBP467	Fire (Dover Township)	CS
155.775R	KNBY446	Sewerage Authority	
39.98	KRH354	Township units	

Brick Township

453.050R	KUQ731	Police dispatch F1	127.3
453.825R	WYC831	Police info F4, roads, trash	127.3
453.375R		Police F2	127.3
453.750M	KUQ731	Police mobiles F3	127.3
46.10	KNCP464	Fire dispatch F1	
46.06	KNCP464	Fire fireground F2	
45.16	KVM311	Fire dispatch F3	
453.450M	WNQU397	Fire mobiles	
453.400M	WNQU397	Fire mobiles	
453.250R	WNQU397	Fire operations	
460.5125R	WPAM421	Fire	
460.5375R	WPAM421	Fire	
460.525R	WNRM841	First Aid	
158.775	KUL795	Water/sewer	
458.2125M	KD51217	Housing Authority	
462.625	KAE0919	Township units	

Dover Township

155.655R	KDT377	Police dispatch F1	114.8
154.085R	KDL864	Police F2	114.8
154.815R	KDT377	Police F3	114.8
158.940M	KDL864	Police	114.8
460.550R	WNMJ873	Police	
154.145R	WNCP530	Fire dispatch F1	136.5
154.190	WNCP530	Fire F2	136.5
154.445	WNCP530	Fire fireground F3	136.5
33.78	KNFZ575	Fire dispatch F1	CS
33.72	KNFZ575	Fire fireground F2	CS

33.64	KYY978	Fire mutual aid F3	CS
460.5625R	WNCP530	Fire operations	
460.5875R	WNCP530	Fire operations	
460.6125R	WNCP530	Fire operations	
460.6375R	WNCP530	Fire operations	
460.625R	WNZW394	Fire operations	
37.32	KZR427	First aid dispatch	
155.220		First aid car to car	
155.205	WNGX557	Silverton First Aid Squad local	
155.220	WNGX557	Silverton First Aid Squad	
150.995R	KNCC804	Roads Department	114.8
151.010R	KNCC804	Roads Department	114.8
156.165R	KNCC804	Roads Department	114.8
453.7125R	KA60630	Roads Department	
453.8625R	KA60630	Roads Department	
453.8875R	KA60630	Roads Department	
453.9125R	KA60630	Roads Department	
453.9375R	KA60630	Roads Department	
453.9625R	KA60630	Roads Department	
451.7875R	KD35964	Toms River Water Co.	
451.8125R	KD35964	Toms River Water Co.	
451.8375R	KD35964	Toms River Water Co.	
151.415R	WPBG522	Parks	
45.60	KFK569	Township units	
46.54	KDL864	Township units	
453.350R	WQO413	Township units	
464.350	WNNB233	Township units	

Eagleswood Township

39.06	WNNA648	Police local	

Harvey Cedars Borough

33.06	WNUE266	Roads Department	

Island Heights Borough

154.995	WNFW555	Township units	

Jackson Township

500.9125R	KNP856	Police F1 dispatch	156.7
501.2875R	KNP856	Police F2	156.7
33.80	WYK506	Fire dispatch	CS
153.830M	KNHZ944	Fireground	
154.430	KNHZ944	Fire (Mercer County)	
460.2375R	WPAJ314	Fire operations	
460.4625R	WPAJ314	Fire operations	
155.235	WZU228	First aid dispatch	
155.160	KNEJ677	First aid squad	
155.295	KTD351	First aid squad	
158.745	WNML266	Township units	

453.475R	KVP802	Township units	

Lacey Township

460.400R	WNUZ667	Police	
37.14	WQN857	Police local	156.7
33.70	KRO266	Fire local	CS
39.82	WPAW878	Municipal Utilities Authority	

Lakehurst Borough

37.04	KGX944	Police	156.7
460.3125R	KD49299	Police operations	
453.600R	WPCH364	Police	
45.72	WPBF862	Roads Department	
507.0375R	WIK848	Borough units	

Lakewood Township

453.325R	KAR824	Police F1	127.3
453.375R		Police F2	127.3
46.12	WNZS909	Fire/ambulance dispatch	
45.12	WPAC577	Public works	
155.985	WQV867	Municipal Utilities Authority	
155.025	KAX615	Township units	
155.055	WPAC577	Township units	
507.0375R	WIK848	Township units	

Lavallette Borough

155.865		Police dispatch	
37.02M	KEA278	Police local	156.7

Little Egg Harbor Township

37.28	KQP507	Police local	156.7
460.3625M	KQP507	Police handhelds	
460.4125R	WNZN655	Police	
33.44	KQP474	Fire	CS
33.58	KWP474	Fire	CS
153.860	WNNE357	Municipal Utilities Authority	
45.52	KMK383	Township units	

Long Beach Township

460.300R	WNCK627	Police	
155.145	WXP423	Sewage Authority	
46.00	WNIK219	Ambulance	
37.10	KFN677	Township units	
39.10	KFN677	Township units	
39.18	KFN677	Township units	

Manchester Township

158.790R	WZJ450	Police	162.2
159.150	WNLJ493	Police	
453.1625R	KD26896	Police operations	
453.6125R	KD26896	Police operations	
154.250	KNIQ539	Fire local	

453.300R	WNYY419	Township units	
39.50	WPCS290	Township units	

Mantoloking Borough

37.06	KNGS302	Police dispatch	156.7
453.375	WNNN712	Borough units	

Ocean Township

37.36	KLG541	Police dispatch F1	156.7
37.18	KLG541	Police county F2	156.7
453.8375R	WNXK957	Police	
460.475R	WNXK957	Police (new)	
33.48	WNKR607	Waretown Fire Co. No. 1 local	
155.160	WNVT206	Rescue	
155.745	KFE366	Township units	
855.9625R	KNJT752	Township units	

Ocean Gate Borough

37.34	WNRV794	Police local	
460.2625M	WNRV794	Police mobile repeaters/portables	

Pine Beach Borough

37.30	KLY878	Police local	156.7
33.68	WXB862	Fire local	CS

Point Pleasant Borough

460.425R	KVR715	Police dispatch F1	107.2
460.400R	KVR715	Police information F2	107.2
39.46	KEC894	Police (Monmouth County)	151.4
45.20	KNJM908	Fire/ambulance dispatch F1	
154.355	WYK598	Fire officers F2	
33.02	WNVI967	Fire local	
155.775	KNBH981	Borough units	

Point Pleasant Beach Borough

155.490	KNDH928	Police mutual aid F2	
155.010	KEB926	Police detectives F3	
154.725M	KNDH928	Police mutual aid F4	
154.755R	KNDH928	Police dispatch F5	94.8
154.875	KEB926	Police (Monmouth County)	151.4
39.46	KNDH928	Police (Monmouth County)	151.4
154.980	KBQ395	Fire/ambulance dispatch F1	94.8
155.820	WNAV332	Borough units/police	94.8
33.02	WNVJ414	Rescue	

Plumstead Township

155.265M	WYK458	New Egypt First Aid Squad	

Seaside Heights Borough

460.350R	KEB403	Police dispatch F1	DPL
460.175R	KEB403	Police F2	DPL
465.350M	KEB403	Police F3 car to car	DPL
37.42	KEB403	Police local/ambulance	

453.0125R	WNWT535	Borough units	

Seaside Park Borough

37.26		Police dispatch	156.7
37.94	KHL667	Tri-Boro First Aid Squad	
150.775M	KB94184	First aid portables	
150.790M	KB94184	First aid portables	
155.175M	KB94184	First aid mobiles	
39.90	WNDC551	Borough units	

Ship Bottom Borough

460.300BM	KBB200	Police F1 dispatch
460.125R	KBB200	Police F2
453.725R	WNST440	Borough units

South Toms River Borough

37.20	WPBX292	Police local
45.68	WNVG723	Roads Department

Stafford Township

460.275R	KFK647	Police	123.0
153.860	KNGN328	Municipal Utilities Authority	
451.0625M	WPDD666	Municipal Utilities Authority	
453.225R	WPCV650	Township units	

Surf City Borough

37.22	KEC771	Police local	156.7
460.250R	WPDD336	Police dispatch	
462.950R	WNRW253	Rescue	
45.64	WNDD296	Borough units	

Tuckerton Borough

154.040	KNDB956	Borough units

SALEM COUNTY

Police

156.210		F1 Dispatch/Sheriff/Prosecutor	203.5
155.700M	KD28536	F3 Car to car (Pennsville/	203.5
		Prosecutor's office)	
155.625	WPBM359	F2 Prosecutor's office operations	
156.150		F2 Prosecutor's office	

Fire

33.86	KEE873	F1	
33.84	KEE873	F2	
33.88	KEE873	F3	
154.265	KEE873	South Jersey mutual aid	
154.430	KEE873	Dispatch	186.2
159.375		Forest fire coordination F6	

Ambulance

155.295	WRU898	EMS-1 Dispatch
155.340	WRU898	EMS-2 Ambulance to hospital/HEAR
155.280	WRU898	Statewide mutual aid
463.150B		Paramedics primary
468.150M		Paramedics primary
463.000B		Paramedics secondary
468.000M		Paramedics secondary

County operations

154.995	KIK846	County units
37.94	KEF272	Roads Department
33.06	various	Emergency Management F2
33.08	various	Emergency Management F1
460.175R	WNYZ967	County units F1
460.175M	WNYZ967	County units car to car F2
460.200M	WNYZ967	County units car to car F3
854.9875R	WNXF589	County units

Municipalities

Carneys Point Township

156.210	KEC736	Police F1 dispatch
155.370	KEC736	Police F2
155.100		Police F3
156.225M	WNVB859	Roads Department
37.26	WZJ578	Township units

Elmer Borough

156.210		Police F1 dispatch

Lower Alloways Creek Township

155.595	KVR896	Police F2
156.210	KVR896	Police F1 dispatch
154.430	KQG743	Fire
154.085	WYR816	Emergency Management
453.7375R	KB64839	Roads Department

Penns Grove Borough

156.210	KNBU377	Police F1 dispatch
155.100		Police F2

Pennsville Township

156.210	KNJP481	Police F1 dispatch
155.910		Police F2
155.700		Police F3
155.880	KIT631	Sewerage Authority

Pilesgrove Township

151.130	WNMI731	Roads Department

Salem City

156.210		Police F1 dispatch
155.430	WNCW528	Police F2
153.635	WXL915	Water Department
156.240		Roads Department

Woodstown Borough

156.210	KNFY941	Police F1 dispatch
155.100	KNHA791	Police F2
155.295	WNUA371	American Legion Ambulance Assn.

WARREN COUNTY

Police
155.760R	KDT244	Prosecutor/sheriff	131.8

Fire
46.14	Dispatch

Ambulance
155.235	WNML300	Dispatch

County operations
155.760R	KDT244	Roads Department	162.2
453.875R	KVV865	County units (old)	
453.5875M	KB78421	County units	
155.820R	KVV865	County units	
155.835M	KVV865	County units	
155.025	WNWJ829	Pollution Control Authority	

Municipalities
Allamuchy Township
46.14	KNGT972	Fire
155.295	WNCN707	Allamuchy-Greenwich First Aid Squad
453.250R	WNCY387	Township units F1
453.250M	WNCY387	Township units F2

Alpha Borough
155.655R	WNCA969	Alpha-Pohatcong police	114.8
45.08	KFT586	Police old	
45.22M	KA55262	Police old (Lopatcong)	
46.14	WNWE913	Fire	

Belvidere Town
453.950R	KUG724	Police
46.14		Fire
46.56	KDV734	Ambulance

Blairstown Township
158.775R	WNBR610	Police dispatch
45.14	WYE399	Police (old)
45.28	KLR386	Fire
46.44	WNXJ450	Fire operations
37.98	KAR319	Ambulance
37.90M	KB65512	Ambulance mobiles

Franklin Township
45.40	WNYD500	Township units	100.0

Greenwich Township

45.40	WNYA682	Township units

Hackettstown Town

154.875R	WNGB201	Police
45.54	KNFZ531	Police
46.52	KDC316	Fire
153.830M	KB31771	Fire police
47.50	KEE826	Rescue squad
151.130	KQL874	Streets Department
153.695	KBV584	Municipal Utilities

Harmony Township

154.130	KBO580	Fire	100.0
156.165	WNJK710	Roads Department	

Hope Township

46.14	KLS450	Fire
45.48	KNJL320	Township units

Independence Township

NOTE: See West Morris network list for frequencies

154.800R	WQY212	Police local
46.52	KBS313	Fire/rescue/roads
155.265	WNGY652	First Aid Squad
151.100R	WNGV424	Roads Department

Knowlton Township

45.62	KLV237	Police (not used)
46.14	KSK483	Fire
45.48	KKC982	Township units

Lopatcong Township

45.22	WZX921	Police	203.5
46.12	WNCN662	Delaware Park Fire Co. local	
46.14	KBN939	Delaware Park Fire Co.	
46.54	KJD311	Township units	

Mansfield Township

NOTE: See West Morris network list for frequencies

45.98	KVD571	Police (not used)
46.14	KQW280	Fire
46.54	KRB426	Roads Department

Oxford Township

158.940M		Police (Washington Borough)
46.14	KZR519	Fire
158.745	KEO254	Rescue dispatch
47.50	KYL738	Rescue squad

Phillipsburg Town

155.190R	KEB424	Police	85.4
153.770	WRB463	Fire	85.4
153.845	KLD667	Fire	

155.265	WYX503	Emergency Squad	85.4

Pohatcong Township

155.655R	WNCA969	Alpha-Pohatcong police	114.8
45.08	KRI667	Police (not used)	
45.22M	KA5763	Police (not used)	
154.725M	WPCS773	Police car to car	
46.14	KLG548	Fire	

Washington Borough

158.745R	WNMC894	Police dispatch	186.2
158.940	KDB389	Ambulance/fire dispatch	
46.14	KYL779	Fire	
46.06	WNQG622	Fire operations	

Washington Township

158.745R		Police dispatch (Wash. Borough)	186.2
158.940	KFR611	Police (Washington Borough)	
39.90	KBI725	Roads Department	

White Township

45.84	WNMG624	Roads Department	

West Morris Communications Network

Operated by Washington Township (Morris County) for the following towns: Mansfield, Chester Borough, Chester Township, Washington Township (Morris County) and Independence Township

Police

154.085R	WQS844	F1 - Tac 1	192.8
155.415R	WQS861	F2 - Dispatch	192.8
154.965R	WQS844	F3 - Hunterdon County coord.	192.8
154.085M	WQS844	F4 - Tac 2 car to car	192.8
154.680	WQS861	F5 - SPEN 1	131.8
155.475	WQS861	F6 - SPEN 2	131.8
154.725	WQS861	F7 - SPEN 3	131.8
153.785	WQS844	F8 - SPEN 4	131.8

Fire

154.085R	WQS844	F1 - Tac 1	192.8
154.325	WQN244	F2 - Dispatch	192.8
154.965R	WQS844	F3 - Hunterdon County coord.	192.8
154.085M	WQS844	F4 - Tac 2 mobiles	192.8
---.---		F5 - blank	
---.---		F6 - blank	
---.---		F7 - blank	
153.785	WQS844	F8 - SPEN 4	131.8

Rescue

154.085R	WQS844	F1 - Tac 1	192.8
155.265	WQP769	F2 - Dispatch	192.8
154.325	WQN244	F3 - Fire	192.8
154.085M	WQS844	F4 - Tac 2 mobiles	192.8
155.340	WQP769	F5 - HEAR ambulance to hospital	
154.965R	WQS844	F6 - Hunterdon County coord.	192.8
155.280	WQP769	F7 - Statewide mutual aid	
153.785	WQS844	F8 - SPEN 4	131.8

FACTOID:

In Warren County, most two-way radio systems are located atop Harmony Mountain. There are several towers atop the mountain that support many types of communications systems.

STATE OF NEW JERSEY

New Jersey State Police

NOTE: New Jersey State Police have been implementing a statewide trunked 800 MHz radio system over the past half-dozen or so years. Frequencies have been reconfigured within the system several times and it is hard to keep current with frequency usage. Former VHF low band, high band and UHF frequencies also are listed after the trunked frequencies because these former frequencies occasionally are found in use, however, most operations are conducted on the 800 MHz trunked frequencies. The following details are current as of this book's presstime. In addition to the state police, other agencies operating on the trunked system include the Division of Gaming Enforcement, Office of Emergency Management, Department of Corrections, State Police Marine Police, Northstar and Southstar medical helicopters, Executive Protection Bureau, Atlantic City Expressway, Department of Criminal Justice, Meadowlands stadium complex, New Jersey Turnpike, Attorney General's office and Statehouse security.

800 MHz Trunked System
Troop A - South
Frequencies used:
855.2125 855.4625 855.7125, 856.4375 856.9375 857.4375,
857.9375 858.4375 858.9375, 859.4375 859.9375 860.9375
Guard tone: 76.60

Troop B - North
Frequencies used:
856.4625 856.9625 857.4625, 857.9625 858.4625 858.9625,
859.4625 859.9625 860.4625, 860.9625 866.5625 867.2375
Guard tone: 90.00

Troop C - Central
Frequencies used:
856.7125 857.2125 857.7125, 858.2125 858.7125 859.2125,
859.7125 860.2125 860.7125, 867.2125 867.6625 868.1375
Guard tone: 83.72

Statewide link frequencies:
866.3125 867.3125

Miscellaneous state police

44.94	F1 Troop A - South/old freq	131.8
44.62	F2 Troop C - Central/old freq	131.8

44.66	F3 Troop B - North/old freq	131.8
44.98	F4 Alternate dispatch/old freq	131.8
44.78M	F5 Car to car, radar/old freq	131.8
45.00	F6 Detectives, DEPE/old freq	131.8
44.70	F7 Bordentown I-295/old freq	131.8
44.82	F8 Tactical/old freq	131.8
154.920	Point to point	131.8
155.445	Marine police F1	179.9
156.850	Marine police F2 (Marine Ch. 17)	CS
155.445	Statehouse security/Trenton	131.8
39.76	EMRAD (Emergency Mgt.) statewide	
39.80	EMRAD (Emergency Mgt.) Central	
39.92	EMRAD (Emergency Mgt.) South	
39.84	EMRAD (Emergency Mgt.) North	
460.050R	Confidential squad - Central	131.8
460.075R	Confidential squad - North	131.8
460.100R	Confidential squad - South	131.8
460.500R	Narcotics - statewide	131.8
460.475R	Special operations - Flemington	131.8
453.7875M	WNUG884	Low-power units, Mercer County
173.075	various	Lojack stolen vehicle recovery

Lojack sites: Atlantic City, Bayville, Hackettstown, Lawrenceville, Little Falls, Sayreville, Voorhees

State police barracks
Division Headquarters - West Trenton
Troop A Headquarters - Hammonton
Stations: Absecon, Atlantic City Expressway (Hammonton),
              Bridgeton (Seabrook), Bellmawr, Berlin,
              Mays Landing, Port Norris, Red Lion (Vincentown),
              Tuckerton (West Creek), Woodstown

Troop B Headquarters - Totowa
Stations: Blairstown, Hackensack, Hainesville, Hope, Little Falls,
              Netcong, Perryville (Union Township, Hunterdon
              County), Somerville (Bridgewater),
              Washington (Washington Twp., Warren County)

Troop C Headquarters - Princeton
Stations: Allenwood, Bordentown, Edison, Flemington (Raritan Twp.),
              Fort Dix (Wrightstown), Hightstown (East Windsor),
              Keyport (alcoholic beverages), Wilburtha (Ewing)

Troop D Headquarters - New Brunswick
New Jersey Turnpike patrol
Stations: Carteret, Moorestown (Mount Laurel), Newark

Troop E Headquarters - Woodbridge
Garden State Parkway patrol
Stations: Avalon (Swainton), Bass River (New Gretna), Bloomfield,
            Holmdel, Pleasant Plains

Marine Police
Stations: Atlantic City, Avalon, Lake Hopatcong, Monmouth Beach,
            Point Pleasant Beach, Wildwood

State Police Emergency Network (SPEN)

*Almost all municipal and county law enforcement agencies in the state
are licensed, authorized or in the process of obtaining equipment to
operate on these four statewide mutual aid channels.*

154.680	SPEN-1	131.8

Common channel for emergency use and bulletins.

155.475	SPEN-2	131.8

*Nationwide police emergency channel; used as secondary channel to
SPEN-1.*

154.725	SPEN-3	131.8

Common channel for non-emergency police activity.

153.785	SPEN-4	131.8

Common channel for all public safety agencies.

Toll Highways
New Jersey Turnpike

155.190	KEC469	State police dispatch N of Exit 14 and S of Exit 7A Channel RED	131.8
155.580R	KEC469	State police dispatch Exit 7A to Exit 14 Channel AMBER	131.8
154.935M	KA9655	State police car to car GREEN	131.8
155.460M	KA9655	Radar operations	131.8
154.680M	KA9655	Off-turnpike talk, SPEN-1	131.8
159.180R	KBE469	Maintenance	
453.875R	KLW300	Road service units	131.8
453.2125M	KB25067	Data to signs	
453.2875M	WNUN391	Statewide units	
453.3125M	various	Data to signs	
453.4375M	various	Data to signs	

453.4625M	various	Data to signs	
453.6875M	various	Data to signs	
453.9875M	KB23898	Data to signs	
458.2125M	KB25067	Signs to operations data	
458.3125M	various	Signs to operations data	
458.4375M	various	Signs to operations data	
458.4625M	various	Signs to operations data	
458.6875M	various	Signs to operations data	
458.9875M	KB23898	Signs to operations data	
866.925R	WNSS306	Future use - south turnpike	
868.4375R	WNSS306	Future use - south turnpike	
866.925R	WNNM898	Future use - north turnpike	
866.0125M	WNNM898	Future use - mutual aid - calling	156.7
866.5125M	WNNM898	Future use - mutual aid - Tac 1	156.7
867.0125M	WNNM898	Future use - mutual aid - Tac 2	156.7
867.5125M	WNNM898	Future use - mutual aid - Tac 3	156.7
868.0125M	WNNM898	Future use - mutual aid - Tac 4	156.7
1610 kHz	WPAS758	Travelers Information Station broadcasts, Moorestown	

Garden State Parkway

154.905R	KEE283	F1 dispatch	151.4
155.505R	KEE283	F2 alternate dispatch	151.4
154.950M	KC5366	F3 car to car	151.4
154.680	KC5366	F4 off-parkway talk, SPEN-1	131.8
154.920		F5 Point to point	131.8
155.460M	KC5366	F6 Radar ops	131.8
155.475	KC5366	F7 off-parkway talk, SPEN-2	131.8
851.1625R	WSB630	State police	151.4
851.3375R	WSB626	State police/north	151.4
852.1625R	WSB626	State police/south	151.4
852.7375R	WSB626	Maintenance/north	151.4
852.7875R	WSB623	State police	151.4
852.8125R	WSB626	State police	151.4
853.8625R	WSB626	Maintenance/south	151.4
853.8625R	WSB626	Garden State Arts Center NJSP patrols, Holmdel	151.4
156.120R	KEJ808	Maintenance	151.4

Atlantic City Expressway

453.900R	KDV781	State police	156.7
453.700R	KJF717	Maintenance	156.7
72.50		Emergency call boxes	
154.45625	WNUK721	Signaling	

Department of Transportation

47.14	F1	CS
47.26	F2	CS
47.36	F3	CS
47.40	F4	CS

Transmitters:

KEE887	Cherry Hill
KEH823	Somers Point
KEE883	Trenton
KEE886	Trenton
KEE888	Vineland
KEE888	Glassboro
KNGE742	Hammonton
KEE885	Toms River
WNVA870	Bordentown
WPBX515	Burleigh

Miscellaneous:

453.2875M	WNUN391	Low-power use statewide
453.7875M	KD37543	Low-power use
506.9375R	WII408	Trenton operations
465.6125M	WNUI481	Low-power use
151.1225R	WNDC568	ACSB system - Cherry Hill

NJ Transit

NOTE: NJ Transit has installed a statewide 800-MHz radio system for its buses. It's believed that the only trunked groups used by NJ Transit buses at present are 856.2375T and 856.4875T.

852.4625R
854.1625R
854.2875R
854.4875R
856.2375T
856.3875T
856.4125T
856.4875T
861.9875T

Transmitter sites:

KNCM735	Wildwood
KNCM736	Atlantic City
KNCM737	Camden

Other:

453.625R	WRG28	Mercer Metro buses	110.9
453.6125M	KB81180	Bus operations	
453.7375M	KB81180	Bus operations	

453.8375M	KB81180	Bus operations
458.6125M	KB81180	Bus operations
458.7375M	KB81180	Bus operations
458.8375M	KB81180	Bus operations
151.625M	KD24712	Bus operations (itinerant)
161.400		Rail operations
		(High Bridge, Point Pleasant)
929.1125P	WNIA607	Paging
		Mays Landing, Bordentown, Berlin,
		Brass Castle, Toms River
929.1125P	WNIA608	Paging
		Woodbine, Barnegat

Department of Corrections

NOTE: The Department of Corrections is another state agency that has switched to its own 800 MHz system, as well as using the state police statewide system.

154.845	KNFL552	Midstate Correctional Facility, Fort Dix
	KNHY434	Youth Correctional Facility, Bordentown
	KEC460	Youth Correctional Facility, Annandale
	KNGQ801	Edna Mahan Corr. Facility, Clinton
	KNIQ394	Southern State 1&2, Maurice River Twp.
154.860	KKG980	Youth Correctional Facility, Bordentown
	WYG328	Southern Correctional Inst., Leesburg
	KZF851	Wharton Tract Hampton Gate,
		Tabernacle
	KNCG432	Knight Farm, West Trenton
	KNCG431	Youth Reception Center, Yardville
	KZF850	Youth Reception Center, Yardville
155.070	WYX411	Bayside State Prison, Ancora Unit
	WYG328	Bayside State Prison, Leesburg
	KMA254	NJ State Prison, Trenton 131.8
	KKG981	NJ State Prison, Vroom Bldg Readjust.
	WQD680	NJ State Prison Jones Farm, W.Trenton
	KNIQ394	Southern State 1&2, Maurice River Twp.
155.070R	KNGK773	New Jersey State Prison, Trenton
453.0875M	WNUJ423	Youth Correctional Facility, Bordentown
453.7875M	WNUG884	Youth Reception Center, Yardville
453.9625R	KB86538	Midstate Corr. Facility, Wrightstown
855.7375R	KNJH417	Youth Correctional Facility, Annandale
	KNJH418	Youth Correctional Facility, Bordentown
855.9875R	KNJH414	Youth Correctional Facility, Bordentown
856.2125R	KNJH426	Bayside State Prison, Leesburg
	KNJH423	Midstate Corr. Facility, Wrightstown

856.2625R	KNJH421	Edna Mahan Corr. Facility, Clinton
	WNRU760	New Jersey State Prison, Trenton
858.2625R	KNJH424	Riverfront Correctional Facility, Camden
	KNJH425	Southern State 1&2, Maurice River Twp.
859.2625R	KNJH412	New Jersey State Prison, Trenton
860.2625R	KNJH415	Youth Reception & Corr. Ctr, Yardville
929.0625P	various	Statewide paging

Department of Human Services

152.300	KNFV828	New Jersey Memorial Home for Disabled Soldiers, Vineland
153.920	KNDD674	Katzenback School for Deaf, W. Trenton
154.130	KNCW540	Trenton Psychiatric Hospital Fire Dept.
154.295	KNCW540	Trenton Psychiatric Hospital Fire Dept.
154.340	KNCW540	Trenton Psychiatric Hospital Fire Dept.
154.385	KNCS215	Ancora Psychiatric Hospital Fire Dept.
154.430	KNCW540	Trenton Psychiatric Hospital Fire Dept.
155.085	KEL512	Ancora Psychiatric Hospital
	KDZ338	Katzenback School for Deaf, W. Trenton
155.895	KUZ605	Johnstone Training Center, Bordentown
	KGE805	New Lisbon Development Center
	WSR216	Trenton Psychiatric Hosp. Forensic Unit
	KWF900	Vineland Development Center
	KTS554	Woodbine Development Center
	KRT678	Hunterdon Development Center, Clinton
	KKR497	Hagedorn Center for Geriatrics, 156.7 Mount Kipp (Lebanon Township)
	KNDL893	New Jersey Memorial Home for Disabled Soldiers, Vineland
157.450P	KNGN969	Woodbine Development Center
500.9875R	KXB910	Trenton Psychiatric Hospital police
460.625R	WNKX260	Trenton Psychiatric Hospital fire
460.575R	WNKX260	Trenton Psychiatric Hospital fire link to Trenton Fire Department
460.600R	WNKX260	Trenton Psychiatric Hospital fire link to Trenton Fire Department
855.4875R	WNSM920	Ancora Psychiatric Hospital

Law enforcement agencies

460.175R	WXK657	Division of Gaming Enforcement 131.8
460.250R	WYK657	Division of Gaming Enforcement 131.8
154.665M	KA60719	State Commission of Investigation
154.695M	KA60719	State Commission of Investigation
155.445	KEA832	Statehouse security 131.8

155.655M	KB62789	Law enforcement units
453.0875M	WNUJ411	Low-power law enforcement

State government operations

153.815M	KB28362	Agriculture Dept. Sire Stakes racing
153.815	KNAB312	Agriculture Department, Trenton
155.895	KRF526	Treasury Department, Trenton
154.47875	WNLZ727	Data, Camden
154.965P	WNUM998	State paging, Dover Township
156.000M	WNVU925	Mobiles, Mercer County
453.1125M	WPDY423	Low-power units, Mercer County
453.1125M	WPDD339	Low-power units, Camden County
453.2875R	KD31197	Low-power state units
453.5125R	KD31197	Low-power state units
453.5625M	WPCT588	Low-power state units, Mercer County
453.6125R	KD81180	Low-power state units
453.7375R	KD81180	Low-power state units
453.7625R	KD31197	Low-power state units
453.8375R	KD81180	Low-power state units
453.750R	WNMA977	State units, Atlantic City
458.475M	KD22453	State units
458.925M	KD31552	State units
851.3375R	WNKH531	State units, Trenton
853.8625R	WNKA642	State units, Trenton
530 kHz	WNPX698	Travelers Information Station broadcasts, I-80, Allamuchy Twp.

Department of Environmental Protection and Energy

Department systemwide channelization

151.190R	F1 Emergency response	179.9
159.300M	F2 Mobile to mobile	179.9
151.325R	F3 Fish and game	179.9
159.345M	F4 Fish and game mobiles	179.9
159.465	F5 Parks	179.9
159.375	F6 DEPE common	179.9
151.415R	F7 Forestry - north	179.9
151.475R	F8 Forestry - central	179.9
151.265R	F9 Forestry - south	179.9
159.285	F10 Mid-Atlantic Fire Net	CS

Division of Parks and Forestry

151.415R	F1 Division A - North	179.9
151.475R	F2 Division B - Central	179.9
151.265R	F3 Division C - South	179.9
159.375	F4 Emergency	179.9

159.465		F5 Parks coordination	179.9
159.285		F6 Mid-Atlantic fire net	CS
159.300		F7 Mobile to mobile DEPE	179.9
159.345		F8 Fish and Game coordination	179.9
151.370		Forestry, Trenton	179.9
159.435		Forestry, Trenton	179.9

Bureau of Parks

| 159.465 | F1 Dispatch | 179.9 |
| 159.375 | F2 Emergency | 179.9 |

Division of Fish and Game

| 151.325R | F1 Dispatch | 179.9 |
| 159.375 | F2 Emergency | 179.9 |

Bureau of Air Pollution

| 151.190R | F1 Dispatch | 179.9 |
| 159.375 | F2 Emergency | 179.9 |

Bureau of Radiation Protection

151.190R	F1 Dispatch	179.9
159.375	F2 Emergency	179.9
44.98	F3 State police dispatch (old)	131.8
45.00	F4 State police coordination (old)	131.8

Bureau of Specialized Services (Water)

| 151.190R | F1 Dispatch | 179.9 |
| 159.375 | F2 Emergency | 179.9 |

Division of Water Resources - Port Spill

156.650	F1 Marine navigational	CS
156.800	F2 Marine calling	CS
157.175	F3 Coast Guard coordination	CS
155.445	F4 Marine police coordination	179.9
151.190R	F5 Dispatch	179.9
159.375	F6 Emergency	179.9
164.640	F7 U.S. EPA coordination	CS

Division of Solid Waste Management

| 151.190R | F1 Dispatch | 179.9 |
| 159.375 | F2 Emergency | 179.9 |

New Jersey Water Supply Authority

173.3125	various	Data - Spruce Run Reservoir
462.575R		Spruce Run, Round Valley reservoirs
159.465		Reservoir security

Miscellaneous units

31.90	KEA733	Trenton
	KEH924	Vincentown
462.550R	KAA8061	Trenton

Thomas H. Kean New Jersey State Aquarium

Camden

464.8875R	WNYW608	Operations
464.8625R	WNYW608	Operations
464.7875R	WNYW608	Operations
464.6875R	WNYW608	Operations

FACTOID:

New Jersey has become a popular place for filmmakers. Try taking your scanner along when there is a film shoot in your area. In 1992 alone, the following films were shot either entirely or partly in the Garden State: "Home Alone 2: Lost in New York," "The American Wife," "Boomerang," "Scent of a Woman," "The Age of Innocence," "Home of Angels," "Music by Chance," "Chamber Music," "Nothing and Nowhere," "Zero Cool," "Hot Heads," "Being Human," "A Bronx Tale," "Taking Gary Feldman," "The Night We Never Met," "The Thing Called Love," "Philadelphia," "Naked in New York," "Manhattan Murder Mystery" and "Life with Mikey." "Home of Angels" was filmed in Voorhees and Deptford, while "Chamber Music" was filmed in Atlantic City.

NEW CASTLE COUNTY

Police

156.165R	KNAU522	F1 Dispatch	103.5
156.165M	KNAU522	F2 Car to car	103.5
155.115R	KNAU522	F3 Car to car primary	173.8
155.115M	KNAU522	F4 Car to car	103.5
155.490	KNAU536	F5 Operations/Detectives	103.5
154.860	KGF268	F6 Statewide emergency net	
155.475		F7 Nationwide police emergency	CS
154.755	KGF268	Police	
158.805M	KNAU522	Police	103.5

Fire

33.78	KGE831	F1 Statewide dispatch	CS
33.94	KGE831	F2 County fireground	CS
33.68	KGE831	F3 County fireground	CS

Local Fire

33.70M		Aetna Hose	
460.625R		Aetna Hose	
465.575M	WNXH760	Aetna Hose	
460.600		Brandywine Hundred	179.9
33.58		Brandywine Hundred	
460.575M		Cranston Heights	88.5
453.900		Elsmere	192.8
460.525		Elsmere	
33.90M		Hockessin	
33.96M		Hockessin	
33.82		Odessa	
460.600R		Talleyville	CS
154.340		Port Penn	

Ambulance

155.235	WXF898	Dispatch	
462.950R	WRY278	Paramedics	
462.975R	WRY278	Paramedics dispatch	192.8
463.050B		Paramedics primary	
468.050M		Paramedics primary	
463.025B		Paramedics secondary	
468.025M		Paramedics secondary	
463.125B		Paramedics backup	
468.125M		Paramedics backup	

County operations

45.16	KBJ979	Public works	103.5
154.115	KQU202	County units	
453.325	KXD290	New Castle Airport units	
47.62	WRX649	Special emergency	
856.4375T	KNIA880	Public safety (future fire system)	
852.6125R	KNIA880	Public safety	
853.0625R	KNIA880	Public safety	
853.3875R	KNIA880	Public safety	
854.1375R	KNIA880	Public safety	
854.5125R	KNIA880	Public safety	

Municipalities

Elsmere Town

155.010R	KAY931	Police dispatch
154.860M	KA48196	State police emergency net
155.535M	KA48196	Police
155.745	WQH723	Town units

Middletown Town

155.775	WRB477	Town units

Mill Creek Town

151.685M	WPDN995	Mill Creek Fire Co. Safety House

New Castle City

154.800	KZB327	Police dispatch	
154.860M	KA41726	State police emergency net	
460.050R	WNUX222	City units	141.3
47.78	KGE376	Water utility	

Newark City

155.250R	KGE351	Police F1 dispatch	141.3
154.755	KGE351	Police F2	141.3
156.030M	KGE351	Police F3 car to car	141.3
154.860M	KGE351	Police F4 state police emergency net	
158.970M		Police surveillance	
154.040	KAZ662	City units/police F5 "Data"	131.8
173.210	WGS902	Water utility data	

Newport Town

154.665R		Police dispatch by state	123.0

Odessa Town

33.82	KCH734	Fire mutual aid

WILMINGTON CITY

856.2625R	KNIA879	Trunked public safety - police/fire	
857.2625R	KNIA879	Trunked public safety - police/fire	
856.7625T	KNIA879	Trunked public safety - police/fire	
155.310	KGA819	Police F1 (old)	103.5

155.130R	KGA819	Police dispatch (old)	103.5
155.610	KGA819	Police operations (old)	103.5
155.640	KGA819	Police operations (old)	103.5
154.860	KGA819	State police emergency net	
154.755	KGA819	State police system	
154.965R	KDL981	Fire F1 dispatch (old)	
155.055R	KDL981	Fire F2	
155.055M	KDL981	Fire F3 car to car	
155.925	WXF791	City units	
155.280M	KV2984	Ambulances to hospitals	179.9
155.340M	KV2984	Ambulances to hospitals	179.9
462.625R	KAC8169	Housing authority	

FACTOID:
The city of Wilmington was the first city in the Delaware Valley to switch public safety communications to an 800-MHz trunked system. Both police and fire departments use the seven-channel system.

STATE OF DELAWARE

Delaware State Police

154.665R	KGA814	F1 North (Bellefonte)	123.0
	KGA815	New Castle "Recom"	
		Troops 1, 2, 6, 9	
154.935R		F2 Central (Kent)	123.0
		Troop 3	
154.755R		F3 South (Sussex)	123.0
		Troops 4, 5, 7	
154.695	KGA814	F4 Data/information (Bellefonte)	123.0
	KGA815	New Castle	
155.460M	KA4953	F5 surveillance/strike force	123.0
155.850M	KA4953	F6 surveillance/strike force	123.0
155.475		F7 Nationwide police emergency	CS
154.860M	KA4953	F8 Statewide emergency net SWEN	
465.475M	KA4953	Mobile extenders	
154.650	WNGB337	Operations, Blackbird	
154.710	WNLQ406	Operations, Dover	
154.770	WNLQ406	Operations, Dover	
460.500M	KA4953	Surveillance	
465.125M	KA4953	Surveillance	
465.225M	KA4953	Surveillance	
465.500M	KA4953	Surveillance	
39.50	KGA814	Bellefonte	
		SERT, hazmat, aircraft, tactical, traffic	
44.86M	KA4953	F1 mobile to base (old with 45.02B)	
45.02		F2 AVCOM (state police aircraft)	CS
45.24	KCT604	F3 Emergency Management	

New 800 MHz trunked system - future use
866.075 866.100 866.425 866.5875 866.700, 868.375 868.6625
868.725 868.9125 868.975

	WNSS436	Talleyville

Department of Transportation

47.22		F1 New Castle County
	KJY892	Wilmington
	KGE666	Odessa
	KGG901	New Castle
	KCV371	Delaware City
		F1 Sussex County
47.34		F2 Kent County

	KJY892	Wilmington	
	KGE666	Odessa	
	KGG901	New Castle	
	KCV371	Delaware City	
151.100M	KD43762	Operations	
156.135	KJI391	Delaware Turnpike maintenance	192.8
1610 kHz	WNZP450	Delaware Turnpike Travelers Information Station, Wilmington/Newark	
530 kHz	WNRZ656	Travelers Information Station, temporary	

Department of Natural Resources and Env. Control

44.68		F1 Parks
44.72		F2 Marine Police
45.28M	KD30556	F3 Park Service
151.175		Forestry and Agriculture operations
151.385		Forestry and Agriculture operations
159.225R	KXQ694	Dept. of Natural Resources, Dover
159.420R	KXQ693	Dept. of Natural Resources, Milton
44.92M	KE7049	Forestry
31.98M	KE7049	Forestry

State government

35.90	WXR411	Gov. Bacon Health Center, Del. City	
45.24	KCT604	Emergency Management, Del. City	
47.62P	KUQ744	Bissell Hospital, Wilmington	
153.995M	KA70289	Superior Court, Wilmington	
155.100	WXT835	State offices, Wilmington	123.0
155.100	KQP602	Capitol Building, Dover	
155.130R	WPDC226	Christiana Hospital security, Wilm.	82.5
155.400	KFT454	State Hospital, New Castle	123.0
155.835	WNKG246	State units, Dover	
155.880M	KD45109	State units	
155.895M	KD49465	State units	
157.450P	KNEE311	State Hospital, Newark	
158.895M	KD49465	State units	
452.325R	KNHS559	DART Buses, Wilmington F1	
452.425R	KNHS559	DART Buses, Wilmington	
452.775R	WPCK610	DART Buses, Kirkwood	
452.850R	KNHS559	DART Buses, Wilmington F2	
452.875R	KNHS559	DART Buses, Wilmington	
453.525R	WXR380	Corrections vans, New Castle F3	88.5
453.7875M	KD51398	State units	
453.8125M	KD50305	State units, New Castle County	

453.8125R	KD50305	State mobile repeaters, New Castle County	
453.950R	WXR379	State units, Dover	
458.050M	KD21365	State units	
458.100M	KD21365	State units	
458.450M	KD30005	State units, New Castle County	
460.025R	WNVK316	State prison, Smyrna	
460.025R	WPBY565	Gander Hill Prison, Wilmington	114.8
861.3875T	WNJJ677	State units	

FACTOID:
The Delaware Memorial Bridge, which connects the New Jersey Turnpike and Interstate 295 in New Jersey with Interstate 95 in Delaware, is 4.63 miles long, including the approaches on each shore. The main span over the Delaware Bay is 2,150 feet long.

REGIONAL AGENCIES

Delaware River Port Authority

154.100R		Electrical and maintenance	77.0
156.120R		Bridge maintenance	
156.700		Port operations - marine	CS
453.425R		Administration	
460.375R		Police north (Ben Franklin, Betsy Ross bridges)	77.0
460.425R		Police south (Walt Whitman, Commodore Barry bridges)	77.0
159.690	WPCC836	Shipping	
530 kHz	WPBN697	Travelers Information Station broadcasts - Camden/Philadelphia	

Delaware River Joint Toll Bridge Commission

151.010R		Maintenance and police (old)	
151.010M	WNWZ312	Car to car	
158.985B		Toll booths (old)	118.8
158.985M	WNWZ312	Car to car	
151.100M	WNWZ312	Car to car	
156.120R	WNWZ312	Operations, Bethel Twp. PA	71.9
	WNWZ312	Operations, Morrisville NJ	71.9
156.135R	WNWZ312	Operations, Easton PA	71.9
156.2250R	WNWZ312	Operations, Milford NJ	71.9
	WNWZ312	Operations, Lambertville NJ	71.9
	WNWZ312	Operations, Milford PA	71.9
	WNWZ312	Car to car	
468.3375M	KD51847	Data	
468.5625M	KD51847	Data	
468.6875M	KD51847	Data	
469.2375M	KD51847	Data	
469.3625M	KD51847	Data	
469.4125M	KD51847	Data	
469.6875M	KD51847	Data	
469.9625M	KD51847	Data	

Delaware River and Bay Authority

155.310		Del Mem Bridge police Ch A	123.0
156.350		Police Channel B (marine)	CS
154.860M		Del. Mem Bridge - police SWEN/DE	
151.070		Del. Memorial Bridge maintenance	141.3
453.9625R		Del. Memorial Bridge maintenance	CS
453.0375M	WNWN414	New Jersey and Delaware units	

Southeastern Penna. Transportation Authority

502.4875R		F2 Buses, City Transit Division	131.8
502.5125R		F3 Buses, City Transit Division	131.8
502.5375R		F4 Buses, City Transit Division	131.8
502.5625R		F5 Buses, City Transit Division	131.8
502.5875R		F6 Buses, City Transit Division	131.8
502.6125R		F7 Buses and trolleys, supervisors - Market Street Subway, Suburban Transit Division	131.8
502.6375R		F8 Telemetry	131.8

502.6625R		F9 Surface supervisors, buses, City Transit Division	131.8
502.6875R		F10 Security - subways, SEPTA police	131.8
502.7125R		F11 Buses, Suburban Transit Division	131.8
502.7375R		F12 Buses, universal emergencies - supervisors	131.8
502.7625R		F13 Subway supervisors	131.8
502.7875R		F14 Surface supervisors	131.8
504.1375M		F15 Operations supervisors	131.8
30.82		Old F4, supervisors, West Phila., Northeast Phila.	
30.94	WNIM250	Broomall PA	
30.98		Old F1, Red Arrow Division, trolleys and supervisors	
31.02	WNIM250	Broomall PA	
31.10		Old F3, City Transit Division maintenance	
31.14		Old F2, City Transit Division maintenance	
457.425M		Security units	
463.575R		Transit units (West Caln Township)	
935.925R	WNXU787	Trunked system (Malvern PA, Phila.)	
936.975R	WNXU787	Trunked system (Malvern PA, Phila.)	
937.9125R	WNXU787	Trunked system (Malvern PA, Phila.)	
937.9875R	WNXU787	Trunked system (Malvern PA, Phila.)	
938.000R	WNXU787	Trunked system (Malvern PA, Phila.)	
939.9625R	WNXU787	Trunked system (Malvern PA, Phila.)	
937.9875R		SEPTA units	
938.000R		SEPTA units	
939.9625R		SEPTA units	

Miscellaneous

Philadelphia Port Corp.
151.895, 151.955, 463.325, 463.525, 463.825, 464.900, 464.950, 464.975

South Jersey Port Corp.
154.540M, 154.570M

Philadelphia Regional Port Authority
151.250, 151.280, 453.225M, 453.275M, 453.475M, 453.525M, 453.625M, 453.675M

Greater Philadelphia Chamber of Commerce
466.4125M,. 466.4375M

RAILROADS

Southeastern Pennsylvania Transportation Authority

160.350	F1 Road (primary)	CS
161.400	F2 Point to train	
160.395	F3 Roberts Avenue Yard, Powelton Avenue Yard	
	(railcars, supervisors)	
161.460	F4 Alternate road; Wayne Junction, Wind Tower	
CTCSS NOTE: Trains CS, bases 141.3		
160.800	Road - Amtrak coordination	
160.275	Police/Suburban Station-Broad Tower to MU car inspectors	167.9
161.325	MU car inspectors to Broad Tower Suburban Station	
160.935	Maintenance	
160.290	Maintenance of way/signal department	

Amtrak - Northeast Corridor

160.920	F1 Road-1 Northeast Corridor
CTCSS NOTE: Trains 141.3, bases 210.7	
160.800	Nationwide road
161.070	F2 Road-2 (Metro North)
160.635	F3 Maintenance of Way, Philadelphia only
160.280	F3 Road - Metro North
160.350	F3 SEPTA Road, train managers
160.515	F4 Maintenance of way, outside of Philadelphia
161.295R	Police dispatch
161.205M	Police car to car
457.900M	Police vehicular repeaters
161.505R	Car Department - 30th Street Yard, Maintenance of Way, Philadelphia
452.900	Station administration, Philadelphia
160.260	Pinup crew, Race Street yardmaster
160.455	Work trains and yard
452.900	Shop operations, Wilmington DE
161.280R	Maintenance of equipment, Wilmington DE shops
161.400	Pennsauken NJ, Berlin NJ, Winslow NJ, Absecon NJ
154.515M	Portables
851.1875R	Bear DE operations

Conrail

160.800	F1 Road	
161.070	F2 Road and Yard	
161.130	F3 Maintenance of Way/Signal Department	
161.130R	F4 Maintenance of Way/PBX	
160.860	F3 Yard & Road, South Philadelphia yard	
160.980	F4 Yard & Road, industrial switching	
160.680M	F3 Police car to car, Philadelphia	CS
160.560	F4 Police dispatch, Philadelphia	
161.205M	Coordination with Amtrak police	
155.475M	Nationwide police emergency	
161.520R	Car Department, Philadelphia	
160.830	Shops, coal pier, Philadelphia	
161.430M	Right of way, Philadelphia	
457.9375M	End of train telemetry	
161.220	Yard, Philadelphia	
160.350	Coordination with SEPTA trains	
161.400	Signal Department trouble desk, Wayne Junction	

160.470	Pennsylvania Truck Lines, Morrisville
160.980M	Pennsylvania Truck Lines, Morrisville
457.5375M	Real estate operations
457.5625M	Real estate operations
457.5875M	Real estate operations
461.3875M	Real estate operations
461.6625M	Real estate operations
461.8125M	Real estate operations
467.7625M	Real estate operations
467.7875M	Real estate operations
467.8125M	Real estate operations
467.8375M	Real estate operations
467.8625M	Real estate operations
467.8875M	Real estate operations
467.9125M	Real estate operations

NJ Transit rail operations

161.355	Philadelphia, Trenton NJ, Atlantic City NJ
161.400	Raritan Valley, Shore lines
160.830	Raritan Valley, Shore lines
160.890	Bayhead NJ
161.235	Raritan Valley Line

Chessie System

160.230	F1 Police/Road
160.320	F2 Dispatch
160.530R	F3 Yard, Wilsmere Yard, Philadelphia
160.530R	F3 Yard, Yardmaster, Wilmington DE
160.425	Yard, Wilmington DE
161.160	F4 Yard
160.290	F5 Yard
160.410	F6 Yard (Maintenance of Way in Philadelphia)
160.740	F7 Yard
160.785	F8 Maintenance of Way/Signal Department
160.875	F9 Police
161.400R	F10 Car Department
160.470	Channel Y - Waterfront terminals, Yard, Philadelphia
160.890	Channel Y1 - Waterfront terminals, Yard

Port Authority Transit Co. High-Speed Line

453.675	Lindenwold NJ yard	
500.8125R	F1 Police dispatch	107.2
500.8375R	F2 Power director, maintenance of way/trackmen	107.2
500.8875R	F3 Administration (trains secondary)	107.2
500.9125R	F4 Road (trains primary)	107.2

Miscellaneous rail lines

New Hope and Ivyland Railroad

161.475R	Operations

Pennsylvania-Reading Seashore Line

161.160	F1 Road
161.190	F2 Road

Philadelphia, Bethlehem and New England

160.575	Road and yard

160.695	Supervisory
161.565	Maintenance of way
161.280	Operations
466.2125M	Operations
466.2625M	Operations
466.3625M	Operations
466.4125M	Operations
466.4625M	Operations
466.5125M	Operations
466.5625M	Operations
466.6125M	Operations
466.6625M	Operations
466.7125M	Operations

Upper Merion and Plymouth Railroad
160.485	Operations

Five-Mile Beach Electric Railway
44.54	Operations, North Wildwood NJ

Octorara Railroad
160.545	Operations, Kennett Square PA
160.605M	Operations

Tyburn Railroad Co.
161.385R	Penndel PA

Wilmington and Western Railroad
160.530	Tourist line
160.755	Not in use
462.700	Operations

Historic Towne of Smithville Railroad
463.525R	Tourist Line, Smithville NJ

Bethlehem Steel Co. railroad
158.430	Fairless Works line, Fairless Hills PA

141.3

Black River & Western Railroad
502.0375R	Train to office, Ringoes NJ
502.0375M	On-train use
161.085	Operations

Reading, Blue Mountain & Northern Railroad
161.310	Operations, Hamburg PA
161.370	Hamburg PA
161.250	Hamburg PA
160.470	Hamburg PA
160.770	Hamburg PA

Brandywine Valley Railroad
462.7625R	Channel A, Operations, Coatesville, PA
464.5625R	Channel B, Operations
467.7875M	Philadelphia operations

Delaware Coast Line
160.455	Operations, Lincoln DE

Landisville Railroad
160.485	Operations, Landisville PA

Shore Fast Line
160.335	Road, Pleasantville NJ
161.385	Switching

Winchester and Western Railroad Co.
161.310	Bridgeton NJ

West Jersey Shore Line
161.025	Operations, Salem NJ

Strasburg Railroad Co.

161.235	Operations, Strasburg PA

Bristol Industrial Terminal Railway Inc.

160.935	Bristol PA

National Railways Historical Society

151.925M	Lancaster chapter, Quarryville PA, excursions

Trains Tower Service

464.100R	Runnemede NJ
852.9375R	Philadelphia
936.225BM	Philadelphia

Association of American Railroads

935.8875R	Automated rail control signaling
935.9375R	Automated rail control signaling
935.9875R	Automated rail control signaling
936.8875R	Automated rail control signaling
936.9375R	Automated rail control signaling
936.9875R	Automated rail control signaling

FACTOID:

The railroad station at 30th and Market streets in Philadelphia is the second busiest in the nation, right behind New York City's Pennsylvania Station. More than 4.8 million passengers use the station for both Amtrak and SEPTA trains every year.

MAJOR AIRPORTS AND MILITARY AIR BASES

Philadelphia International Airport

133.400	ATIS (recording)	
125.400	Approach	
126.600	Approach	
127.350	Approach	
128.400	Approach	
281.300	Approach (military)	
307.200	Approach (military)	
343.600	Approach (military)	
118.500	Tower	
263.000	Tower (military)	
121.900	Ground	
348.600	Ground (military)	
119.750	Departure	
124.350	Departure	
320.100	Departure (military)	
118.850	Clearance	
348.600	Clearance (military)	
121.650	Pre-taxi	
125.300	Clearance delivery (small airfields)	
162.300	FAA wind shear telemetry	
453.450R	Airport police/operations	107.2
453.850R	Airport operations	107.2
500.3875R	Airport Parking Authority	79.7
27.47	Atlantic Aviation	
35.88	Thrifty Rent A Car	
42.96	Sheraton Airport Inn	
122.825	Business Express	
122.950	Gateway Pace Aviation	
129.425	United Parcel Service flight operations	
130.400	Atlantic Aviation operations	
151.625M	Park 'N' Go valet parking	118.8
151.655	Ground Services	
151.685	APCOA Parking	
152.300B	Rapid Rover Airport Shuttle	
154.515	Airport Inn, Essington PA	
157.560M	Rapid Rover Airport Shuttle	
411.550R	US Postal Service Express Mail operations	D223
452.800R	Flite Line Service	
460.650R	Continental	110.9
460.675R	TWA	
460.700R	Com Air	
460.700R	Commuter airline	123.0
460.725R	United	203.5
460.750BM	Allegheny Commuter Airlines	
460.775R	American	114.8
460.800R	Northwest	
460.825R	Delta	
460.825R	Bar Harbor Airways	
460.850R	Piedmont	
460.875R	Delta Air Lines	
461.0625R	Ogden Allied Aviation	186.2
461.150R	Globe Airport Parking	
461.1875M	Pilot Freight Carriers	
461.225R	PHL Airline Service	
461.2375R	United Parcel Service operations	D143

461.7125M	USAir operations	
461.7625R	United Parcel Service operations	D143
461.9125M	USAir operations	
461.9375M	Dollar Rent A Car	
461.9875M	USAir operations	
462.025M	Airport Taxicab Dispatcher	
463.2125M	American Airlines	
463.3625M	American Airlines	
463.4375R	United Parcel Service operations	D143
463.4875M	American Airlines	
463.5375M	American Airlines	
463.6375R	United Parcel Service sorting operations	D143
463.8625M	Dollar Rent A Car	
463.9375R	United Parcel Service feeder trucks	D143
463.950R	Ground Services Inc.	
464.1875R	United Parcel Service ramp operations	D143
464.325R	Flying Car Port	
464.375R	Aircraft Service International	
464.475R	Continental Airlines	
464.4875M	American Airlines	
464.525R	Avis Rent A Car	
464.525R	TW Express Airlines	
464.525R	Delaware Aviation	
464.525R	Atlantic Aviation	
464.575R	National Car Rental	
464.575M	Avis Rent A Car	
464.6625R	United Parcel Service feeder trucks	D143
464.675R	Ogden Allied Aviation	
464.725R	Atlantic Aviation	
464.725R	APCOA Parking attendants	
464.750R	Philadelphia Airport Shuttle	
464.775R	Budget Rent A Car	
464.825R	Ogden Allied Aviation	
464.9125R	United Parcel Service aircraft ramp operations	D143
464.925R	Holland Bus Co. parking lot shuttle buses	
464.975R	Hertz	
464.975R	Continental Airlines	
464.9875M	Budget Rent A Car	
465.750M	Business Express	
466.0125M	Budget Rent A Car	
466.1125M	Federal Express	
466.6625M	Budget Rent A Car	
466.5375M	TW Express Airlines	
467.7875M	American Airlines	
468.5375M	Budget Rent A Car	
469.8625M	Budget Rent A Car	
851.0875R	Hudson General Aviation Services	
851.9625R	Federal Express	
852.5125R	Federal Express	
854.5375R	1st Class Airport Transportation	
856.2875T	USAir operations	
858.8625R	Federal Express	

Northeast Philadelphia Airport

123.000	Unicom
121.150	ATIS (recording)
112.000	Philadelphia Radio (transmit)
122.000	Philadelphia Radio
122.200	Philadelphia Radio

122.600	Philadelphia Radio
255.400	Philadelphia Radio (military)
123.800	Approach/Departure
291.700	Approach/Departure (military)
126.900	Tower
349.000	Tower (military)
27.47	Delaware Aviation

Allentown-Bethlehem-Easton International Airport

121.900	Ground ops
118.200	Approach/departure
119.650	Approach/departure
124.450	Approach/departure
120.500	Tower
122.950	Unicom
122.950	Suburban Airlines
453.625R	Airport operations/fire
453.925R	Airport operations
460.225R	Airport police
460.650R	Suburban Airlines
460.700R	USAir
460.725R	United Airlines
460.775R	American Airlines
460.775M	Northwest Airlines

Atlantic City International Airport

122.950	Unicom/Butler Aviation
108.600	ATIS (recording)
118.350	Approach
124.600	Approach
239.000	Approach (military)
385.500	Approach (military)
396.000	Approach (military)
120.300	Tower
133.600	Tower (helicopters)
239.000	Tower (military)
385.500	Tower (military)
121.900	Ground
284.600	Ground (military)
119.550	Clearance
124.600	Radar
385.500	Radar (military)
396.000	Radar (military)
151.955	Butler Aviation
154.600M	Atlantic City Group Services
460.700BM	USAir
460.750R	Continental Airlines

Dover Air Force Base

126.350	Tower
128.000	Approach
138.045	Flight lines
138.275	Freight ops
138.405	Aircraft maintenance
173.5875	Fire/crash
225.400	Ground control
273.500	ATIS (recording)

289.400	Clearance delivery	
324.500	Departure control	
327.000	Tower	
339.100	Approach control	
342.500	Metro (weather)	
130.650	Command post	
349.400	Command post	
359.300	Radar service	
372.200	Pilot to dispatcher	
163.5875	Post engineers/maintenance	
165.1125	Base "common"	
173.9125	Security police	173.8
173.4375	Base police	
173.5625P	Medical paging	
413.200	Base "operator"	

Greater Wilmington Airport

122.950	Unicom	
123.950	ATIS (recording)	
118.350	Philadelphia Approach/Departure	
323.100	Philadelphia Approach/Departure (military)	
126.000	Tower	
305.400	Tower (military)	
121.700	Ground	
275.800	Ground (military)	
453.325	Airport operations	
343.000	Air National Guard C-130 ops ("Seabee")	
38.60	National Guard	
46.90	Army National Guard helicopters	
148.200	Air National Guard security	
149.325	Air Force Reserves security	
150.250	Air Force Reserves fire	
34.15	Air Force Reserves crash fire-rescue	
43.76	Airport Shuttle Service	CS
129.000	DuPont Co. flight operations	
151.625M	Delaware Wing, Civil Air Patrol	
464.525BM	Atlantic Aviation	162.2
43.76	Airport Shuttle Service	CS

McGuire Air Force Base

265.500	ATIS (recording)
112.600	ATIS (recording)
110.600	Approach
120.250	Approach
127.500	Approach
259.300	Approach
363.800	Approach
388.200	Approach
120.600	Tower
236.600	Tower
255.600	Tower
121.800	Ground
275.800	Ground
120.250	Departure
127.500	Departure
259.300	Departure
363.800	Departure
135.200	Clearance

335.800	Clearance	
130.650	Command Post (commercial)	
319.400	Command Post (military)	
120.000	Radar	
318.200	Radar	
239.800	Pilot to Metro Service	
30.50	Army operations	
36.90	Walson Army Hospital ambulance	
38.85	Army Military Police	
36.85	Air Force Military Police (liaison)	
41.35	Army operations	
138.075	Air Force Office of Special Investigations	
138.165	Air Force Office of Special Investigations	
139.300	Army operations	
143.775R	Air Force MARS (hams)	
143.950	Air Force MARS (hams)	
148.065	Air Force operations	
148.075	Air Force ramp control	
148.100	Air Force transportation	
148.175R	Air Force 21st Command primary phone	179.9
148.215	Air Force aircraft line maintenance 438th primary	
148.225	Aircraft maintenance	
148.475	Air Force aircraft maintenance 170th	
148.515	Air Force aircraft fueling operations	
148.675	Medical net	
149.000	Air National Guard security	
149.175	Strategic Air Command alert units	
149.200	Air Force aircraft maintenance	
149.215	Air Force aircraft maintenance	
149.225	Air Force POL trucks	
149.265	Air Force aircraft maintenance 438th secondary	
149.300	Air National Guard law enforcement	
149.400	Air Force aircraft maintenance	
149.500	Air National Guard law enforcement	
150.175	Air Force MMS	
150.200	Air National Guard aircraft maintenance	
150.225	Air Force aerial port cargo control	
150.275	Air National Guard medical net	
150.325	Air Force civil engineers	
150.345	Air Force civil engineer	
151.775	McGuire ALERT Team	
163.4625	Air Force flight line defense security	CS
163.4875	Air Force base security	118.8
163.5375	Air Force clinic and ambulance medics	
163.5625	Air Force security	
165.0125	Air Force base taxi dispatcher/motor pool	
165.1125R	Air Force 21st Command F3 phone	118.8
166.200	Air Force POL trucks	
173.5375	Air Force Crash Fire Rescue common	
173.5875	Air Force fire/crash	
407.450R	Fire Department dispatch/operationss	114.8
412.800	Crash crew	
413.200	Air Force civil engineers	
413.450P	Air Force alert pagers	

Mercer County Airport

123.000	Unicom
119.450	ATIS (recording)
123.800	Philadelphia Approach/Departure

291.700	Philadelphia Approach/Departure (military)	
120.700	Trenton Tower	
257.800	Trenton Tower (military)	
121.900	Ground	
257.800	Ground (military)	
121.900	Clearance	
257.800	Clearance (military)	
111.300	ILS	
41.00	New Jersey National Guard	
CTCSS note: base CS; aircraft 148.0		
155.115	Airport operations	71.9

Reading Municipal Airport

119.900	Tower
119.250	Approach-north
125.150	Approach-south
121.900	Ground operations
127.100	ATIS (recording)
151.745	USAir Express
453.425R	Airport operations

Warminster Naval Air Warfare Center

123.800	Philadelphia Approach
291.700	Philadelphia Approach (military)
126.200	Navy Tower
340.200	Navy Tower (military)
359.600	Navy Tower (military)
139.500	Military Police
CTCSS note: mobile CS; base 123.0	
140.100	Runway access
140.900	Fire Department

Willow Grove Naval Air Station

123.800	Philadelphia Approach	
266.800	Radar - GCA	
291.700	Philadelphia Approach	
325.200	Radar - GCA	
119.350	Radar (airshow control)	
134.675	Philadelphia radar	
340.200	Navy Tower	
121.800	Ground	
340.800	Ground	
121.800	Clearance	
344.600	Pilot to Metro Service (weather)	
141.800	PA Air National Guard (AM mode) OA-10	
143.800	PA Air National Guard (AM mode)	
343.000	PA Air National Guard OA-10	
138.900	Air Force Reserve (AM mode) C-130	
351.200	Air Force Reserve C-130 "Shortstop"	
139.500	Military Police; fire dispatch	
CTCSS note: mobile CS; base 123.0		
140.100	Runway access F2	
141.000	Fuel operations	
CTCSS note: mobile CS; base 123.0		
143.715	Flight line operations	
148.250P	Paging	CS
165.1375	Military police	103.5

30.55	Army (airshow use)
34.55	Army UH-1
52.50	Marine Reserves A-4M
49.75	PA Air National Guard OA-10 "Sandy ops"
119.600	Tower
138.800	Police dispatch
138.300	PA Air National Guard air to air (AM mode) OA-10
138.500	PA Air National Guard air to air (AM mode) OA-10
127.550	Radar
275.600	ATIS
306.800	Base operations
320.100	Philadelphia approach/departure
299.600	Radar - GCA
323.500	Radar - GCA
325.200	Radar - GCA
314.800	Radar - GCA (airshow control)
226.500	Army U-H1
273.000	Navy VP-64 P-3C
370.050	Navy P-3C
345.950	Navy P-3C
362.800	Navy VP-64 P-3C
382.800	Navy VR-52 C-9 "Home Plate"
383.500	Navy SH-2 "Goldensword"
283.000	Marine Reserves H-53 "Hustler"/A-4M "Viper"
310.200	Aircraft maintenance

FACTOID:

The following airlines use Philadelphia International Airport: American, American Eagle, British, Air Jamaica, SwissAir, AMC, USAir, USAir Express, Midwest Express, Mohawk, Continental, Continental Express, United, United Express, Northwest, Northwest Airlink, TWA, TW Express, Delta and Delta Connection. In addition, the following cargo operators also operate at Philadelphia International Airport: Federal Express, United Parcel Service, Emery Worldwide, DHL, Airborne Express, Zantop, U.S. Postal Service and Burlington Express.

WEATHER

162.400	KHB38	Atlantic City NJ
	WXL39	Allentown PA
	KEC83	Baltimore MD
162.475	**KIH28**	**Philadelphia PA**
162.550	KWJ94	Lewes DE
	WXL40	Harrisburg PA
	KWO35	New York City NY

MARINE

156.300	Channel 6	Intership safety
156.350	Channel 7	Commercial
156.400	Channel 8	Commercial
156.450	Channel 9	Commercial
156.500	Channel 10	Commercial
156.550	Channel 11	Commercial
156.600	Channel 12	Port operations/U.S. Coast Guard
156.650	Channel 13	Navigational
156.700	Channel 14	Port operations/U.S. Coast Guard
156.750	Channel 15	Environmental/hydrographic
156.800	Channel 16	Distress and calling
156.850	Channel 17	State control
156.900	Channel 18	Commercial
156.950	Channel 19	Commercial
161.600R	Channel 20	Port operations
157.050	Channel 21	U.S. Coast Guard
157.100	Channel 22	U.S. Coast Guard
157.150	Channel 23	U.S. Coast Guard
161.800R	Channel 24	Marine phone calls
161.850R	Channel 25	Marine phone calls
161.900R	Channel 26	Marine phone calls
161.950R	Channel 27	Marine phone calls
162.000R	Channel 28	Marine phone calls
156.275	Channel 65	Port operations
156.325	Channel 66	Port operations
156.375	Channel 67	Commercial
156.425	Channel 68	Non-commercial
156.475	Channel 69	Non-commercial
156.525	Channel 70	Non-commercial
156.575	Channel 71	Non-commercial
156.625	Channel 72	Non-commercial
156.675	Channel 73	Port operations
156.725	Channel 74	Port operations
156.875	Channel 77	Commercial
156.925	Channel 78	Non-commercial
156.975	Channel 79	Commercial
157.025	Channel 80	Commercial
157.175	Channel 83	U.S. Coast Guard Auxiliary
161.825R	Channel 84	Marine phone calls
161.875R	Channel 85	Marine phone calls
161.925R	Channel 86	Marine phone calls
161.975R	Channel 87	Marine phone calls
157.425	Channel 88	Commercial

AMERICAN NATIONAL RED CROSS

47.42	WSV436	Eagleville PA	
	KMK205	Langhorne PA	
	KLL699	Philadelphia PA	
	KKD443	Philadelphia PA	
	KUE532	Allentown PA	
	KUS573	Allentown PA	
	WNYD916	Bethlehem PA	
	KNFM396	Easton PA	
	KGE755	Reading PA	
	KAA774	Toms River NJ	
	KNHL460	Camden NJ	
	KAA764	Cape May Courthouse NJ	
	KUI719	Trenton NJ	
	WNXV840	Vineland NJ	
	WNHQ486	Dover DE	
	KLM690	Delaware City DE	
47.46	KRM271	Langhorne PA	
	WNKC824	West Hempfield Township PA	
	WYG334	Wilmington DE	CS
	WNHQ486	Dover DE	
47.62	WNUG880	Lancaster PA	
	WNUG880	West Hempfield Township PA	
	WNVM336	Princeton NJ	
453.0125R	KD48132	Berks County PA	
	WNKC824	West Hempfield Township PA	
462.675R		Philadelphia PA	
	KAE1805	Newtown Square PA	
462.9875R	KUS573	Allentown PA	
	WPAA256	Philadelphia	
467.9875M	KUS573	Allentown PA	
502.1625R	WIJ897	Woodbury NJ	
851.6125R	WNVW358	Wilmington DE/Philadelphia	

TOWNWATCH GROUPS

39.18	KGA260	Abington Township PA	162.2
27.205		Paulsboro NJ (CB Channel 20)	
27.47	WSC698	Kensington, Philadelphia	
154.515	KNFS910	Haverford Township PA	
154.515		Prospect Park PA	
154.600M	KD52189	Yeadon Town Watch Assn. Inc., Yeadon PA	
462.550M	KAC2914	Olney CB Townwatch, Philadelphia	
462.575	KAD8761	Upper Darby PA	
462.600	KAD4239	Society Hill, Philadelphia	
462.625R	KAD1169	Bustleton-Bowler, Philadelphia	
462.625R	KAD5737	Charlestown, Malvern PA	
462.650	KAB8964	Torresdale, Philadelphia	
462.650R	KAB5134	Delaware County, Media PA	
462.650R	KAB5135	Delaware County, Holmes PA	
462.650R	KAB5136	Delaware County, Alden PA	
462.700	KAD1272	Kensington, Philadelphia	
462.700R	KAD7519	Nottingham, Bensalem PA	
861.8875T		Guardian Angels, Philadelphia	
461.650R	WPBK540	East Falls Town Watch, Phila.	
463.700R	WPEG697	West Phila. Coalition of Neighborhoods	
151.625M	WNZG735	Glasgow Pines Community Watch, Newark DE	
151.685	WPDX279	Glasgow Pines Community Watch, Newark DE	
463.775R	WPAI964	21st Ward Central Town Watch, Phila.	
154.515	WNUW652	Reading Volunteer Crime Watch Inc., Reading PA	
464.525R	WNUD848	Pennsbury Watch Inc., Chadds Ford PA	
151.715M	WPDJ580	Neighborhood Watch, Burlington County NJ	
151.805M	WPDJ580	Neighborhood Watch, Burlington County NJ	
154.600M	KD29438	Hilltown Township Town Watch Inc., Bucks County PA	
464.1125R	KD49192	Haverford Township Townwatch Inc., Delaware County PA	

RADIO ORGANIZATIONS

462.5625M	various	Philadelphia Notification Network	100.0
462.000R	WPAJ806	Philadelphia Fire Films	123.0
155.265	WRZ699	Greater Philadelphia Search and Rescue	
45.92M	KA69109	Greater Philadelphia Search and Rescue	
33.10M	KA69109	Greater Philadelphia Search and Rescue	
462.675R	KAD3391	Suburban REACT	
462.675M	KAB4920	Eastern Pennsylvania REACT	
462.675M	KAB6438	PA Emergency & Communications Council	
462.675M	KAB9344	Delaware Valley REACT	
462.675M	KAC2691	North Penn Valley REACT	
462.675M	KAB4490	Commonwealth Monitors REACT	
462.675R	KAD5025	Mid-Atlantic Amateur Radio Club	
155.160M	KA48357	PA Emergency Communications Association	
155.220M	KA48357	PA Emergency Communications Association	
155.280M	KA48357	PA Emergency Communications Association	
155.340M	KA48357	PA Emergency Communications Association	
462.600R	KAC8633	LEMA REACT, Allentown PA	
462.675	KAD5982	Lancaster County REACT	
462.675R	KAD8722	Berks Emergency Repeater Association, Reading PA	
462.675R	KAC7950	Daniel Boone REACT, Reading PA	
462.675R	KAE1940	Greater Philadelphia Search and Rescue	
462.675R	KAD1699	Roving Knights REACT, Philadelphia	
462.675R	KAC8633	LEMA REACT, Allentown PA	
462.700R		Overbrook Amateur Radio Club, Philadelphia	
151.625M	WPDZ482	Delaware Wing, Civil Air Patrol	
462.700R		Law Enforcement Assistance Radio Network (LEARN)	

NOTE: This system operates in western suburbs. West CTCSS tone is 82.5; south CTCSS tone is 136.5. Many police officers operate on this system.

155.325	WPBW578	New Jersey Search and Rescue Inc.
151.715	WNYF617	McGuire ALERT Team, Browns Mills NJ

FACTOID:
While organizations no longer can license themselves in the general mobile radio service from 462.550 to 462.725 MHz, they still can use the eight repeater channels and seven splinter channels if each member or family who belongs to their organization obtains a license.

NEWS MEDIA

TV stations

Note: As of presstime, there are anticipated network affiliation changes that may alter which TV stations use which news media frequencies. KYW-TV Channel 3 is to switch from NBC to CBS. WCAU-TV Channel 10 probably will become the new NBC affiliate. The other stations should retain their affiliations.

KYW-TV Channel 3 (News 3)

450.550R	KGJ812	F1 Primary	107.2
450.550M	KGJ812	F2 Car-to-car	107.2
450.650M	KGJ812	F3 KYW-AM coordination	107.2
450.1875	KGJ812	F4 Cues	107.2
450.1875	WYR221	F5 Trenton bureau	
450.1875	WHE708	F6 Atlantic City	
450.1875R	KGJ812	Skycam 3 copter	107.2
455.4375	KGJ812	IFB	107.2

WPVI-TV Channel 6 (Action News)

455.450R	KEH411	F1 News vans	156.7
455.0875	KEH411	F2 Engineering	156.7
450.450	KEH411	F3 Trenton bureau	156.7
455.1125	KEH411	F4 Special events	156.7
450.4875	KEH411	F5 New Jersey units	156.7
455.2375	KEH411	IFB	156.7
455.1125	KPK520	Harrisburg bureau	
455.1125	KPK520	Atlantic City bureau	
161.640	KJV904	News cars	
455.2625	KPK520	Smyrna DE, Wilmington DE remote sites	
455.4625	KPK520	Chester County remote site	
450.2375	KPK520	Chester County remote site	

WCAU-TV Channel 10 (Channel 10 News)

455.050	KEH242	F1 News dispatch	114.8
455.150	KEH242	F2 Engineering	114.8
455.3875	KEH242	F3 Camera	
455.5125	KEH242	F4 Talent	141.3
455.4125	KEH242	F5 Directors	many
450.3875	KEH242	F6 Camera minitor	
450.5125	KEH242	F7 Talent minitor	
450.4125	KEH242	F8 Camera, studio	
455.2125	KEH242	IFB	103.5
153.170	KSQ556	VHF-1	
154.570M	KC4780	VHF-2 portables	

WHYY-TV Channel 12

461.825R	WNHK628	Philadelphia operations	
463.675R		Wilmington operations	
463.675R	WNHK628	Avondale PA repeater	
464.850R	WNCX214	WDPB-TV 64 Seaford DE operations	

WNJS-TV Channel 23 (New Jersey Network News)

455.3875	KSO239	Camden base	110.9
462.575M	KAD9788	New Jersey Public Broadcasting	
467.575M	KAD9788	New Jersey Public Broadcasting	

WTXF-TV Channel 29 (The 10 O'Clock News)

450.2875R	KPH649	News crews	118.8
153.170M	KJ9420	Operations	

WWOR-TV Channel 9 (Secaucus NJ)

| 450.4875M | | Trenton bureau |

WGAL-TV Channel 8 Newscenter 8 (Lancaster PA)

| 450.4125 | | IFB |
| 450.650 | | News |

WBOC-TV Channel 16 (Dover DE/Salisbury MD)

| 161.640 | KPG528 | F1 alternate |
| 161.700 | KPG528 | F2 engineering |

WTVE-TV Channel 51 (Reading PA)

| 464.625R | KNDY370 | Operations |

WGCB-TV Channel 49 (Red Lion PA)

| 151.955 | WNDZ331 | Operations |

Philadelphia radio stations

KYW Newsradio 1060 AM / WMMR-FM 93.3

450.750R	KGJ811	F1 Remote relays KYW	107.2
450.750M	KGJ811	F2 car to car KYW	107.2
450.650M	KGJ811	F3 KYW-TV coordination	107.2
161.730M		Mobile repeaters KYW	
161.640		WMMR-FM events	
450.800		WMMR-FM remotes	

WGMP-AM 1210 / WOGL-FM 98.1

450.350R	KKA206	F1 Remotes, audio	114.8
450.250	KKA206	F2	
455.350M	Traffic copter		DPL

WIP-AM 610 Sportsradio / WYSP-FM 94.1

450.050	KQA894	F1 News, special events	
450.150	KQA894	F2 News, special events	
450.850R	KQA894	F3	
161.760	KPJ300	WIP sports remotes	79.7

WPHY-AM 560 / WBEB-FM 101.1

| 450.1125M | KE5630 | Remotes |
| 450.1875M | KE5630 | Remotes |

WIOQ-FM 102.1

| 450.900M | | Remotes |
| 455.925M | | Remotes |

WRTI-FM 90.1 Jazz 90 Temple Public Radio Network

| 450.700M | | Remotes |
| 455.700M | | Remotes |

WFLN-FM 95.7

450.700M	KB96802	Remotes
450.750M	KB96802	Remotes
450.800M	KB96802	Remotes
455.700M	KB96802	Remotes
455.750M	KB96802	Remotes
455.800M	KB96802	Remotes
852.2125R	WYA204	Operations

WPLY-FM 100.3 (Media PA)

450.6125	KPM479	Remotes
455.6125	KPM479	Remotes
161.730	KC23223	Remotes
161.670	KC23223	Remotes

Philadelphia traffic reporting services
Metro Traffic Control

450.800		Operations	141.3
455.800		WJBR airborne reports F3	141.3
450.1625	KPL585	Alternate airborne reports F4	
450.700M		Operations	
455.700M		Operations	
450.850R	KPH252	Shadow aircraft, copter reports F2	97.4
455.850	KPH252	Shadow copter, aircraft	97.4
450.5875R	KPJ827	Shadow reporters F1	162.2
450.5875M	KPJ827	Shadow car to car	162.2
450.1125		Shadow future use	162.2
450.875		Shadow operations	
123.050		Aircraft operations	
135.750		Aircraft operations	
122.900		Copter aero use	

Express Traffic

450.2625		Traffic spotters	CS
461.625R	WNYF955	Operations	
935.675		F1 car to car	
939.2625R		Trunked system F1	
939.275R		Trunked system F1	
939.2875R		Trunked system F1	
939.300R		Trunked system F1	
939.3125R		Trunked system F1	
939.325R		Trunked system F2	
939.3375R		Trunked system F2	
939.350R		Trunked system F2	
939.3625R		Trunked system F2	
939.375R		Trunked system F2	

Other radio stations

151.625M		WKDN-FM, Camden NJ	
151.715	KWT351	WCOJ-AM, Coatesville PA	
153.050	KFH744	WDAC-FM, Lancaster PA	
153.230	KJK815	WBUD-AM, Trenton NJ	
153.290	KJK815	WBUD-AM, Trenton NJ	
153.350	KJK815	WBUD-AM, Trenton NJ	
161.640	KJR586	WCHR-FM, Trenton NJ, church service remotes	CS
161.640		WTTM-AM, Trenton NJ remotes	
161.640		WDEL-AM/WSTW-FM, Wilmington DE traffic reports	CS
161.670	KKN776	WAWA-AM, Chester PA	
161.670	KVH331	WNAP-AM, Norristown	
161.670	KJB601	WOND-AM, Pleasantville, NJ	
161.670		WBUX-AM, Doylestown PA sports/events	CS
161.670		WDEL-AM/WSTW-FM, Wilmington DE	
161.670	KC27680	WWFM-FM, Ewing NJ	
161.700		WTNJ-AM, Trenton NJ sports remotes	
161.700		WBUD-AM, Trenton NJ, church service remotes	
161.700		WMID-AM, Atlantic City NJ copter	
161.700		WKXW-FM, Trenton NJ remotes	CS
161.700M	KJ6230	WPAZ-AM, Pottstown PA	
161.700	WRI280	WRNJ-AM, Hackettstown NJ cue	100.0
161.730	KVD492	WHWH-AM, Princeton, NJ plane	
161.730	KVD492	WPST-FM, Trenton NJ remotes	CS

	KVD492	WPST-FM, Trenton NJ remotes	110.9
161.730	KKN776	WAWA-AM, Chester PA	
161.730	KVH331	WNAP-AM, Norristown	
161.730	KFH744	WDAC-FM, Lancaster PA	
161.760	KVH331	WNAP-AM, Norristown PA	
161.760		WBCB-AM, Levittown PA, sports remotes	
161.760M	KD4138	WCOJ-AM, Coatesville PA	
450.010	WSM718	WLAN AM-FM, Lancaster, PA	
450.050	KUI487	WSNJ-FM, Bridgeton NJ	
450.1125M		WDEL-AM, Wilmington DE, Beachwatch plane	
450.2125	WHE840	WILM-AM, Wilmington DE traffic plane	
450.250	KUI487	WSNJ-FM, Bridgeton NJ	
450.450	KQB218	WRNJ-AM, Independence NJ	
450.700		WGMD-FM, Rehoboth Beach DE, F1 portable	
450.750		WRNJ-AM, Hackettstown NJ remotes	
450.800		WGMD-FM, Rehoboth Beach DE, F1 remotes	
450.950		WDRE-FM, Jenkintown PA	
455.2625		WILM-AM, Wilmington DE	
455.700		WRDV-FM, Warminster PA remotes	
455.700		WGMD-FM, Rehoboth Beach DE, F2 portable	
455.700	KPL764	WGLS-FM, Glassboro NJ	
455.800		WGMD-FM, Rehoboth Beach DE, F2 remotes	
455.900		WDRE-FM, Jenkintown PA	
455.900	KPL764	WGLS-FM, Glassboro NJ	
462.725R	KAC9746	WDVR-FM, Ocean City NJ operations	
464.300R		WLEV-FM, Easton PA events	
852.6125R	WPBE516	Traffax Traffic Network, Harrisburg, Lancaster, Reading units	

Newspapers
The Philadelphia Inquirer / Philadelphia Daily News

173.325	WNFQ458	Photographers	CS
452.975R	KNHR949	Circulation	114.8
453.000R	KNHR949	Circulation	114.8
464.3125M	KB86492	Operations	
464.325M	KZ5232	Broad Street building security	
464.3375M	KB86492	Operations	
464.5125R	KB86492	Operations	
464.750R	WQY774	South Jersey circulation	114.8
502.0125R		Daily News city desk	
851.7625R	WNLK853	Operations	
852.0875R	WNPM314	Bucks County PA operations	
852.6375R	WNLK853	Operations	
464.3125M	WPAX507	Upper Merion PA printing plant	
464.3375M	WPAX507	Upper Merion PA printing plant	
467.7625M	WPAX507	Upper Merion PA printing plant	
467.7875M	WPAX507	Upper Merion PA printing plant	
467.8125M	WPAX507	Upper Merion PA printing plant	
467.8375M	WPAX507	Upper Merion PA printing plant	
467.8625M	WPAX507	Upper Merion PA printing plant	
467.8875M	WPAX507	Upper Merion PA printing plant	
467.9125M	WPAX507	Upper Merion PA printing plant	
464.5125R	WPAX507	Upper Merion PA plant operations	
952.0625R	WNJT616	Data, Philadelphia	
952.48125R	WNTQ987	Data relay, Malvern PA	
953.150B	WNTQ989	Data relay, Malvern PA	
956.750B	WNTQ988	Data relay, Malvern PA	

Other newspapers

35.94	KZL943	The Mercury, Pottstown, PA	
173.275	KNIG389	Daily Local News, West Chester PA	
173.375	KER671	The Morning Call, Allentown PA	114.8
465.000P	WPDT670	The Morning Call, Allentown PA paging	
173.225	WNIQ992	The Morning Call, Easton PA bureau	
173.375	WNIQ992	The Morning Call, Easton PA bureau	
462.150R		Express-Times, Easton PA	
463.275R	KJD477	Bucks County Courier Times, Levittown PA circulation	
501.0875R	KNR669	The Reporter, Lansdale PA	
808.2625M	WNSE641	The Reporter, Lansdale PA	
502.3125R	WIE921	The Daily Intelligencer, Doylestown PA	
502.3625R	KNR671	The Reporter, Lansdale PA	
856.1875T		The Times-Herald, Norristown PA	
861.6125T		The Times-Herald, Norristown PA	
173.275	KLQ705	Lancaster New Era, Lancaster PA	
453.000R	WNGJ531	Patriot-News, Harrisburg PA	
461.875R	WNJP824	Reading PA Eagle	
464.450R	WNPG771	Evening Phoenix, Phoenixville PA	
502.1625R	WII383	The Record, Horsham PA	
453.000R	WNKN252	Times Leader, Wilkes-Barre PA	
173.275	WNUA385	Scranton Times, Scranton PA	
173.225	KCL620	Courier Post, Cherry Hill NJ	
173.275	WNHV665	The Times, Trenton NJ	DPL
463.275R	WQE263	Burlington County Times, Willingboro NJ	136.5
464.025R	KNAJ632	The Press, Atlantic City NJ	167.9
502.4125R	KNQ490	Courier Post, Cherry Hill NJ circ	
453.000R	KGC868	Asbury Park Press, Neptune NJ	
452.700R		Asbury Park Press photographers	
452.9875R	WNDF230	Asbury Park Press	
458.000M	KP4604	The Associated Press, NJ units	
936.5625M	WNZU845	The Associated Press, NJ units	
173.225	KZY571	The Morning News/Evening Journal, Wilmington DE, dispatch, reporters	
463.825R	WXR829	The Morning News/Evening Journal, Wilmington DE, trucks, loading	
463.950R	WNPK227	The Morning News/Evening Journal, Wilmington DE, USA Today circ.	
457.5625M	KD34051	The Morning News/Evening Journal, Wilmington DE operations	
461.6625R	KD42273	The Morning News/Evening Journal, Wilmington DE operations	

Video

463.700R	WNIR708	NFL Films, Camden NJ	
462.000R	WPAJ806	Philadelphia Fire Films F1 dispatch	123.0
462.000M	WPAJ806	Philadelphia Fire Films F2 fireground	123.0
462.575R		Philadelphia Fire Films F3	
462.875P	KNCU277	Philadelphia Fire Films	
154.540		Philadelphia Fire Films	
462.675R		Philadelphia Fire Films	162.2
462.725R		Philadelphia Fire Films	
154.540	WNNG823	Camden County Fire Video, Pine Hill NJ	
464.400R	KNAG683	Photo Research, Philadelphia	
464.550M		EJ Stewart Video, sports events	

Cable TV

464.350M	KD24153	PRISM Production Center, Phila.
464.925R	WNJF591	QVC Network studios, West Chester PA
464.775R	WPBR292	QVC Network studios, West Chester PA
154.570M	WNWX584	QVC Network studios, West Chester PA
154.600M	WNWX584	QVC Network studios, West Chester PA
464.375M	WNXC314	QVC Network studios, West Chester PA
464.6625R	WPCY769	QVC Network studios, West Chester PA
464.925BM	WNQR926	QVC Network warehouse, Lancaster PA
461.7125R	WPBM450	QVC Network warehouse, Lancaster PA
161.730		Service Electric Cable, Allentown PA TV shows
450.450		Service Electric Cable, Allentown PA "Super 2" events and cameras
151.805	KUV535	Service Electric Cable, Allentown PA Service Center F1
151.715	KNEB320	Service Electric Cable, Allentown PA Service Center F2

Magazines

154.600M	KZ8392	TV Guide, Radnor PA
464.425R	WRZ214	TV Guide, Radnor PA
464.675R	WRZ214	TV Guide, Radnor PA
464.925R	WRR626	TV Facts of North Wilmington (DE)

FACTOID:

While many news organizations use two-way radios for their routine news operations, cellular telephones also are used widely. While SMRS radio systems in the 800 and 900 MHz band don't seem to be used by any news media in the Philadelphia area, they are used quite extensively in other Pennsylvania cities.

ENTERTAINMENT AND RECREATION

Pennsylvania

501.8875R	KNM639	Philadelphia Zoo Society
463.7125R	WPCU934	Zoological Society of Philadelphia
464.3125R	WPCU934	Zoological Society of Philadelphia
151.655	WQC674	Philadelphia Zoo
151.685	WQC674	Philadelphia Zoo
151.805	WNCV255	Zoological Society of Philadelphia
463.4875R	KD22965	Zoological Society of Philadelphia
463.5375R	KD22965	Zoological Society of Philadelphia
464.325R	KVC315	Kimberton Rollerama, Devon PA
154.600M	KQ9637	Franklin Institute research, Phila.
154.570M	KL4210	Philadelphia Zoo monorail (old)
151.805	WPDP202	Philadelphia Zoo Safari Monorail
461.875R	WQI616	Pt. Pleasant Canoe, Pt. Pleasant PA
35.92	KQX725	Merion Golf Club, Ardmore PA
464.3375R	WPAJ299	Merion Golf Club, Ardmore PA
462.9125R	WPAJ299	Merion Golf Club, Ardmore PA
467.900M	WNYV623	Merion Cricket Club, Merion PA
461.375M	KD42989	Merion Cricket Club, Merion PA
151.835	WNYI680	Saucon Valley Country Club, Bethlehem PA
151.685	WNYI680	Saucon Valley Country Club, Bethlehem PA
464.475	WQG779	Highpoint Racquet Club, Chalfont PA
464.300	WXQ681	Longwood Gardens, Kennett Square PA
464.325	WXQ681	Longwood Gardens, Kennett Square PA
464.800R	WPDA641	Longwood Gardens, Kennett Square PA
461.450R	KNAM737	Northbrook Canoe, Malvern PA
461.425R	WNGQ451	Northbrook Canoe Co., Wagontown PA
501.9625R		Northampton Valley Country Club, Holland PA
463.3375R	WNVE805	State Theater, Newtown PA
463.8875R	WNVE805	State Theater, Newtown PA
464.550M	WPBM380	Penn National Racetrack Offtrack Wagering, Harrisburg PA
464.375M	WPBM380	Penn National Racetrack Offtrack Wagering, Harrisburg PA
464.250M	WPAQ864	Pocono Downs, Luzerne County PA
463.875M	WPAQ864	Pocono Downs, Luzerne County PA
469.250M	WPAQ864	Pocono Downs, Luzerne County PA
468.875M	WPAQ864	Pocono Downs, Luzerne County PA
469.9375M	WNWK911	Grandview Speedway, Berks County PA
151.655	WNFW321	Chester Valley Golf Course, Malvern PA
463.875R	WZH202	D&G Amusements, Philadelphia
464.950	KNFG495	Specta-Guard, Phila. Spectrum security
151.775M	KY5041	Philadelphia Eagles
464.775M		Philadelphia Eagles cheerleaders choreographers wireless microphones
151.895M	KA73526	Golf Association of Philadelphia
153.350M	KU3840	Valley Forge Music Fair
461.4625M	KD30378	Valley Forge Music Fair
464.325	WNHX957	Historic Strasburg, Strasburg PA
154.570M	KB48580	The Phillies, Philadelphia
154.540M		The Phillies, Philadelphia
151.715	WNFK931	Ogden Co., Philadelphia
151.745	WNFK931	Ogden Co., Philadelphia
461.825R	WNQO870	Supercade Amusements, Philadelphia
463.400R	KNHA490	Home Theater Inc., Philadelphia
464.875R	WNUY970	Philadelphia Museum of Art

154.570M	KR2670	Franklin Institute, Philadelphia. F1	
154.600M	KR2670	Franklin Institute, Philadelphia, F2 lab	
154.600M	KZ8354	Spectrum, Philadelphia	
461.900M	KA96125	West Point Park, West Point PA	
464.875M	KO7160	Academy of Natural Sciences, Phila.	
464.0625R	WPBK851	Academy of Natural Sciences, Phila.	
463.3125R	WPBK851	Academy of Natural Sciences, Phila.	
151.835M	WPDZ366	Wyncote Golf Club, Wyncote PA	
151.745M	WPDZ366	Wyncote Golf Club, Wyncote PA	
464.825M		Reading Fairgrounds, Reading PA	
151.835M	WPAA749	Sesame Day Camp, Montgomery County PA	
151.805M	WPAA749	Sesame Day Camp, Montgomery County PA	
151.655		Outdoor World/Lake Gaston, Lancaster PA	
154.515		Penn Warner Club, Tullytown PA	
461.175	WNJU721	Penn Warner Club, Tullytown PA	
151.715	KNGB561	Sesame Place, Langhorne PA	
151.685M	KD21176	Sesame Place, Langhorne PA	
464.275R	WNGM659	Spectrum, Philadelphia	
464.950	KNFX871	Spectrum, Philadelphia	
467.750M	KN7460	Spectacor Management, Philadelphia	
467.1625M	KB48083	Spectacor Management, Philadelphia	
467.7625M	KN7460	Spectacor Management, Philadelphia	
154.600M	KA30792	General Security, Veterans Stadium, Phila.	
463.4375M	KB80959	Boyertown USA, Boyertown PA	
463.400R	KNAR368	Eastern Penn Relay, Philadelphia	
469.8125M	KB76779	Daniel Boone Homestead, Berks County PA	
151.715	KGR708	Dutch Wonderland, Lancaster PA	
154.570M	KA75469	Pocono Action Park	
151.775M	KA92065	Pocono Vacation Park	
461.275R	WNGT945	Bertil Roos School of Motor Racing at Pocono Raceway, Long Pond PA	
464.425R	WNHJ233	Pocono Raceway, Long Pond PA	
856.7875R	WNGT901	Stavola Brothers Racing, Long Pond PA	
154.570M	KB74698	Lancaster Country Club, Lancaster PA	
464.150R		Hersheypark, Hershey PA security F1	
464.275R		Hersheypark, Hershey PA maintenance	
464.400P		Hersheypark, Hershey PA paging	
464.325R		Hersheypark, Hershey PA operations	
464.975R		Hersheypark, Hershey PA operations	
464.425BM	WNZX245	Hersheypark, Hershey PA security F2	
464.375BM	WNZX246	Hersheypark, Hershey PA first aid	
463.200R		Larry Holmes Enterprises, Easton PA	118.8
151.655	KNGC764	Dorney Park, Allentown PA security F2	
154.515M	KB73377	Dorney Park, Allentown PA maint. F5	
154.540M	KD29836	Dorney Park, Allentown PA portables F6	
154.570M	KA61905	Dorney Park, Allentown PA ops F1	
462.750P	WNQK472	Dorney Park, Allentown PA	
154.600M		Dorney Park Wildwater Kingdom, Allentown PA	
151.805		Dorney Park, Allentown PA ops F3	
151.625M	KB93607	Musikfest, Bethlehem PA F1	
151.685	WPBF349	Musikfest, Bethlehem PA F2	
464.550M		Musikfest, Bethlehem PA	
151.865	WNDG904	The Great Allentown Fair, Allentown PA, security F1	
151.475M		The Great Allentown Fair, Allentown PA gate control F2	
151.415M		The Great Allentown Fair, Allentown PA parking control	

151.685M		The Great Allentown Fair, Allentown PA, operations
151.715		Terry Hill Water Park, Breinigsville PA
154.570M	KD47583	Coatesville Country Club, Coatesville PA
154.600M	KD47583	Coatesville Country Club, Coatesville PA
154.600M	KD23992	Lehigh Country Club
154.600M	KB72797	Media Heights Country Club
467.125M	KB95285	Llanerch Country Club, Llanerch PA
461.4375M	WNWS776	Lancaster Family YMCA, Lancaster PA
464.000R	WNWS776	Lancaster Family YMCA, Lancaster PA
461.175M	WPDA595	Little League Baseball, Williamsport PA
464.375M	WPDA595	Little League Baseball, Williamsport PA
152.930		Blue Mountain Ski Area, Palmerton PA
155.220	WNIX723	National Ski Patrol, Spring Mount PA
155.295	WNIX723	National Ski Patrol, Spring Mount PA
155.340	WNIX723	National Ski Patrol, Spring Mount PA
154.540	WNHY610	Spring Mountain Winter Sports ski area, Spring Mount PA
463.225R	WNGG605	Shawnee Canoe Trips, Stroudsburg PA
464.925M	WNWL978	Hershey Country Club Golf, Hershey PA
464.675R	WNWL978	Hershey Country Club Golf, Hershey PA
154.600M	WPCF593	Gwynedd Club Management Corp., Gwynedd Valley PA
154.600M	WNUG730	Tree Top Golf Course, Lancaster County PA
151.625M	WNWU633	PA State Women's Golf Association
151.865M	WNZR868	North Hills Country Club, North Hills PA
151.715M	WNZR868	North Hills Country Club, North Hills PA
154.600M	WPDF520	Blue Mountain Quarter Midget Racing Assn., Northampton County PA
151.835	WNUR370	Mountain Springs Camping Resort, Shartlesville PA
464.1625R	WPAF969	Bent Creek Country Club, Lancaster County PA
464.1875R	WPAF969	Bent Creek Country Club, Lancaster County PA
464.0875R	WPAF969	Bent Creek Country Club, Lancaster County PA
463.900R	WNXC661	Keystone State Games, Allentown PA
154.570M	WPAH804	Waynesboro Country Club, Chester County PA
154.600M	WPAH804	Waynesboro Country Club, Chester County PA
464.575BM	WPAZ458	Camp Swatara, Bethel Township PA
461.1125R	WNSK341	Spring Gulch Resort Campground, Lancaster County PA
464.925M	KD27580	Waterloo Gardens, Downingtown PA
463.7875M	KD40482	Hershey Professional Soccer Club, Hershey PA
154.570M	KB91583	United Parachute Club, Montgomery County PA
154.570M	KD34061	Tel Hai Campground Association, Chester County PA
30.80	KD30751	Huntingdon Valley Country Club, Huntingdon Valley PA
30.84M	KD30751	Huntington Valley Country Club, Huntingdon Valley PA
154.600M	KD34060	Village Greens Miniature Golf Course, Lancaster County PA
151.895M	KB94890	Berkleigh Country Club, Berks County PA
154.570M	WNSR439	Explorer Post 2123
154.600M	WNSR439	Explorer Post 2123
154.540	WNSR439	Explorer Post 2123
461.9125R	KB92071	Great Valley Girl Scout Council, Frazier PA
154.515M	KD43585	Torresdale-Frankford Country Club, Philadelphia
463.800M	KD51483	Indian Valley Country Club, Bucks County PA
151.925	WNLM946	Country Club of Harrisburg PA

New Jersey

154.600M	KA61773	Wading Pines Campground, Pleasantville, NJ
151.955	WYN884	Pine Barrens Canoe, Chatsworth NJ
461.825R	KNBF983	American Sightseeing, Hamilton NJ
151.715	WSO257	Oak Ridge Campground, Marmora NJ
158.460P	WZL337	Atlantic City Racetrack, McKee City NJ
154.570M	KB54433	Atlantic City Racetrack, McKee City NJ
464.525R	WNSZ480	Atlantic City Racetrack, McKee City NJ
855.0375R	KNHY638	Garden State Park, Cherry Hill NJ
855.2625R	KNHY637	Garden State Park, Cherry Hill NJ
855.3375R	KNHY617	Garden State Park, Cherry Hill NJ
855.5125R	KNHY616	Garden State Park, Cherry Hill NJ
467.8625M	WNZX224	Riverton Country Club, Riverton NJ
154.600M	KB73326	Hopewell Vallley Golf Club,Hopewell NJ
154.600M	KD22008	YMCA Camp Bernie, Warren County NJ
463.200R	KNJR606	Pineland Canoes, Toms River NJ
464.550M		New Jersey Special Olympics
469.550M		New Jersey Special Olympics
502.4125R	WIF666	Harrison Aire hot-air ballooning, Ringoes NJ
154.540	WNPZ364	Skydive East, Pittstown NJ
154.515	KVW426	Pine Haven Campground, Ocean View NJ
151.955M	WNZR359	Westwood Golf Club, Gloucester County NJ
464.2875M	WPBT924	Sea Pirate Light Campsite, Ocean County NJ
463.525R		Historic Towne of Smithville (NJ)
154.600M	KA80009	New Jersey State Golf Association
154.540M	WPCZ546	Delaware RIver Family Campground, Warren County NJ
154.600M	KM8702	Seaview Country Club, Linwood NJ
461.9625M	WPAU689	Marriott Seaview Golf Resort, Absecon NJ
464.575BM	WPAU689	Marriott Seaview Golf Resort, Absecon NJ
463.225M	KD44513	Marriott Seaview Golf Resort, Absecon NJ
463.6375M	WPBQ797	Linwood Country Club, Linwood NJ
151.835	WNGA911	Driftwood Campground, Cape May Courthouse NJ
154.570M	WNXH675	King Mummy Campground, Cape May County NJ
154.540	KVW509	Great Adventure, Jackson NJ safari gates/road service

154.600M	KS6934	Great Adventure, Jackson NJ safari	
462.725R	KAB6419	Great Adventure, Jackson NJ food/concessions	179.9
464.675R	WQP950	Great Adventure, Jackson NJ security F1	179.9
464.425R	WNMF812	Great Adventure, security F2	179.9
464.975R	WNGL707	Great Adventure, maintenance	179.9
464.825R	WNLF952	Great Adventure, services,	179.9
469.325M		Great Adventure safari trucks	179.9
464.325R	WNGL726	Great Adventure, Jackson NJ	179.9

154.570M	KB83646	Tavistock Country Club, Tavistock NJ
154.600M	KB83646	Tavistock Country Club, Tavistock NJ
154.600M	KO2166	Boy Scouts of America (NJ)
151.775M		Forsgate Country Club
151.955M		Forsgate Country Club
151.805M		Hidden Acres Campground
151.925M		Clementon Amusement Park, Clementon NJ
151.625M	WNWI662	Beaver Brook Country Club, Clinton NJ
154.570M		Delsea Campground
461.1125R	WPBI232	Four Seasons Camp Ground, Salem County NJ
154.570M	WPDE738	Gambler Ridge Golf Club, Burlington County NJ
154.515	WNNX379	Hunterdon Ballooning, Flemington NJ
152.420	WNQB614	Avalon Development and Golf, Cape May Court House NJ

463.900R	WNQS630	Brigantine Beach Club, Brigantine NJ
154.540	WNNZ593	Pleasant Valley Campground, Estell Manor NJ
464.6875M	KD45621	Holly Shores Girl Scout Council, Cumberland County NJ
154.570M	WNSM520	Acorn Campground, Cape May County NJ

Delaware

151.715M	KS3535	US 13 Dragway (DE)
151.715	WXD993	Brandywine Raceway, Wilmington DE
151.655	KEU349	Delaware Racing Assn., Stanton DE
151.805	KEU349	Delaware Racing Assn., Stanton DE
151.835M	KD20676	Winterthur Museum (DE)
464.825	WNAC332	Du Pont Country Club, Wilmington DE maintenance
154.515	WZK642	Wilmington Country Club, Wilmington DE
157.740P	KSH600	Brandywine Raceway, Wilmington DE
151.895	KRL694	Dover Downs Race Track, Dover DE
464.325	WNGU495	Grand Opera House, Wilmington DE

MUSHROOM FARMING

43.28	KYA583	Ontelaunee Mushroom Farms, Temple PA
451.9875R	WNYZ577	Jen Mar Mushroom, Berks County PA
158.385	KLB223	C&C Carriage Mushroom, Toughkenamon PA
43.48	WNNA343	Alpha Mushroom Farm, PA statewide
35.48	KXW874	RCA Mushrooms, Kennett Square PA
151.925	WPBW971	Giorgi Mushroom Co., Temple PA
463.675R	KNIL380	C&C Carriage Mushroom, Lincoln University PA
151.955	WNVN486	VJ Mushrooms, Temple PA
464.4375R	WPBN578	Elite Mushroom, Chester County PA
464.7875R	WPBN578	Elite Mushroom. Chester County PA
464.375R	WNWP348	Hy Tech Mushroom Compost, West Grove PA
151.775	WNZJ859	Giorgi Mushroom Co., Temple PA
154.600M	KJ9881	Moonlight Mushrooms, PA statewide
151.745	WPDG499	Rain Fresh Mushrooms, Fleetwood PA
463.475R	WNUM314	JD Mushroom Inc., Cochranville PA
464.325M	KB39025	M&J Mushroom Co., PA statewide
463.400R	WNNG923	Kaolin Mushroom Farms, Avondale PA
463.350R	WNQW447	Giorgi Mushroom Co., Wayne Township, Schuylkill County PA
464.275R	WNSD967	Remos Mushroom Service, Cochranville PA

UTILITIES

PECO Energy Co.
Formerly Philadelphia Electric Co.
800 MHz system
Divisions:

Philadelphia	851.8875T, 851.4125R, 853.4875R	
Systemwide	854.3875R, 854.3875M	210.7
Conowingo	854.3875R	
Eastern (Warminster, Newtown, Oreland, North Wales)		
	851.2125R, 851.8625R, 852.7625R, 853.1125R, 853.7625R	
Schuylkill	851.9125T	
Main Line (Ardmore)		
	856.3625T	
Delaware	856.3375T	
Western	856.3125T	
Sanatoga trunked:	852.9625R, 853.8125R, 854.9125R, 855.9125R	

Electric

37.64	Coatesville PA
37.68	Doylestown PA, Eagleville PA, Hillside PA, Langhorne Manor PA, Media PA, North Wales PA, Warminster PA
37.78	Ardmore PA, Bristol PA, Bryn Mawr PA, Carversville PA, Chester PA, Coatesville PA, Cromby PA, Eddystone PA, Langhorne Manor PA, Morton PA, Plymouth Meeting PA, Plymouth Township PA, Valley Forge PA, Warminster PA, West Grove PA, West Norriton PA, Phoenixville PA, Limerick PA (nuclear plant)
37.80	Bryn Mawr PA, Eagleville PA, Valley Forge PA
37.86	Media PA

Gas

47.90	Media PA, Morton PA	
48.00	Ardmore PA, Langhorne Manor PA, Warminster PA, Willow Grove PA	CS
48.26	Ardmore PA, Chester PA, Coatesville PA, Eagleville PA, Langhorne Manor PA, Morton PA, Valley Forge PA, Warminster PA, West Conshohocken PA, Willow Grove PA	
48.32	Berwyn PA, Coatesville PA, Valley Forge PA	

Miscellaneous PECO Energy Co.

154.570M	Pole-Line intercom
151.925	Mark Controls - Limerick nuclear power plant
154.46375	Data
158.235M	Portables
173.20375	Data
451.075	Limerick nuclear plant
451.1125M	Limerick nuclear plant
451.1625R	Load dispatcher, Eagleville PA
451.1625M	Coatesville PA
451.1875M	Portables
451.4375M	Portables
451.625P	Valley Forge PA, Limerick PA
451.6375M	Portables - Chester County PA
457.6625M	Portables - Chester County PA
457.6875M	Portables - Chester County PA
460.9625M	Portables (also 461.0875M, 465.9625M, 466.0875M)
467.750M	Portables (also 467.800M, 467.850M, 467.900M)
507.3125R	Limerick nuclear plant

507.3375R	Limerick nuclear plant
507.3625R	Limerick nuclear plant
507.3875R	Limerick nuclear plant
507.4125R	Limerick nuclear plant
507.4625R	Limerick nuclear plant
928.53125	Data
928.73125	Data
952.53125	Data
952.73125	Data

UGI Corp.

48.02	Reading PA
48.38	Reading PA
451.050	Gas - Souderton, Salisbury Township PA
451.150	Gas - Souderton, Salisbury Township PA

Pennsylvania Power & Light Co.

37.62	Systemwide
37.30	Systemwide
37.86	Systemwide
37.54	Systemwide
37.56	Systemwide
37.70	Systemwide
37.74	Systemwide
37.46	Systemwide
451.200R	Systemwide

Systemwide = Telford, Allentown, Easton, Slatington, Wernersville, Columbia, Kinderhook PA

37.76	Columbia PA
451.200R	Holtwood PA

Philadelphia Suburban Water Co.

48.10	Bryn Mawr PA, Janney PA, Media PA, Phoenixville PA, Wyncote PA, Valley Forge PA
153.500	West Chester PA
851.2625R	Operations
48.32	Valley Forge PA, Bryn Mawr PA
451.125R	Valley Forge PA

Other utilities

Pennsylvania American Water Co.

48.34	Yardley PA
158.220	Norristown PA

Audubon Water Co.

48.40	Audubon PA

GPU Service Corp.

464.675R	Reading PA

North Penn Water Authority

153.455	Lansdale PA
158.145	Lansdale PA

Great Valley Water Co.

153.500	West Chester PA

Citizens Utilities Home Water Co.

153.635	Upper Providence PA
452.175R	Royersford PA

Chester Water Authority

153.680	Thornbury PA

Octoraro Water Co.

502.9625R	Londonderry PA

Lower Bucks County Joint Sewer Authority

153.515	Levittown PA

Valley Forge Sewer Authority

154.995	Valley Forge PA

Metropolitan Edison

New 900 MHz trunked system:
936.000R, 936.900R, 937.8875R, 937.900R, 937.9375R, 937.950R,
937.9625R, 937.975R, 939.950R
Transmitter sites: Bally, Pine Grove, Reading, Easton
New 800 MHz trunked system:

856.7625T	Wind Gap PA, Phillipsburg NJ, Riegelsville PA, Krumsville PA, Reading PA
856.3875T	Boyertown PA, Krumsville PA, Reading PA
Other:	
37.52	Reading, Topton PA
37.54	Reading, Topton PA
37.56	Reading, Topton PA
451.025R	Reading, Topton PA
451.100R	Reading, Topton PA

Western Berks Water Co.

48.20	Sinking Spring PA

MCI Telecommunications

451.500R	Philadelphia, Boyertown PA
451.300R	Philadelphia
451.350R	Elwood NJ

AT&T

451.325R	Chester PA, Lionville PA, Oxford PA, Wyndmoor PA, Buckingham PA, Lynnport PA
451.400R	Cedar Brook NJ
456.225M	Cherryville relay tower operations (Hunterdon County NJ)

Bell Telephone Co. of Pennsylvania

New 900 MHz trunked system:
Philadelphia:
935.3875R, 935.400R, 935.4125R, 935.425R, 935.4375R, 935.450R,
935.4625R, 935.475R, 935.4875R, 935.500R, 936.3875R, 936.400R,
936.4125R, 936.425R, 936.4375R, 939.8875R, 939.900R, 939.9125R,
939.925R, 939.9375R
Doylestown PA, Allentown PA:
935.450R, 935.4625R, 935.475R, 935.4875R, 935.500R
Coatesville PA:
936.3875R, 936.400R, 936.4125R, 936.425R, 936.4375R,
939.8875R, 939.900R, 939.9125R, 939.925R, 939.9375R
Valley Forge PA, Reading PA:
939.8875R, 939.900R, 939.9125R, 939.925R, 939.9375R
Itinerant use:
936.6375M, 936.6625M

Other:	
451.400R	Philadelphia (also 451.425R, 451.450R, 451.475R, 451.500R, 451.550R, 451.575R, 451.600R, 451.650R)
35.12	Philadelphia, Valley Forge PA
35.16M	Statewide PA
43.16M	Statewide PA
469.550M	Statewide PA

151.985	Upper Darby PA

Conestoga Telephone and Telegraph Co.

451.350R	Boyertown PA
151.775M	Berks County PA

United Telephone Co. of Pennsylvania

451.400R	Columbia PA

Sprint

462.475R	Philadelphia, Berkeley NJ, Pleasantville NJ
463.225R	Philadelphia, Carrcroft DE

Atlantic States Microwave Transmission Corp.

451.300R	Elizabethtown PA
451.350R	Philadelphia PA

Easton Suburban Water Co.

153.455	Operations
158.145	Operations

Blue Mountain Consolidated Water

153.635	Pen Argyl PA

Atlantic Electric Co.

37.60	Beesley Point NJ, Pennsville NJ, Pleasantville NJ
47.98	Atlantic City NJ, Cape May Courthouse NJ, Carlls Corner NJ, Clementon NJ, Germania NJ, Hammonton NJ, Minotola NJ, Ocean City NJ, Paulsboro NJ, Pleasantville NJ, Salem NJ, Wildwood NJ, Williamstown NJ, Woodstown NJ, Mays Landing
48.04	Atlantic City NJ, Salem NJ, Hammonton NJ, Mays Landing NJ
48.12	Same as 47.98
48.36	Same as 47.98
153.470	Beesley Point NJ
154.46375B	Data - Ocean County, Cape May County, Cumberland County NJ
158.145M	Salem County NJ
451.0375R	Operations (Salem County NJ)
451.0875M	Cape May County NJ
451.1875M	Cape May County NJ
451.5875R	Operations
456.4875M	Operations (Salem County NJ)
851.1375R	Cape May Courthouse NJ, Carlls Corner NJ, Egg Harbor Twp. NJ, Pleasantville NJ
852.4375R	same as 851.1375R
853.3375R	Pleasantville NJ
855.1625R	same as 851.1375R
855.3875R	same as 851.1375R
855.6625R	same as 851.1375R
855.8625R	same as 851.1375R
855.9375R	same as 851.1375R

Public Service Electric & Gas Co.

New 900 MHz trunked systems:
937.3875R, 937.400R, 937.4125R, 937.425R, 937.4375R, 937.450R,
937.4625R, 937.475R, 937.4875, 937.500, 938.8875R, 938.900R,
938.9125, 938.925R, 938.9375R, 938.950R, 938.9625R, 938.975R,
938.9875R, 939.000R
Transmitter sites: Bordentown, Lawrence Township, Moorestown NJ

936.200R, 936.2125R, 936.9125R, 936.925R, 937.000R
Transmitter sites: West Deptford, Moorestown, Bordentown,
                 Springfield Township (Burlington County),
                 Lawrence Township NJ

938.250R (non-trunked)
Transmitter sites: Bellmawr, Hamilton Township, Burlington NJ

Other:
Electric

48.14	Bellmawr NJ, Moorestown NJ, Winslow Township NJ	

CTCSS note: base CS, mobiles 114.8

48.16	Hamilton NJ, Lawrence Township NJ	
48.28	Lawrence Township NJ, Moorestown NJ, Winslow Township NJ, Hamilton Township NJ (Mercer County)	
48.56	Lawrence Township NJ	
48.70	Moorestown NJ	
154.570M	Statewide	
154.600M	Statewide	
173.20375M	Data - Salem County NJ	
451.575R	Lower Alloways Creek NJ	
851.9375R	Burlington NJ, Moorestown NJ, Trenton NJ	
852.0125R	Burlington NJ, Moorestown NJ, Trenton NJ	
854.3375R	Operations	
861.8875T	Operations	
938.950R	Operations	
938.9625R	Operations	

Gas

153.545	Burlington Township NJ, Audubon NJ	
153.620	Burlington Township NJ, Audubon NJ	CS/162.2
	also: Springfield Twp. (Burlington County NJ), Bordentown NJ, Moorestown NJ, West Deptford NJ, Pemberton Township NJ	
153.440	Pemberton Township NJ	
158.130	Audubon NJ	
451.100R	Lawrence Township NJ	CS
451.275R	Harmony Township NJ	
173.2375B	Data - Harmony Township NJ	
33.14M	Portables	
451.0375M	Portables (also 451.0625M, 451.0875M, 451.1375M, 451.1625M, 456.0375M, 456.0625M, 456.0875M, 456.1625M, 469.500M, 462.5125M, 467.5125M, 464.325M, 464.375M)	

Trunked
937.3875R, 937.400R, 937.4125R, 937.425R, 937.4375R, 937.450R, 937.4625R, 937.475R, 937.4875R, 937.500R 938.8875R, 938.900R, 938.9125R, 938.925R, 938.9375R, 938.950R, 938.9625R, 938.975R, 938.9875R, 939.000R

PSE&G Artificial Island
(Salem 1&2 / Hope Creek Nuclear Generating Stations)

Operations

451.050R	F1 Salem Unit 1
451.100R	F2 Salem Unit 2
451.375R	F3 Hope Creek
451.050M	F4 Talkaround 1
451.100M	F5 Talkaround 2
451.375M	F6 Talkaround 3

Radiation Protection

451.050R	F1 Salem Unit 1
451.100R	F2 Salem Unit 2
451.375R	F3 Hope Creek
451.150R	F4 Outages

Security

158.205	F1 Salem
158.250	F2 Hope Creek

156.210	F3 Salem County police F1

Fire Department

33.86	F1 Salem County fire F1
33.84	F2 Salem County fire F2
33.88	F3 Salem County fire F3
33.08	F4 Salem County Emergency Management
451.050R	F1 Salem Unit 1
451.100R	F2 Salem Unit 2
451.375R	F3 Hope Creek
451.050M	F4 Talkaround 1
451.100M	F5 Talkaround 2
451.375M	F6 Talkaround 3

Technical Support Centers (TSC)

158.205	F1 Salem security
158.250	F2 Hope Creek security
156.210	F3 Salem County police F1
153.470	F4 Site services

Site Services

158.205	F1 Salem security
158.250	F2 Hope Creek security
none	F3 none
153.470	F4 Site services

Material Control Center

464.325	F1
469.325M	F2

Contractors

151.625	AC&S F1, Stone & Webster F1,
	Bechtel Power Corp. F1, United Engineers F1
151.505	Bechtel Power Corp. F2, United Engineers F2
151.775	AC&S F2
158.460P	United Engineers paging
465.675M	Williams Power F1
464.200	Williams Power F2
464.375M	Chambers Cogeneration

Miscellaneous

173.2875B	Emergency sirens
173.3375B	Emergency sirens
465.000P	PSE&G paging
72.02	Industrial controls (also 72.06, 72.1, 72.3, 72.34, 72.38)

Jersey Central Power & Light Co.

153.425	Hightstown NJ, N. Hanover NJ, Flemington NJ	103.5
	Delaware Township NJ (also 153.605, 153.665, 153.710)	
154.570M	Portables - Ocean County	
30.84M	Operations	
35.02M	Itinerant operations	
154.45625B	Data - Howell Township NJ	
451.075M	Portables (also 451.125M, 451.150M, 456.075M, 456.125M, 456.150M)	
467.7875M	Operations - Ocean County NJ	

New Jersey Natural Gas Co.

48.64	Barnegat NJ, Toms River NJ
48.84	Barnegat NJ
153.485	Swainton NJ
153.530	Swainton NJ
501.4375R	Toms River NJ
451.5375R	Operations
451.6875R	Operations, Ocean County NJ
451.7375R	Operations
451.7625R	Operations
456.1375M	Operations, Ocean County NJ

461.8375M	Operations	
463.9625M	Operations	

United Telephone System of New Jersey
451.400R	Cherryville NJ	100.0
451.400R	Belvidere NJ	

Williams Telecommunications Group
451.350R	Cherryville NJ (Hunterdon County NJ)

New Jersey American Water Co.
173.39625	Data - Cape May County NJ, Atlantic County NJ
451.0375R	Cape May County NJ
451.475R	Washington NJ
451.2125M	Somers Point NJ
461.2375R	Ocean County NJ
462.0375R	Ocean County NJ
463.3625R	Ocean County NJ
464.2625R	Ocean County NJ
464.8625R	Ocean County NJ
855.1875R	Haddon Heights NJ

South Jersey Gas Co.
153.515	Folsom NJ	
153.650	Millville NJ, Folsom NJ	CS
153.695	Glassboro NJ, Folsom NJ	CS

GPU Nuclear Corp.
173.2875B	Data - Ocean County NJ
173.3375B	Data - Ocean County NJ

Elizabethtown Water Co.
47.70	Princeton Township NJ

Garden State Water Co.
153.575	Blackwood NJ, Hamilton Square NJ

New Jersey Water Co.
37.58	Camden NJ, Hi-Nella NJ
47.84	Delran NJ
855.1875R	Cherry Hill NJ

South Jersey Water Co.
462.125R	Malaga NJ

Vincentown-New Egypt Water Co.
506.3125R	Vincentown NJ

New Jersey Bell Telephone Co.
Trunked (statewide)
938.3875R, 938.400R, 938.4125R, 938.425R, 938.4375R, 938.450R, 938.4625R,
938.475R, 938.4875R, 938.500R, 939.3875R, 939.400R, 939.4125R, 939.425R,
939.4375R, 939.450R, 939.4625R, 939.475R, 939.4875R, 939.500R

939.975R	Itinerant use (mobile also)	
939.9875R	Itinerant use (mobile also)	
451.300R	Atlantic City NJ, Cape May Courthouse NJ, Folsom NJ	
151.985	Haddonfield NJ, Vineland NJ	
451.500R	Medford NJ, Trenton NJ	CS
151.715M	New Jersey statewide	
151.745M	New Jersey statewide	
154.600M	New Jersey statewide	
462.625	Atlantic City NJ	
464.500M	New Jersey statewide	
464.550M	New Jersey statewide	
469.500M	New Jersey statewide mobile repeaters	
469.550M	New Jersey statewide	

Delmarva Power & Light Co.
New 900 MHz trunked system:
935.900R, 935.9125R, 936.7125R, 936.725R, 936.7375R,
936.750R, 936.950R, 937.2375R, 939.225R, 939.7375R
Transmitter sites: Tybouts Corner DE, Wilmington DE

Other:

37.62	Wilmington DE
37.76	Wilmington DE
851.1125R	Delaware City DE
851.6875T	Delaware City DE
30.84M	Itinerant operations
35.02M	Itinerant operations
451.0375R	Operations
451.0625R	Operations
451.0875R	Operations
451.1125R	Operations
851.6875R	Hockessin DE, Newark DE, Wilmington DE
852.1375R	Hockessin DE, Newark DE, Wilmington DE
851.6875R	Hockessin DE, Newark DE, Wilmington DE, F1 North - Electric system operations
852.6875R	Hockessin DE, Newark DE, Wilmington DE, F2 North - Transmission and distribution
853.6875R	Hockessin DE, Newark DE, Wilmington DE, F3 North - Wilmington district
854.6875R	Hockessin DE, Newark DE, Wilmington DE, F4 North - Gas system operations
854.9375R	Hockessin DE, Newark DE, Wilmington DE
855.6875R	Hockessin DE, Newark DE, Wilmington DE, F5 North - Fleet common channel

Artesian Water Co.

47.78	Wilmington DE
451.3625R	Newark DE
451.8375R	Operations
451.8625R	Operations
461.5625R	Operations
461.7625R	Operations
461.8375R	Operations
461.9375R	Operations
461.9625R	Operations
461.9875R	Operations
462.0625R	Operations
462.0875R	Operations
463.5625R	Operations
463.8625R	Operations
463.9125R	Operations
463.9375R	Operations
464.2875R	Operations
464.6125R	Operations
854.8625R	Operations 123.0

Wilmington Suburban Water Co.

158.160	Claymont DE, Wilmington DE
153.590	Wilmington DE
451.8375R	New Castle County DE
451.8625R	New Castle County DE
452.0625R	New Castle County DE
452.0875R	New Castle County DE

Diamond State Telephone Co.

35.16	Wilmington DE

COLLEGES AND UNIVERSITIES

Pennsylvania

464.475R	Penn State University Ogontz Campus, Abington PA	
468.6625M	Penn State University Ogontz Campus, Abington PA	
154.515	Penn State University, Reading PA	
151.835	Penn State University, Reading PA	
464.375	Penn State University, Allentown PA	
154.540	Montgomery County Community College, Blue Bell PA	
464.075R	Bryn Mawr College, Bryn Mawr PA	
464.0625M	Bryn Mawr College handhelds, Bryn Mawr PA	
154.600M	Bryn Mawr College, Bryn Mawr PA	
461.0125R	Bryn Mawr College, Bryn Mawr PA	
461.3125R	Bryn Mawr College, Bryn Mawr PA	
461.5375R	Bryn Mawr College, Bryn Mawr PA	
464.325R	Widener College Auxiliary, Chester PA	
460.725R	Widener College, Cheyney PA	
463.8625R	Widener College, Cheyney PA security	110.9
464.4625M	Widener College handhelds	
453.100R	Cheyney University, Cheyney PA	
151.835	Ursinus College, Collegevlle PA	
151.715M	Penn State University, Delaware County Campus	
464.075R	Beaver College, Glenside PA	162.2
151.895	Gwynedd Mercy College, Gwynedd Valley PA	
152.480P	Haverford College, Haverford PA	
154.515	Haverford College, Haverford PA	
461.375R	Haverford College, Haverford PA	
463.6375R	Haverford College, Haverford PA	
457.5875M	Haverford College, Haverford PA	
461.0125M	Haverford College, Haverford PA	
461.5625M	Haverford College, Haverford PA	
468.5625M	Haverford College, Haverford PA	
464.9375R	Haverford College, Haverford PA	
461.9125R	Haverford College, Haverford PA	
463.6375M	Haverford College, Haverford PA	
464.575M	Haverford College, Haverford PA	
464.425M	Pierce Junior College, Jenkintown PA	
464.975R	University of PA School of Veterinary Medicine, Kennett Square PA, Philadelphia	
154.600M	Philadelphia College of the Bible, Langhorne PA	
151.865	Lincoln University, Lincoln University PA	
461.375R	Lincoln University, Lincoln University PA	
464.425R	Lincoln University, Lincoln University PA	
151.655	Bucks County Community College, Newtown PA	
154.980	Bucks County Community College, Newtown PA	
154.540	Bucks County Community College, Newtown PA	
464.0875R	Keystone Junior College	
464.425M	Pierce Junior College	
154.570M	LaSalle University, Philadelphia	
154.600M	LaSalle University, Philadelphia	
151.745	LaSalle University, Philadelphia	
154.540	LaSalle University, Philadelphia	
463.625R	St. Joseph's University, Philadelphia	
464.250R	St. Joseph's University, Philadelphia	
464.750R	St. Joseph's University, Philadelphia	
463.300R	St. Joseph's University, Philadelphia	
151.715M	University of Pennsylvania, Philadelphia	
151.775	University of Pennsylvania, Philadelphia	

154.600M	Philadelphia College of Art, Philadelphia	
154.600M	Drexel University, Philadelphia	
462.000R	University of Pennsylvania security, Philadelphia	
506.9875R	University of Pennsylvania police, Philadelphia	203.5
462.050R	Drexel University, Philadelphia	
462.0125R	Drexel University, Philadelphia	
462.1625R	Drexel University, Philadelphia	
453.100R	University of Pennsylvania, Philadelphia	
464.725R	University of Pennsylvania, Philadelphia	
502.1625R	University of Pennsylvania, Philadelphia	
502.9625R	University of Pennsylvania, Philadelphia	
506.9625R	University of Pennsylvania, Philadelphia	
507.2625R	University of Pennsylvania police, Philadelphia	
508.9125R	University of Pennsylvania police, Philadelphia	
936.1375R	University of Pennsylvania, Philadelphia	
151.835	Albright College, Reading PA	
151.745M	Temple University, Philadelphia	
460.400R	Temple University police, Philadelphia	173.8
460.400R	Temple University police, Ambler PA campus	
463.3625M	Temple University, Philadelphia	
464.0375M	Temple University, Philadelphia	
464.050R	Temple University, Philadelphia	
464.700R	Temple University, Philadelphia	
463.900R	Temple University, Philadelphia	
463.4375M	Temple University police, Philadelphia	
464.0375M	Temple University police, Philadelphia	
463.650R	Campus Apartments, Philadelphia	
154.570M	St. Joseph's University, Philadelphia	
154.600M	Lancaster (PA) Bible College	
461.1125R	Philadelphia College of Textile, Philadelphia	
461.4625R	Philadelphia College of Textile, Philadelphia	
461.6625R	Philadelphia College of Pharmacy & Science, Philadelphia	
463.4625R	Philadelphia College of Pharmany & Science, Philadelphia	
464.8125R	Philadelphia College of Pharmacy & Science, Philadelphia	
464.575M	Pennsylvania Academy of Fine Arts, Philadelphia	
464.575R	Girard College, Philadelphia	
464.875	Girard College, Philadelphia	
464.325R	Holy Family College, Philadelphia	
507.8875BM	University of the Arts, Philadelphia	
508.2625R	University of Pennsylvania physical plant, Philadelphia	
154.570M	Pennsylvania College of Optometry, Philadelphia	
464.675R	Cabrini College, Radnor PA	
151.655	Rosemont College, Rosemont PA	
464.875R	Rosemont College, Rosemont PA	71.9
151.805	Eastern College, St. David's PA	
463.2875R	Eastern College, St. David's PA	
463.3625R	Eastern College, St. David's PA	
463.4875R	Eastern College, St. David's PA	
151.715	Swarthmore College, Swarthmore PA	
462.650R	Swarthmore College, Swarthmore PA	
463.725R	Swarthmore College phone patch, Swarthmore PA	
33.02	Villanova University, Villanova PA	
464.2125R	Villanova University, Villanova PA	
464.4125M	Villanova University, Villanova PA	
463.9125R	Villanova University, Villanova PA	
464.925R	Villanova University, Villanova PA	
464.325R	Villanova University, Villanova PA	
464.475M	Villanova University, Villanova PA	
469.475M	Villanova University, Villanova PA	
464.725M	Villanova University, Villanova PA	

464.425R	Villanova University, Villanova PA
154.515	Allentown College of St. Francis de Sales, Allentown PA
154.515	Thomas Jefferson University, Philadelphia
461.700R	Thomas Jefferson University, Philadelphia
463.625R	Thomas Jefferson University, Philadelphia
464.350R	Thomas Jefferson University, Philadelphia
464.625R	Thomas Jefferson University, Philadelphia
155.865R	West Chester University, West Chester PA
453.375R	West Chester University, West Chester PA
464.350M	West Chester University, West Chester PA
462.600R	Philadelphia College of Osteopathic Medicine, Phila.
501.8625	University of Pennsylvania, Philadelphia
462.0375R	St. Charles Seminary, Wynnewood PA
463.7625R	St. Charles Seminary, Wynnewood PA
464.575R	St. Charles Seminary, Wynnewood PA
453.875R	Millersville University, Millersville PA
158.820R	Millersville University, Millersville PA
464.425M	Millersville University, Millersville PA
464.325M	Millersville University, Millersville PA
464.775R	Millersville University, Millersville PA
464.875M	Millersville University, Millersville PA
453.900R	Kutztown University, Kutztown PA
155.415	Kutztown University police, Kutztown PA
464.575M	Kutztown University Foundation, Kutztown PA
155.025	Penn State University, Media PA
151.745	Northampton County Area Community College, Bethlehem PA
464.675	Northampton County Area Community College, Bethlehem PA
151.715	Lebanon Valley College, Annville PA
151.745	Moravian College, Bethlehem PA
463.850R	Moravian College security, Bethlehem PA
151.745	Lehigh County Community College, Schnecksville PA
154.600M	Lehigh County Community College, Schnecksville PA
151.805	Lehigh County Community College, Schnecksville PA
464.575R	Elizabethtown College, Elizabethtown PA
462.8375M	University of Pennsylvania, Philadelphia
464.725R	University of Pennsylvania, Philadelphia
154.570M	Community College of Philadelphia, Philadelphia
154.600M	Community College of Philadelphia, Philadelphia
463.8375R	University of Pennsylvania escort service, Philadelphia
151.775	Lehigh University, Bethlehem PA
154.650M	Lehigh University police, Bethlehem PA
154.540	Lehigh University transportation service, Bethlehem PA
463.3625M	Eastern College, St. Davids PA
463.4875M	Eastern College, St. Davids PA
151.865	Cedar Crest College, Allentown PA
463.5375R	Cedar Crest College, Allentown PA
463.6375R	Cedar Crest College, Allentown PA
151.865	Muhlenberg College, Allentown PA
151.865	Lafayette College, Easton PA
461.375R	Lafayette College security, Easton PA
462.8375R	Lafayette College, Easton PA
464.525R	Franklin & Marshall College, Lancaster PA
464.575R	Franklin & Marshall College, Lancaster PA
151.655	Lehigh University, Bethlehem PA
151.895M	Lehigh University, Bethlehem PA
154.540	Lehigh University, Bethlehem PA
154.515M	Lehigh University, Bethlehem PA
151.895M	Lehigh University, Bethlehem PA
151.835	Lehigh University auditorium, Bethlehem PA
464.875M	Delaware Valley College, Doylestown PA

156.7

464.975M	Delaware Valley College, Doylestown PA
464.425M	Delaware Valley College, Doylestown PA
464.775M	Delaware Valley College, Doylestown PA
461.3625R	Delaware Valley College, Doylestown PA
464.575R	Harrisburg Area Community College, Harrisburg PA
154.600M	Lancaster Bible College, Lancaster PA

New Jersey

464.775R	Rutgers University housing, Camden NJ	
155.820	Rutgers University emergency services, Camden NJ	
35.02M	Rutgers University, statewide use NJ	
461.9625M	Rutgers University, statewide use NJ	
461.0625M	Rutgers University, Camden NJ	
462.175	Rutgers University, Camden NJ	
464.6375M	Rutgers University, Camden NJ	
461.0125M	Rutgers University, Camden NJ	
468.9125M	Rutgers University, Camden NJ	
155.895	Rowan College of New Jersey, Glassboro NJ	
154.515	Rowan College of New Jersey, Glassboro NJ	
154.515	Atlantic Community College, Mays Landing NJ	
30.84M	Burlington County College, Pemberton NJ	
155.415	Stockton State College, Pomona NJ	
156.000	Stockton State College, Pomona NJ	
155.895	Stockton State College, Pomona NJ	
151.775	Princeton University, Princeton NJ	
462.825P	Princeton University, Princeton NJ	
463.5625R	Princeton University, Princeton NJ	
856.1375T	Princeton University, Princeton NJ	
151.745	Princeton University, Princeton NJ	
151.715	Princeton University, Princeton NJ	
462.150BM	Princeton University, Princeton NJ	
154.540	Princeton University, Princeton NJ	
154.600M	Princeton Charter Club, Princeton NJ	
151.805	Camden County College, Blackwood NJ	
151.835	Camden County College, Blackwood NJ	
861.4625T	Princeton Theological Seminary, Princeton NJ	
464.825R	Princeton Theological Seminary, Princeton NJ	
461.7125R	Rider College phone patch, Lawrenceville NJ	
462.7625M	Rider College, Lawrenceville NJ	
462.650	Rider College, Lawrenceville NJ	
464.0625R	Rider College, Lawrenceville NJ	
461.9875R	Rider College, Lawrenceville NJ	
151.805	Georgian Court College, Lakewood NJ	
155.415	Princeton University police	107.2
35.04M	Princeton University geological (NJ)	
154.600M	Mercer County Community College, West Windsor NJ	
501.8625R	Mercer County Community College	
155.895	Raritan Valley Community College, Branchburg NJ	186.2
506.3375R	Trenton State College, Ewing NJ	
155.895	Trenton State College, Ewing NJ	
464.575R	Cumberland Community College, Vineland NJ	
155.805	Burlington County College, Burlington NJ	
154.570M	Centenary College, Hackettstown NJ	

Delaware

45.36	University of Delaware, Newark DE
151.805	University of Delaware, Newark DE
151.925	University of Delaware, Newark DE

152.480P	University of Delaware, Newark DE	
453.625R	University of Delaware, Newark DE, Dover DE, Lewes DE	
154.600M	University of Delaware, Newark DE	
151.655	Brandywine College, Wilmington DE	
461.3875R	University of Delaware, Newark DE	
461.4375R	University of Delaware, Newark DE	
461.5375R	University of Delaware, Newark DE	
463.3375R	University of Delaware, Newark DE	
154.980R	University of Delaware, Newark DE	
501.6625R	Univ. of Delaware, Newark/Wilmington DE police	123.0
501.5125R	Univ. of Delaware, Newark/Wilmington DE transportation/maint.	123.0
463.200M	University of Delaware, Newark DE	

AMATEUR RADIO

With the "no-code" technician class ham license available, many scanner enthusiasts are getting their ham licenses to operate on the VHF and UHF bands. Because the two hobbies go together hand in hand (with many repeaters frequently sporting talk about scanning), here is a list of ham bands on the VHF and UHF bands, as well as an idea where to find repeaters. Other portions of ham bands might be used for operations such as moonbounce, single sideband, satellites and packet (data) communications.

10 meters

28.000 to 29.700 - repeaters from 29.620 to 29.680. Nationwide simplex calling frequency is 29.600.

6 meters

50-54 - repeaters from 53-54 and nationwide simplex on 52.525.

2 meters

144-148 - repeaters on 145.110 to 145.500, 146.610 to 147.390. Nationwide simplex on 146.520.

222 MHz

222-225 - repeaters on 223.600 to 224.980. Nationwide simplex on 223.500.

420–450 MHz

420-450 - repeaters typically on 440-450 MHz with nationwide simplex on 446.000.

902 MHz

902-928 - repeaters on 919 to 922 with nationwide simplex on 906.500.

1.2 GHz

1240-1300 MHz - repeaters on 1282 to 1288 with nationwide simplex on 1294.500.

SHOPPING MALLS

Pennsylvania

464.825R	Cheltenham Square Mall, Cheltenham PA	
464.575R	Exton Square Mall, Exton PA	
464.9125R	Exton Square Mall, Exton PA	
154.515	King of Prussia Plaza, King of Prussia PA	
464.300R	King of Prussia Plaza, King of Prussia PA	
461.8875R	King of Prussia Plaza, King of Prussia PA	
151.865	The Court at King of Prussia, King of Prussia PA	
464.625R	The Court at King of Prussia, King of Prussia PA	
464.325R	Oxford Valley Mall, Langhorne, PA	
464.1375R	Oxford Valley Mall, Langhorne PA, security	141.3
151.955M	Langhorne Square Shopping Center, Langhorne PA	
464.325R	Granite Run Mall, Media PA	
35.70	Newtown Square, Newtown Square PA	
154.540	Montgomery Mall, North Wales PA	123.0
151.955	Northeast Shopping Center, Philadelphia	
151.955	Head House Square, Philadelphia	
154.570M	Head House Square, Philadelphia	
464.675R	The Market Place, Philadelphia	
154.515	Plymouth Meeting Mall, Plymouth Meeting PA	
457.5625M	Plymouth Meeting Mall, Plymouth Meeting PA	
461.7375R	Plymouth Meeting Mall, Plymouth Meeting PA	
461.7875R	Plymouth Meeting Mall, Plymouth Meeting PA	
154.540	Springfield Mall, Springfield PA	
461.175R	Springfield Mall, Springfield PA	
464.775R	Willow Grove Park, Willow Grove PA, F1 security	88.5
464.875R	Willow Grove Park, Willow Grove PA (old)	88.5
464.675R	Willow Grove Park, Willow Grove PA F2 maintenance	88.5
151.685M	Suburban Square	
154.515M	Coventry Mall, North Coventry PA	
462.175R	Bala Plaza, Bala Cynwyd PA	
151.805	Park City Mall, Lancaster PA	
154.515	Westgate Mall, Bethlehem PA	
154.515	Berkshire Mall, Wyomissing PA	
464.6625M	Berkshire Mall, Wyomissing PA	
464.325R	Lehigh Valley Mall, Whitehall PA	
461.175R	Lehigh Valley Mall, Whitehall PA	
463.300R	Lehigh Valley Mall, Whitehall PA	
151.685M	Hamilton Mall, Allentown PA	
151.775M	Hess's Hamilton Mall, Allentown PA	
151.655	Whitehall Mall, Whitehall PA	
151.655	Palmer Park Mall, Easton PA	
151.745M	Village Mall, Horsham PA	
501.0625R	The Gallery at Market East, Philadelphia	
464.4125R	Franklin Mills, Philadelphia, security/maintenance	
463.4125R	Franklin Mills, Philadelphia, entertainment	123.0
463.3625	Franklin Mills, Philadelphia, 49th Street Galleria	
463.0375	Franklin Mills, Philadelphia, maintemamce/electrical	
461.9375	Franklin Mills, Philadelphia, detectives	
461.175R	The Bourse, Philadelphia	
463.300R	Old York Road Atrium, Abington PA	
463.425M	Old York Road Atrium, Abington PA	
463.375M	Old York Road Atrium, Abington PA	
463.475M	Old York Road Atrium, Abington PA	
151.805	Peddlers Village, Lahaska PA	
464.675M	Camp Hill Shopping Center, Camp Hill PA	

463.600R	Crown American Corp., New Tripoli PA	
154.600M	Zern's Farmers Market, Gilbertsville PA	
464.2375R	One Reading Center, Philadelphia	
464.325M	One Reading Center, Philadelphia	
461.5875R	Davisville Center, Upper Moreland Township PA	
463.4625M	Davisville Center, Upper Moreland Township PA	
463.2875M	Davisville Center, Upper Moreland Township PA	
466.8375M	Davisville Center, Upper Moreland Township PA	
463.425R	York Galleria Mall, York PA	
467.775M	Zinn's Market, Lancaster PA	
467.850M	Zinn's Market, Lancaster PA	
151.775	Manufacturers Outlet Mall (MOM), Morgantown PA	
464.325R	Harrisburg East Mall, Harrisburg PA	
151.745M	Stroud Mall, Stroudsburg PA	

New Jersey

461.900R	Ocean One, Atlantic City NJ	
154.570M	Black Horse Pike Shopping Center, Audubon NJ	
464.825R	Cherry Hill Mall, Cherry Hill NJ	
464.425R	Deptford Mall, Deptford NJ	
464.775R	Deptford Mall, Deptford NJ	
464.575R	Echelon Mall, Echelon NJ	
464.425R	Quaker Bridge Mall, Lawrenceville NJ	
151.895	Palmer Square, Princeton NJ	192.8
463.625R	Cumberland Mall, Vineland NJ	
464.3875R	Cumberland Mall, Vineland NJ	
464.9125R	Ocean County Mall, Toms River NJ	
464.775R	Princeton Market Fair, West Windsor NJ	
463.2625R	Burlington Center, Burlington NJ	
464.925R	Burlington Center, Burlington NJ	
467.850M	Shore Mall, Pleasantville NJ	
467.775M	Phillipsburg Mall, Phillipsburg NJ	
464.775R	Phillipsburg Mall, Phillipsburg NJ	
154.570M	Rio Mall, Rio Grande NJ	
464.575	Hamilton Mall, Mays Landing NJ	

Delaware

464.9125R	Christiana Mall, Newark DE	141.3
464.775R	Christiana Mall, Newark DE	141.3

ATLANTIC CITY CASINOS

Merv Griffin's Resorts Casino-Hotel

464.675R	Security, paging	DPL
464.275P	Paging	CS
465.000P	Paging	CS
154.570M	Security	
466.2625M	Surveillance	
461.1125M	Surveillance	
463.625R	Operations	
463.650R	Operations	
463.950M	Operations	
464.075	Operations	
464.375R	Operations	
464.525R	Operations	
464.775	Operations	
464.875R	Operations	
469.475M	Operations	
468.950M	Operations	
856.8375T	Trunked system	

Caesar's Hotel-Casino

461.925P	Paging	82.5
461.925M	Security portables	
461.950R	Security	131.8
461.8625M	Surveillance	
461.575R	Operations	
461.675R	Operations	
461.8875M	Operations	
464.425R	Operations	
464.625R	Operations	
464.850R	Operations	
861.3375T	Operations (trunked)	
929.1875P	Paging	
861.5875T	Philadelphia operations (trunked)	

Bally's Park Place Casino Hotel & Tower

463.600R	Paging, security	
464.100R	Security	
462.800P	Paging	
464.325M	Maintenance portables	
464.575M	Surveillance	
461.675R	Maintenance	82.5
157.740P	Paging	
463.4875M	Operations	
463.5875M	Operations	
462.775P	Paging	
464.625R	Operations	

Sands Hotel & Casino

463.325R	Security	
463.325P	Paging	CS
465.000P	Paging	
463.500R	Security	DPL
463.2125M	Operations	
461.525R	Operations	
151.625M	Operations	
154.600M	Country Club	
462.000R	Operations	

463.575R	Operations	
462.100	Operations	
463.5375M	Operations	
464.975R	Operations	
467.775M	Portables	

The Grand - A Bally's Casino Resort

464.125R	Security	
464.375M	Surveillance	
461.6125M	Surveillance	
464.200P	Paging	CS
463.550P	Paging	
464.175R	Operations	
800 MHz	VIP limousines	
460.850	Operations	
465.800M	Bus operations	
463.700	Operations	
463.800	Operations	
464.2125M	Operations	
469.200M	Operations	
464.950R	Operations	
861.4125T	Operations, Philadelphia (trunked)	
861.9375T	Operations, Philadelphia (trunked)	
861.9875T	Operations, Philadelphia (trunked)	

Harrah's Casino-Hotel

463.750R	Buses	
154.600M	Gaming portables	
461.675R	Operations	
463.850R	Operations	
463.950R	Operations	
462.1625M	Operations	
463.425R	Operations	
464.900M	Operations	
464.325R	Operations	
464.425R	Operations	
464.825R	Operations	
464.875R	Operations	
929.0375P	Paging	
461.450M	Operations	
463.825M	Operations	
464.125M	Operations	
462.175M	Operations	
464.700M	Operations	

Claridge Hotel-Casino

464.350R	Security	
464.600R	Maintenance	
462.875P	Paging	CS
465.9375M	Surveillance	
461.550R	Operations	
461.925R	Operations	
463.775R	Operations	
464.2875M	Operations	
464.4375M	Operations	
464.575R	Operations	

TropWorld Casino and Entertainment Resort

464.825R	Operations	
464.725R	Security	DPL
462.900P	Paging	CS

464.175R	Buses	
461.300R	Operations	
464.050R	Operations	
464.800R	Operations	
463.650M	Operations	
464.375R	Operations	
461.425R	Operations	
462.075R	Operations	

Trump Plaza Hotel-Casino

461.5125	Security	136.5
463.350	Security	
462.925P	Paging	
461.825R	Operations	
462.750P	Paging	

The Castle Hotel and Casino

463.200R	Security dispatch	DPL
463.350R	Operations	
463.425R	Security	DPL
464.475R	Maintenance	
462.800P	Paging	
462.925P	Paging	
460.675	Operations	
460.725	Operations	
460.750	Operations	
460.775	Operations	
460.825	Operations	
461.250R	Operations	
464.700M	Operations	
464.800R	Operations	
464.875	Operations	
464.925R	Operations	
861.5875T	Operations, Atlantic City (trunked)	
861.5875T	Operations, Philadelphia (trunked)	

Showboat Hotel-Casino and Bowling Center

461.625R	Security	118.8
461.225R	Operations	
461.700R	Operations	
462.875P	Paging	
460.650	Operations	
464.325	Operations	
464.825	Operations	
464.975	Operations	

Trump Taj Mahal Casino-Resort

460.800R	Operations	
469.3375M	Operations	
468.6125M	Operations	
469.1125M	Operations	
854.7875R	Operations	
854.8125R	Operations	
855.7625R	Operations	
855.8125R	Operations	
856.8125R	Operations	
935.6375R	Operations	
935.6875R	Operations	
935.700R	Operations	
929.0125P	Paging	
929.7375P	Paging	

468.3125M	Operations
897.6375M	Itinerant operations
897.6625M	Itinerant operations

Golden Nugget Marina Hotel and Casino

(under construction)

461.400M	Security
464.125	Operations
464.365M	Operations

Miscellaneous casino-related

Holiday Inn Marina Hotel

462.800P	Paging
464.475	Operations

International Game Technology

464.025R	Operations

International Micorp.

462.900P	Paging

Casino Limousine Service

461.650R	Limousines

Casino Connection Line

157.680	Operations

Boardwalk Corvettes of Atlantic City

467.0875M	Operations

Atlantic Exposition Service

464.475R	Exhibits service

Sen. Farley State Marina

156.275	Marine Channel 65 port operations
156.800	Marine Channel 16 calling
156.925	Marine Channel 78 non-commercial

New Jersey Casino Control Commission

Division of Gaming Enforcement

460.175R	Operations
460.250R	Operations

U.S. GOVERNMENT AND MILITARY

See air bases under airports

30.50	Fort Dix flight detachment helicopters	
36.85	Fort Dix MPs liaison with McGuire AFB	
38.60	Delaware National Guard, Wilmington	
38.71	Fort Dix Fire Department F1	
38.85	Fort Dix MPs courtesy patrol	
38.91	Fort Dix Fire Department F2	
41.00	NJ National Guard aircraft	148.0
41.00B	NJ National Guard Trenton base	CS
122.900	Civil Air Patrol drills (AM mode)	
123.100	Civil Air Patrol search/rescue (AM)	
138.975R	Philadelphia Naval Shipyard police	156.7
139.110P	Fort Dix Fire Department paging	
139.200	Fort Dix MPs F1	
139.500	Lakehurst NAS police/fire	
140.075R	Philadelphia Naval Shipyard Naval Intelligence unit	
140.125	Lakehurst NAS, NAEC	
140.550	Philadelphia Naval Ship Yard police units aboard ships	
140.775M	US Navy Naval Intelligence	
141.050R	Fort Dix staff duty officer	151.4
141.100	Fort Dix MPs	
141.125	Fort Dix crisis net F1/emergency	
141.275	Fort Dix crisis net F2/emergency	
141.200	Fort Dix Fire Department	
141.325	Fort Dix CID	
141.400	Fort Dix MPs F2	
142.325	Fort Dix CID	
142.345	Fort Dix CID	
143.150	Fort Hamilton MPs	
143.450R	Air Force MARS (hams)	CS
143.525P	Lakehurst NAS commander paging	
143.750	Civil Air Patrol mobile	
148.150R	Civil Air Patrol primary	100.0
148.290	Philadelphia Naval Base ambulance	
148.350	Philadelphia Naval Ship Yard police	
148.400	Philadelphia Naval Shipyard fire	
148.625	Fort Dix range control F1	CS
148.675R	Fort Dix EMS	
148.750	Fort Hamilton MPs	
148.875	Fort Dix range safety F2	
148.925	Fort Dix range safety	
148.925P	Fort Dix medical emergency paging	
148.950P	Philadelphia Navy Yard paging	
148.985	Aviation Supply Office, Philadelphia, special events	
149.025	Aviation Supply Office, Philadelphia, public works	
149.650	Fort Dix firing range	
149.925	Civil Air Patrol mobile	
149.950P	Philadelphia Naval Ship Yard paging	
150.100	Philadelphia Naval Shipyard hospital	
150.425	Fort Dix transportation/motor pool	
155.340	Fort Dix Walson Hospital to ambulance	
162.275	Princeton Plasma Physics Lab, Princeton NJ	
162.300	FAA wind shear telemetry, Phila. International Airport	
162.7125R	US Marshal Service F5, Philadelphia	CS
162.7875	US Marshal Service operations, Philadelphia	CS
163.000	C&D Canal, Army Corps of Engineers, Delaware City DE	
163.050P	Veterans Affairs Hospital, Philadelphia	

163.200R	US Marshal Service F1, Philadelphia	CS
163.200M	US Marshal Service F2, Philadelphia	CS
163.225	National Marine Fisheries agents, Cape May NJ	
163.4125	Army Corps of Engineers, Philadelphia	94.8
163.4875	NJ Air National Guard security police F1, Pomona FAA Test Center	
163.5125	NJ Air National Guard, civil engineers, medics, Pomona FAA Test Center	
163.5625	NJ Air National Guard security police F2, Pomona FAA Test Center	
163.650R	Immigration and Naturalization Service, Philadelphia	
163.8125	US Marshal Service, Philadelphia	
163.8875R	FBI, PA surveillance	167.9
163.900R	FBI, PA	167.9
163.9375R	FBI, NJ F5	167.9
164.275	Princeton Plasma Physics Lab EMS, Princeton NJ	
164.325M	FBI bank robberies, PA	167.9
164.375P	Princeton Plasma Physics Lab, Princeton NJ	
164.400	US Secret Service "Papa"	
164.475	Valley Forge National Historical Park	
164.600M	US Marshal Service F3, F4	CS
164.650	US Secret Service "Tango"	CS
164.700	US Postal Service Bulk Mail Center, Philadelphia	
164.725R	Independence National Historical Park maintenance, Phila.	127.3
164.800R	US Secret Service, Philadelphia	CS
164.800M	US Secret Service, Philadelphia	CS
164.8875	US Secret Service "Oscar"	CS
164.9625	Veterans Affairs Hospital, Elsmere DE	
165.0375	NJ Air National Guard ordnance disposal, Pomona FAA Test Center	
165.0375	Defense Personnel Support Center, security police, Philadelphia	
165.0625	Fort Dix facility engineers	
165.1375	NJ Air National Guard aircraft maintenance, Pomona FAA Test Center	
165.2125	US Secret Service "Mike"	CS
165.2375M	US Customs Service car-to-car	100.0
165.2625	US Coast Guard Electronics Engineering Center security F2, Cape May NJ	
165.2875M	US Bureau of Alcohol, Tobacco and Firearms F1	CS
165.2875M	US Bureau of Alcohol, Tobacco and Firearms F3 primary	CS
165.3375	US Coast Guard Electronics Engineering Center security F1, Cape May NJ	
165.375	US Secret Service, "Charlie"	CS
165.4125R	EPA, Philadelphia	CS
165.4375	Valley Forge National Historical Park, PA	
165.4625R	US Customs Service, Philadelphia	100.0
165.5125R	US Secret Service, New Jersey	CS
165.750	National Transportation Safety Board, air crash investigations	
165.7875	US Secret Service, "Baker"	CS
165.900R	FBI operations, bank robberies PA	167.9
165.9125M	US Bureau of Alcohol, Tobacco and Firearms, F5 surveillance	CS
165.950R	US Internal Revenue Service agents	CS
166.000R	US Internal Revenue Service internal affairs	131.8
166.275	US Postal Service trucks, Philadelphia	CS
166.4625	US Treasury Dept. "common" F4, ATF/Secret Service/Customs, etc.	
166.5125	US Secret Service protective details "Sierra"	CS
166.5375	US Bureau of Alcohol, Tobacco and Firearms F2	CS
166.700	US Secret Service "Quebec"	CS
166.825	FBI operations	167.9
166.950R	Delaware Water Gap National Recreation Area	
167.025	US Secret Service "November"	CS
167.050R	Federal Communications Commission	173.8
167.2375	FBI, PA Gold-3	167.9

167.2625	FBI, NJ F3	167.9
167.4375	FBI operations, PA 167.9	
167.500	FBI, PA	167.9
167.525	FBI, NJ F1	167.9
167.5625	FBI, nationwide F4 car to car	167.9
167.5875	FBI operations (input to 163.900)	167.9
167.6125	FBI, NJ F2	167.9
167.6125R	FBI, Delaware operations	167.9
167.7375	FBI operations (also 167.6125R input)	167.9
167.825	Veterans Affairs Hospital, Elsmere DE	
168.375R	FBI, NJ	167.9
168.425R	FBI, NJ	167.9
168.525	Veterans Affairs Hospital, Coatesville PA	
168.725R	FBI, NJ	
168.775R	FBI, Harrisburg PA	167.9
168.850	FBI operations	167.9
168.975	FBI base input to 167.2625	167.9
169.000	US Postal Service Inspectors	82.5
169.600	US Postal Service dispatch, Philadelphia	
169.950	Department of Agriculture, Eastern Research Station, Wyndmoor PA	
169.975R	FBI, PA	167.9
170.400	US Postal Service trucking, Philadelphia	
170.425	Drug Enforcement Administation (418.9 link)	
170.475	Veterans Affairs Hospital, Philadelphia	
170.800	US Marshal Service, Philadelphia	
170.875	Federal Correctional Facilities	
171.525	Department of Agriculture, Plant Protection & Quarantine, Phila.	
171.650R	Independence National Historical Park rangers, Philadelphia	127.3
172.400R	Hopewell Village Nat'l Hist Site, Berks County PA	
172.475M	FBI simplex	167.9
172.8125	NJ Air National Guard ground control (aero)	CS
	Pomona FAA Test Center	
172.9125	NJ Air National Guard fire F2 Pomona FAA Test Center	
173.150R	NJ Air National Guard fire F1 Pomona FAA Test Center	
173.100M	FBI simplex ops	
173.125	input to 168.375R, NJ simplex FBI	
173.3125	US Coast Guard security, Cape May NJ	
173.9125	FBI (encrypted)	
173.9375	FBI (encrypted)	
407.600	US State Department security Net 2	
407.700	US Mint, Philadelphia	
408.000	US Mint, Philadelphia	
408.175	US Mint, Philadelphia	
408.600	US State Department security Net 1	
409.225M	US Postal Service inspectors	
409.625R	US State Department security	151.4
411.025	Princeton Forrestal Campus maintenance, Princeton NJ	
411.200	Princeton Forrestal Campus security, Princeton NJ	
411.400	US Postal Service trucks, Wilmington DE	192.8
411.550	US Postal Service Express Mail operations	D223
	at Philadelphia International Airport	
412.275	US Postal Service Bulk Mail Center, Philadelphia	
412.825R	Aviation Supply Office, Philadelphia, security/fire/medical	
413.875R	US General Services Administration security	CS
414.750R	US Postal Service Inspectors F5	82.5
415.200R	US General Services Administration security	
415.700	Air Force 1, executive aircraft phone patches	CS
415.825	US Coast Guard, Cape May NJ	
415.875	US Mint, Philadelphia	
416.075R	US Postal Service inspectors G-1 operations	110.9

417.200R	US General Services Administration security	
418.300	US Postal Service security, main post office, 30th and Market, Phila.	
418.625R	Drug Enforcement Administration F1	156.7
418.675M	Drug Enforcement Administration F4	156.7
418.750M	Drug Enforcement Administration F3	156.7
418.825R	Drug Enforcement Administration F5	156.7
418.900R	Drug Enforcement Administration F2	156.7
418.950R	Drug Enforcement Administration F6	156.7
461.750R	Environmental Protection Agency, Philadelphia	

SPACE FLIGHTS

259.700	U.S. space shuttle (AM mode)	
296.800	U.S. space shuttle (AM mode)	
279.000	U.S. space shuttle extra vehicular activity (AM mode)	
143.625	Russian MIR orbiting crews - voice	CS
166.135	Russian MIR orbiting crews - data	CS

NEW 800 MHz PUBLIC SAFETY BAND

As the FCC approves regional plans, municipalities, counties, states and regional agencies are able to apply for frequencies in the new 866-869 MHz band. Applicants for the new band must surrender all frequencies they use on lower frequencies such as on VHF and UHF when applying for the new band. A mutual aid system has been set up on five channels and may be used with either repeaters or for simplex. The FCC suggests a CTCSS tone of 156.7 be employed for these mutual aid channels:

866.0125	Calling
866.5125	Tac-1
867.0125	Tac-2
867.5125	Tac-3
868.0125	Tac-4

Regional plans have been approved for southeastern Pennsylvania/southern New Jersey/Delaware and northern New Jersey/New York City as frequencies are being allocated in those areas on this new band.

ITINERANT BUSINESS FREQUENCIES

27.49	110 watts maximum (AM mode)
35.04	110 watts maximum
43.04	special industrial use only
151.505	special industrial use only
151.625	110 watts maximum
158.400	special industrial use only
451.800	special industrial use only
456.800M	special industrial use only
464.500	35 watts maximum (469.500 pair)
464.550	35 watts maximum (469.550 pair)
853.4875	(paired with 808.4875)
936.6375	(paired with 897.6375)
936.6625	(paired with 897.6625)

SPECIALIZED MOBILE RADIO SERVICE

Specialized mobile radio service is a fancy term for trunked 800-MHz radio systems that allow businesses to use the technology without having to build their own systems. In fact, FCC rules now allow even individuals to operate on SMRS, much like the general mobile radio service, or GMRS, in the 462-/467-MHz band.

An entrepreneur or large radio business typically builds an SMRS and offers both dispatch and telephone interconnect (phone patch calls) service to its subscribers. On individual users' license applications to operate on SMRS, the frequency is stipulated as 806-821 MHz for the 851-866 MHz band or 896-901 MHz for the 935-940 MHz trunked band. Following is a list of users who are licensed to operate on 800 MHz and 900 MHz trunked systems in southeastern Pennsylvania, South Jersey and northern Delaware. While the license applications also state the call sign and the owner of the SMRS they intend to operate on, we did not have access to that information for the preparation of this guide. The reason we are publishing this information is to give you an idea where to look for some additional radio users. We suggest you check in the 856-866 MHz and 935-940 MHz ranges to find some of the following users (# after call sign indicates 935-940 MHz band):

Pennsylvania

WNNQ894	American Red Cross
WNKJ459	Arsenal Business Center (Philadelphia)
WNXN336	ATC Philadelphia Shared Ride (Philadelphia)
WNUW539	Berks County Legal Process Service (Berks County)
WNRS945	Bridesburg Civic Association (Philadelphia)
WNKM550	Budget Rent A Car (Philadelphia)
WNGM552	Chester County SPCA (Chester County PA)
WNRP928	Citizens Voice (Wilkes-Barre PA)
WNQT447	The Daily Intelligencer (Doylestown PA)
WNUD677	The Daily Intelligencer (Doylestown PA)
WNZV372	Daily Local News (West Chester PA)
WNPN387	Delaware County Daily Times (Primos PA)
WNJU864	Delaware County
WNRY869	Dollar Rent A Car (Philadelphia)
WPAM748	Exeter Ambulance Association (Berks County PA)
WNWP258	Express-Times (Easton PA)
WNRT367	The Reporter (Lansdale PA)
WNSE642	The Reporter (Lansdale PA)
KB21157	Franklin Mint (Franklin Center PA)
WNHH454	Greater Media Inc. (WPLY-FM, Media PA)
WNRR815	Heidelberg Township (Berks County)
WMYV403	Lancaster Township (PA)
WNIV441	City of Lancaster
WPAA941	Lancaster County Solid Waste Management Authority
WNLM344	The Morning Call (Allentown PA)
WNUD551	The Morning Call (Allentown PA - NJ units)
WNYB884	The Morning Call (Allentown PA)
WNSE568	Muhlenberg Township (Berks County PA)
WNNO573	Myerstown First Aid Unit (Berks County PA)
KNJX399	National Car Rental (Philadelphia)
WNRK414	National Car Rental (Philadelphia)
WNKS408	North Heidelberg Township (Berks County)
WNMR204	North Wales Water Authority (North Wales)
WNZV434	Ogden Government Services (PA)
WNQD617#	Old Town Trolley Tours of Philadelphia Inc. (Phila.)
WNED558	PECO Energy Co. (Philadelphia)
WNJPS61	PECO Energy Co. (Philadelphia)
WNXB390	PECO Energy Co. (Philadelphia)

WNXB391	PECO Energy Co. (Philadelphia)
WNXB392	PECO Energy Co. (Philadelphia)
WNUX795	Pennsylvania American Water Co. (PA)
WNUZ984	Pennsylvania SPCA (Philadelphia)
WNKQ650	The Philadelphia Inquirer
WNLW956	Philadelphia Ranger Corps (Philadelphia)
WNJL302	Philadelphia Water Department
WNQM643	City of Philadelphia
WNZV374	City of Philadelphia
WNIP753	Phillyship (Philadelphia)
WNNJ820#	Pilots Association for Bay and River of Delaware (PA)
WNNW677	The Reading Eagle (Reading PA)
WNHL230	Reading Terminal Market (Philadelphia)
WNPN401	Salvation Army (Philadelphia)
WNXB815	Salisbury Township (Lancaster County PA)
WNZQ419	Selective Subpoena Service Inc. (Philadelphia)
WNRE950	SEPTA (Philadelphia)
WNWT331#	Special Services District of Central Philadelphia
WNFR203	SPCA of Philadelphia
WNPT805	Springfield Township (Delaware County)
KNJK440	Television 69 (WFMZ-TV, Allentown PA)
WNLR307	Temple University (Philadelphia)
WNUE783	Thomas Jefferson University (Philadelphia)
WNMW699	Thrifty Car Rental (Philadelphia)
WNXQ250	Times Herald (Norristown PA)
WPAZ301	Traffax Traffic Network (Harrisburg, Reading PA)
WPAW779	Tulpehocken Township (Berks County PA)
WNNN757	United Parcel Service
WNIZS73	University of Pennsylvania School of Art (Philadelphia)
WNIZ205	WBRE-TV (Wilkes-Barre PA)
KNJK441	WFMZ-FM (Allentown PA)
WNNM377	WHP-TV (Harrisburg PA)
WNZT987#	WPVI-TV (Philadelphia)
WNZS485	WVIA-TV (Scranton PA)
WNSX532	WYOU-TV (Scranton PA)

New Jersey

WNNX728#	American Red Cross
WNZG225#	The Associated Press (NJ units)
WNZT763	Atlantic City Sewerage
WNQW657	Atlantic County Utilities Authority (Atlantic City NJ)
WNKL500	Atlantic County
WNQD579	Beachwood Borough (Ocean County NJ)
WNYT991#	Burlington County Times (Burlington NJ)
WNRV658#	Burlington County Times (Burlington NJ)
WNIS368	Caesars Hotel & Casino (Atlantic City NJ)
WNYM207	Clean Harbors Environmental Services (NJ)
WNJU964	Courier Post (Cherry Hill NJ)
WPAS343#	Courier Post (Cherry Hill NJ)
WNYM262	Gloucester County Assn. for Retarded Citizens
WNXK603	International Game Technology (Atlantic City NJ)
WNPX365	Lakewood Township (Ocean County)
WNHI232	Lower Township (Cape May County NJ)
WNZT581#	Mercer Metro buses (Trenton NJ)
WNIM508	Middle Township (Cape May County NJ)
WNHF930	Princeton University (Princeton NJ)
WNQT333	Showcase Publications
WNQT375	Showcase Publications

WNMP320	Trump Castle Casino (Atlantic City NJ)
WNMO272	Trump Plaza Hotel & Casino (Atlantic City)
WNKU735	Upper Pittsgrove Township (Salem County)
WNAY813	Voorhees Township (Camden County)

Delaware

WNJR780	C&P Telephone Co.
WNJPS63	Delaware Express Shuttle
WNJJ677	State of Delaware
WNKQ700	State of Delaware
WNNJ792	State of Delaware
WNUZ971	Executive Shuttle Service
WNKQ650	The Philadelphia Inquirer
WNKJ805	SW Delaware County Authority
WNLFS85	Winterthur Museum Inc. (Wilmington DE)

GENERAL MOBILE RADIO SERVICE

The GMRS band is available only to individuals over the age of 18 and previously was available to other users as well, including businesses, organizations and local and state governments.

Repeaters and simplex operations can be heard on the following frequencies:

462.550, 462.575, 462.600, 462.625,
462.650, 462.675, 462.700, 462.725

When employing repeaters, mobiles transmit 5 MHz higher in the 467 MHz band. In addition, all individual GMRS licenses also may operate on the following seven frequencies without prior licensing as long as their power output is limited to 5 watts ERP (effective radiated power) or less:

462.5625, 462.5875, 462.6125, 462.6375,
462.6625, 462.6875, 462.7125

PHONES, PHONES, PHONES

Cellular

In each metropolitan and rural area, the FCC has licensed two cellular phone systems. One is licensed to a wireline service, or a firm that also offers landline telephone service, and another is issued to an entrepreneur, a non-wireline service.

To tune in cellular telephone calls, search through the region from 869-894 MHz. You normally will hear both sides of the conversation on this side. Mobile phones transmit 45 MHz lower in frequency than the tower sites.

Typically, non-wireline systems operate from 870-880 MHz and wireline systems operate from 880-890 MHz. The 869-870 and 890-894 MHz ranges are split up with 2.5 MHz for both wireline and non-wireline users. Non-wireline systems utilize the 869-870 and 890-891.5 segments while wireline systems use 891.5-894 MHz.

Control channels that send data to cellular phones transmit from 880-880.650 and 879.360-879.99 MHz. If you find a control channel, you can find all 15 channels at a cellular tower by adding 630 kHz to the control channel. The next channel is found by adding 630 kHz again, etc. For instance, if the control channel is on 880.050, the cell tower uses frequencies as follows: 880.680, 881.310, 881.940, etc. Keep adding until you get to 890 MHz for wireline and keep subtracting until 870 for non-wireline.

We do caution you, however, that the Electronic Communications Privacy Act of 1986, a federal law, prohibits you from listening to cellular phone calls, conventional mobile phone calls, paging and news media remote pickups, as well as any and all encrypted communications (that is if you have the capability to unencrypt them). On the same note, we know of few convictions under this law. It should be added that most are celebrated cases that show blatant violation of the law.

Cordless phones

If you want to tune in your neighbors' phone calls, we can't tell you not to. There is no law that prohibits you from doing so. If you have the desire to snoop, here is a list of channels used for cordless phones available on the commercial market:

> Channel 1 - 46.61 base/49.67 handset
> Channel 2 - 46.63 base/49.845 handset
> Channel 3 - 46.67 base/49.86 handset
> Channel 4 - 46.71 base/49.77 handset
> Channel 5 - 46.73 base/49.875 handset
> Channel 6 - 46.77 base/49.83 handset
> Channel 7 - 46.83 base/49.89 handset
> Channel 8 - 46.87 base/49.93 handset
> Channel 9 - 46.93 base/49.99 handset
> Channel 10 - 46.97 base/49.97 handset

Some older cordless phones transmitted the handset on 49.83, 49.845, 49.86, 49.875 and 49.89 with the base transmitting just above the AM broadcast band on 1695, 1725 and 1755 kHz. Most of these phones have died by now, but you may find a few in use.

It also should be noted that some newer cordless phones being manufactured use the 900-MHz band. These phones operate in the 902-928 MHz band, which is host to a variety of services, including hams. There are no standardized frequency plans for 900 MHz phones as each manufacturer uses its own scheme.

The FCC has proposed allocating several new VHF low band frequencies for cordless phones and they are expected to become in use eventually. These new frequencies for base sets are:

> 43.72, 43.74, 43.82, 43.84, 43.92,
> 43.96, 44.12, 44.16, 44.18, 44.20,
> 44.32, 44.36, 44.40, 44.46, 44.48

Baby monitors
These sensitive microphones can pick up literally everything in a house. The following frequencies feature your favorite criers:
49.83, 49.845, 49.86, 49.875, 49.89

Conventional mobile phones
In the days before cellular phones, if you wanted a mobile phone, you got one of the VHF or UHF variety - if you stayed on the waiting list long enough. These phones still are in use in the following bands that also are shared with paging operations:
152.030 to 152.210
152.510 to 152.810
454.025 to 454.650

Aero phones
Phone calls from persons on board planes can be heard in two places. Phones used on private planes can be easily heard coming down on 459.700 to 459.975 MHz. The ground stations transmit 5 MHz lower on the 454 MHz side, however, unless you are close to one, don't expect to hear anything there. There are no ground stations in the Philadelphia area, however, the planes can be easily heard. If the plane phone's audio is loud enough, you'll hear both sides of the conversation, but typically you'll only hear the side of the conversation from the plane coming down.

On commercial jetliners, pay phones are now in place. You can hear persons on commercial flights placing direct dial calls from 894-896 MHz in the AM mode. If you can search in 1 kHz steps, it is best because the phone channels are 6 kHz apart. Also, the 894-896 MHz phones transmit in the AM mode.

PCS
There's a new cellular-type service that is expected to take to the airwaves soon. PCS, or personal communication service, will allow the user to carry around a simple handset phone to place calls from transmitter sites placed in large buildings, on telephone poles, in subway tunnels and other locations. It is not designed to operate like cellular because there are no handoffs. Calls must be made in the area of the nearest transmitter.

These PCS phones eventually will operate in the following segments:
1850-1890 MHz
1930-1970 MHz
2130-2150 MHz
2180-2200 MHz

RADIO CONTROL TOYS

If you like listening to odd sounds (and that's about all you'll hear) try tuning in remote control cars, airplanes and whatever other kind of similar toys (mind you some of these toys can cost hundreds of dollars):
Model surface or aircraft
26.995, 27.045, 27.095, 27.145, 27.195, 27.255
Model aircraft
There are 50 8-kHz channels every 20 kHz from 72.01 to 72.99 MHz.
Model surface
Things such as cars and boats can be tuned in on 30 8-kHz channels from 75.41 to 75.99 MHz.
Ham use for model crafts
Hams can use the 6-meter band for remote control of model craft on 10 20-kHz channels from 50.800 to 50.980 MHz.

MISCELLANY

154.600M	Franklin Mint, Franklin Center PA
462.425R	Franklin Mint, Franklin Center PA
502.0125R	Franklin Mint, Franklin Center PA
451.475R	Franklin Mint, Franklin Center PA
451.3625R	Franklin Mint, Aston PA
451.425R	Franklin Mint, Aston PA
451.5625R	Franklin Mint, Aston PA
464.575R	Franklin Mint, Franklin Center PA
157.740P	Wistar Institute, Philadelphia
463.850R	Center for Lab Medicine, Philadelphia
464.825R	American Institute for Mental Studies, Vineland NJ
461.850M	American Institute, PA units
469.575M	Institute for Defense Analysis, Princeton NJ
461.7625M	Freedom Valley Girl Scouts, PA
461.525R	Easter Seal Society, Pen Argyl PA
851.1625R	Salvation Army, Philadelphia
852.6125R	Salvation Army, Lancaster PA
154.600M	Salvation Army, Bucks County PA
464.975R	One Liberty Place Tower, Philadelphia
466.5375M	Westminster Choir Co., Princeton NJ
462.650R	Westminster Choir Co., Princeton NJ
464.975R	Philadelphia Stock Exchange, Philadelphia
461.5875M	Pennsylvania Convention Center, Philadelphia
461.7125M	Pennsylvania Convention Center, Philadelphia
461.8625M	Pennsylvania Convention Center, Philadelphia
463.8625M	Pennsylvania Convention Center, Philadelphia
461.9375M	PhillyPride, Philadelphia
464.2875M	PhillyPride, Philadelphia
151.835	Telford Diving Unit, Harleysville PA
464.575M	Direct Truth Anti-Drug Coalition, Philadelphia
502.1875R	Kids Peace, Allentown PA
502.8875R	Habitat for Humanity of Chester County, West Caln PA
153.140	David Sarnoff Research Center, West Windsor Township NJ
154.600M	David Sarnoff Research Center, Princeton NJ
151.715	David Sarnoff Research Center, Princeton NJ
151.625	Phoenixville Jaycees, Phoenixville PA
151.955	Phoenixville Jaycees, Phoenixville PA
151.685	Operating Engineers Local Union 542, Bernville PA
464.375R	HELP, Lakewood NJ
154.600M	Powhatan Indians of Delaware Valley, Burlington County NJ
466.4125M	Philadelphia Psychiatric Center, Philadelphia
461.325R	Occupational Training Center, Mount Holly NJ
461.850M	Fire Service Communications, Trenton NJ
461.025R	Fire Service Communications, Trenton NJ
461.900R	Blue Cross/Blue Shield of Delaware, Wilmington DE
463.400R	National Housing Partnership, Philadelphia
464.375M	Valet Parking at Christiana, Christiana DE
154.570M	Pennsylvania Credit Union League, PA statewide
461.500R	United Cerebral Palsy of Delaware Co., Boothwyn PA
851.0625R	United Cerebral Palsy of Chester County PA
469.5125M	Billy Graham Crusade, PA statewide
469.6125M	Billy Graham Crusade, PA statewide
154.600M	College of Physicians, Philadelphia
154.600M	Reading Elks Lodge, Reading PA
463.6125R	Friends of Israel Gospel Ministry, Gloucester Co. NJ
33.16	Emergency Care Research Inst., Plymouth Meeting PA

151.775	Water Street Rescue Mission, Lancaster PA
461.6125M	Pennsylvania Hand Center, Montgomery County PA
464.325M	Delaware Bay Launch Service, New Castle County DE
154.600M	Eastern Mennonite Board of Missions, Lancaster County PA
151.715M	ARC of Pennsylvania, Lancaster PA
151.955M	First Alert Mobile Unit, Delaware County PA
464.975R	Philadelphia Owners Association, Philadelphia
461.2625R	Blue Cross of Greater Philadelphia, Philadelphia
461.8625R	Blue Cross of Greater Philadelphia, Philadelphia
461.3625R	Blue Cross of Greater Philadelphia, Philadelphia
853.4875M	Phillyship, Philadelphia
156.450	Bridesburg Outboard Club, Philadelphia
156.800	Bridesburg Outboard Club, Philadelphia (calling)

FLEMINGTON SPEEDWAY
Flemington NJ

Racetrack

151.625M	Race coordination

Race teams

469.7625M	WPBU827	Bouchard Motorsports
461.2125R	WNYV227	Miksen Inc.
461.4125R	WNYY733	Loesch Racing
463.8625R	WPCR352	K Racing Inc.
461.6125R	WNZW863	Hughes Racing Ltd.
464.6375R	WPCN916	Jim Wismer Jr.
461.8125R	WPAK643	Robert W. Lammond
464.5375R	WPCW689	Orchard Racing Inc.
461.1125R	WPAK245	Rusty Turbush
464.9625R	WPAR803	Frank Stinson Motorsports
464.4625R	WPDI717	Quality Structures Racing
464.1375R	WPCW688	Thomas F. Kirchman
462.7625R	KD45461	Ken Dot Inc.

ENVIRONMENTAL

151.775	Hancock Recycling, Philadelphia
463.950R	East Coast Pollution Control, Wyndmoor PA
151.775	Jersey Environmental Management, Florence NJ
151.895	South Jersey Pollution, Mickelton NJ
461.075R	Keystone Conservation Service, Charlestown PA
501.8125R	Environmental Corp. of America, Philadelphia
463.375R	Underwater Technics oil spills, Philadelphia
463.300R	Underwater Technics oil spills, Philadelphia
154.515	Rollins Environmental Services chemical incinerator, Bridgeport NJ
463.9375M	Clean Venture spills, Perth Amboy NJ
464.575R	GROWS Inc. landfill, Morrisville PA
501.8125R	J&J Spill Service, Norristown PA
151.925M	Republic Environmental Systems, PA
464.750BM	New Jersey Marine Sciences Consortium, Sandy Hook NJ
461.100R	Environmental Operations Services, Malvern PA
936.175R	Adams Underwater Recovery Inc., Deptford NJ
852.6125R	Real Estate Environmental Services, Penn Township PA

CONVENTION FACILITIES

464.500M		Philadelphia Convention Center security
460.450R	KQR594	Philadelphia Civic Center security
461.5875R	WPDN820	Pennsylvania Convention Center, Phila.
461.7125R	WPDN820	Pennsylvania Convention Center, Phila.
461.8625R	WPDN820	Pennsylvania Convention Center, Phila.
463.5875R	WPDN820	Pennsylvania Convention Center, Phila.
463.7125R	WPDN820	Pennsylvania Convention Center, Phila.
463.8625R	WPDN820	Pennsylvania Convention Center, Phila.
461.4875R	WNXT414	Valley Forge Convention Plaza, King of Prussia PA
466.9875M	WNXT414	Valley Forge Convention Plaza, King of Prussia PA
462.7625R	WNXT414	Valley Forge Convention Plaza, King of Prussia PA
464.0625R	WNXT414	Valley Forge Convention Plaza, King of Prussia PA
469.7625M	WNXT414	Valley Forge Convention Plaza, King of Prussia PA
463.700R	WNLW253	Hershey Lodge and Convention Center, Summerdale PA
464.825R	WNLW254	Hershey Lodge and Convention Center, Hershey PA

HUMANE ORGANIZATIONS

863.6125R		Pennsylvania SPCA, Philadelphia
461.325R		Pennsylvania SPCA, Philadelphia
464.150R		Pennsylvania SPCA, Philadelphia
463.350R		Women's SPCA of Pennsylvania, Philadelphia
461.325R		Women's SPCA of Pennsylvania, Philadelphia
461.075R		Chester County SPCA, Malvern PA
154.540		SPCA, Cape May NJ
31.16		Burlington County SPCA, Mt. Holly NJ
35.02		Animal Welfare, Voorhees NJ
461.500R		Animal Patrol, Turnersville NJ
461.500R		Siemer Animal Radio Rescue, Malaga NJ
461.800BM		Delaware SPCA, Wilmington DE　　　192.8
461.850R	WNZN684	Warren County SPCA, Mansfield Township NJ
151.895	WNHL853	Associated Humane Societies Corp., Forked River NJ

APCO 10 CODES

Different radio users have their own forms of verbal shorthand to use over the air. For instance, police may use "10-codes" and various public safety agencies may use phonetics to spell names and words over the air.

In many larger cities and metropolitan areas, fire and police departments are switching to "plain English" instead of radio codes for dispatching. For instance, instead of telling a police officer to "10-21," the dispatcher will simply tell the officer to "Please call the communications center." Likewise, instead of dispatching units to a "10-50," the dispatcher will advise units to respond to a motor vehicle accident.

A recent study by the Associated Public-Safety Communications Officers of state police codes study showed that while a lot of states use "10-codes," not all codes mean the same thing in every state. For instance, the universal "10-4," which means "affirmative," was used in 35 of the 38 states with codes. Likewise, 36 states use "10-20" to mean "location." While APCO has issued its own standard 10-code for agencies to use, most states use only about a half of the actual code as issued. In fact, a third of all states use less than a half of the APCO 10-codes.

NOTE: The Associated Public-Safety Communications Officials Inc. have produced the following list of standard radio signals that may be used by police and fire departments around the nation for brevity and interagency commonality. While not every municipality, county or state will use this exact list, many do use it with some minor changes.

10-1	Signal weak
10-2	Signal good
10-3	Stop transmitting
10-4	Affirmative (OK)
10-5	Relay (to)
10-6	Busy
10-7	Out of service
10-8	In service
10-9	Repeat (say again)
10-10	Negative
10-11	_____ on duty
10-12	Stand by (stop)
10-13	Existing conditions
10-14	Message or information
10-15	Message delivered
10-16	Reply to message
10-17	En route
10-18	Urgent
10-19	(In) contact
10-20	Location
10-21	Call _____ by telephone
10-22	Disregard
10-23	Arrived at scene
10-24	Assignment completed
10-25	Report to (meet)
10-26	Estimated arrival time
10-27	License or permit information
10-28	Ownership information
10-29	Records check
10-30	Danger or caution
10-31	Pick up
10-32	_____ units needed
10-33	Help me quick
10-34	Time
10-35	through 10-39 (Reserved by APCO)
10-40	upward (To be used on a local basis)

AMERICA ONLINE

The editor of this guide recommends computer users utilize an online service such as America Online to enhance their scanning. Chuck Gysi, N2DUP, this guide's editor, also serves as scanning co-host for America Online's scanning message boards.

America Online is very simple to use if you have a computer and modem and the monthly cost is very reasonable. You can connect with many others also interested in the scanning hobby in America Online's Ham Radio Club section. You'll find fellow scanning enthusiasts from around the nation exchanging frequencies, product reviews and more. There also are many files related to scanning that you can download at no additional charge.

For a free diskette containing the software needed to log onto this service and a free 10-hour trial period, call America Online at (800) 827-6364. In addition, Scanner Master maintains a support area in the Ham Radio Club where you can interact with the publisher or other Scanner Master guide editors. The editor of this guide can be reached on America Online by sending e-mail to SCAN911, or through any Internet connection by sending e-mail to scan911@aol.com.

THE INTERNET

The Internet is a global system that ties together computers all over the world. From most online services such as America Online, CompuServe, Genie and Prodigy, you can send e-mail to anyone with an Internet account.

Another feature of the Internet is newsgroups that contain postings on various topics. While some online services already offer access to newsgroups, others are working to provide this service. Two newsgroups are of interest to scanner users. The primary newsgroup is rec.radio.scanner. On this newsgroup, you'll find up to several hundred messages posted per week from scanner enthusiasts generally around the United States, but also from other countries, too. There also is a newsgroup known as alt.radio.scanner, however, not too many system administrators allow access to the alt. groups and it has been slowly dying from declining use. In fact, many persons post in both newsgroups.

In the Philadelphia area, there also are phl.newsgroups. At presstime, we are trying to convince the newsgroup administrator to start a phl.scanner newsgroup for scanner folks in the Philadelphia area and surrounding areas of Pennsylvania, New Jersey and Delaware. In the interim, a scanning thread has been created in the phl.misc newsgroup. This was done at the suggestion of the phl.newsgroup administrator. If he sees there is a lot of interest in creating a phl.scanner newsgroup, then we'll succeed! If you need more information on this special newsgroup for regional purposes only, e-mail the editor at scan911@aol.com.

SCANNER BBS

The Scanner BBS is a computer bulletin board operated in the Philadelphia suburbs by sysop Carter Ames. This board offers free use to computer modem users who are interested in exchanging information and files with other scanning enthusiasts in the Philadelphia area.

The Scanner BBS carries files oriented to scanning enthusiasts, ham radio operators and more. It currently has more than 150 users, growing every day. It maintains online a CD-ROM (with games) but is studying adding an FCC license database disc. The system has 500 megabytes available on the hard drive, with about 200-plus megabytes of files available for download.

Each user is allowed 120 minutes per call, and there is no charge for the BBS, and there are no upload/download ratios. The board runs the Spitfire BBS program (for now) and has a 14.4 kbps modem.

The Scanner BBS' modem line is (610) 525-4004.

PHILADELPHIA FIRE FILMS BBS

Another computer bulletin board service we can recommend in the Philadelphia area is the Philadelphia Fire Films BBS. This BBS is operated by sysop Jim Bonner, owner of Philadelphia Fire Films. Many of you have monitored their service on 462.000R chasing major fires throughout the Greater Philadelphia and South Jersey areas. While they no longer are providing video to the TV stations, they still are shooting still photos for newspapers and wire services.

Many of the photos they shoot at these fire scenes and accidents are available for download on their BBS. There also is a section for scanning information on the BBS and the editor of this guide, Chuck Gysi, N2DUP, serves as a co-sysop on the BBS in this area.

The Philadelphia Fire Films BBS modem line is (215) 289-6940.

PHILLY PHREQUENCY PHONE (TM)

For those who aren't wired (on a computer) yet, you may try a simpler service provided by the editor of this Scanner Master guide. You can call Philly Phrequency Phone (TM) 24 hours a day to receive updates to this scanner guide.

The recording runs two minutes maximum and is updated approximately the first and 15th of each month. Callers are asked to leave their frequency updates, too, after the tone at the end of the message. These updates left by callers are placed on the outgoing message when it is next updated. Your participation in this special phone service is invited on a bi-monthly basis. Get the hottest frequencies while they still are hot!

Call Philly Phrequency Phone (TM) 24 hours a day at **(215) 552-8940.**

AMERICAN SCANNERGRAM

Serving Ohio, the surrounding area, and NOW the Northeast with the most up-to-date radio monitoring information that is available

*Official publication of the **ALL OHIO SCANNER CLUB**, 50 Villa Road, Springfield OH 45503-1036*

The ALL OHIO SCANNER CLUB is a not-for-profit organization that is dedicated to sharing information and improving the hobby of monitoring radio communications. The AOSC newsletter is staffed by a group of dedicated volunteers who work together to publish a top-notch information exchange and reference source for our members.

The AOSC was founded in 1979 by a scanner enthusiast who wanted to aid in bringing together people interested in the same hobby and to share information such as frequencies, codes and technical knowledge that is helpful to the hobbyist. Since then, the AOSC has grown to include nearly 1,000 members in more than 40 states and Canada, and the newsletter has grown from a mimeographed single sheet to newsletters averaging 40 pages or more that are professionally printed and bound.

The ALL OHIO SCANNER CLUB publishes an information exchange newsletter, called the "AMERICAN SCANNERGRAM," every two months for club members. The newsletter includes regional public safety columns covering all of Ohio, plus Illinois, Indiana, Kentucky, Michigan, Pennsylvania, West Virginia, Ontario, and other areas of North America as well. In the spring of 1995, we will start including the Northeast states from Maine to Virginia, including New Jersey and Delaware (Pennsylvania already is covered). We have articles that help the beginners in the scanning hobby, including topics about antennas and other improved reception techniques, and other subjects that are technical in nature. Other columns include subjects of special interest such as state government; sports, entertainment and auto racing; special events; tourist attractions; aviation, railroads and other modes of transportation; shortwave utilities; and a no-holds-barred column covering federal government and the U.S. military. Many of these columns of "special interest topics" provide information that is of use nationwide.

Also included are occasional columns covering new licenses from the files of the FCC; shortwave broadcast; new products and book reviews; and other special features. All of these columns utilize information sent in by members such as yourself. We are an all volunteer organization - no one receives payment for material written for our publication.

The cost of membership in the ALL OHIO SCANNER CLUB is $18 per year, payable by check or money order. Renewals are $17. Membership dues are non-refundable; a newsletter sample copy is available for $3. New members will receive a booklet containing general information about the club; frequencies, codes, and other statewide information for most states in our coverage area. Your membership will begin with the next regular mailing of the club newsletter, and will expire after you have received six issues. We print the American Scannergram every other month. Issues normally are mailed by third-class bulk rate the last week of February, April, June, August, October and December.

The AOSC holds an annual family-style picnic and business meeting (if necessary) at a central Ohio location. The AOSC hosts a booth for all Association of North American Radio Clubs at the Dayton Hamvention in Dayton, Ohio, each year (normally the last weekend of April), and also participates in the Winter SWL Festival in Kulpsville PA the second weekend of March every year. At the Dayton Hamvention, the AOSC co-sponsors a forum for shortwave and scanner listeners. A social gathering and meeting for AOSC members also is scheduled each year during each of these events. Similar events also will be scheduled for our Northeast members.

The AOSC can be reached on the information superhighway at any Internet connection by sending a message to Dave Marshall at davem0911@aol.com. Join today by sending your check or money order (and specify what county you live in) to the address above, and you will become part of the growing group of scanner buffs that are "in the know"! Please allow as much as 6 to 8 weeks before you receive your first mailing from AOSC.

NEW JERSEY SCANNER LAW

Following is the text of New Jersey's scanner law that went into effect in 1992:

2C:33-21   Any person who intercepts any message or transmission made on or over any police, fire or emergency medical communications system, or any person who is the recipient of information so intercepted, and who uses the information obtained thereby to facilitate the commission of or the attempt to commit a crime or a violation of any law of this State, or uses the same in a manner which interferes with the discharge of police operations, shall be guilty of a crime of the fourth degree.

2C:33-22   Any person who, while in the course of committing or attempting to commit a crime, including the immediate flight therefrom, possesses or controls a radio capable of receiving any message or transmission made on or over any police, fire or emergency medical communications system, shall be guilty of a crime of the fourth degree.

2C:33-23   For purposes of this section, the term "police, fire or emergency medical communications system" shall not include radar devices used to monitor vehicular speed.

PHILADELPHIA SCANNER LAW

Following is the text of Philadelphia's scanner law. While the original law dates back to 1967, it was amended in 1983 as the result of a court case.

10-817.   Police and Fire Radio Broadcasts.

(1) Prohibited Conduct:

(a) No person shall own, possess, sell or transfer any radio equipment or conversion equipment of any nature or type which is capable of transmitting on or otherwise interfering with police or fire radio broadcast frequencies.

(b) No person shall alter any radio equipment in any manner so that the receiver or converter makes it possible to transmit on or interfere with police or fire radio broadcast frequencies.

(c) No unauthorized person who owns or is in possession of any radio equipment or conversion equipment of any type which is capable of receiving signals on frequencies allocated for police or fire radio broadcasts shall transmit on said frequencies or otherwise interfere with any police and fire radio broadcast.

(d) No person shall use any radio equipment or conversion equipment for the purpose of violating the law or for the unlawful purpose of hindering or interfering with police officers or firemen in the performance of their official duties.

(e) No person shall:

(i) Possess on a public street or on public or private property not his or her residence; or

(ii) Equip in a motor vehicle or otherwise carry in a motor vehicle a radio receiver, portable or otherwise, capable of receiving signals on frequencies used by police or fire departments, without first having obtained a permit to install and/or use such radio device from the Department of Licenses and Inspections. The Department of Licenses and Inspections shall issue permits in accordance with the procedure set forth in Section 10-817(4). The enforcement of this subsection shall be vested in the Police Department of the City of Philadelphia

(2) Confiscation:

(a) Any radio equipment or conversion equipment capable of transmitting or interfering with police and fire radio broadcasts shall be presumed to be used for that purpose and any police officer is authorized to impound the equipment and hold it until the owner arranges for it to be re-equipped so that it will not be capable of transmitting on or interfering with police and fire radio broadcasts. If the owner does not make such arrangements within a period of thirty (30) days, the equipment shall be destroyed.

(3) Exemptions:

(a) Sections 10-817(1) and (2) shall not apply to any law enforcement agency or to the Fire Department of the City of Philadelphia.

(b) Sections 10-817(1)(e) shall not apply to any person engaged in the retail or wholesale business of selling or manufacturing radio equipment capable of receiving police or fire broadcasts, as long as the possession and/or carrying of such equipment is for business purposes.

(4) Permits:

(a) The Department of Licenses and Inspections, in cooperation with the Police Department, shall issue permits for use of radio scanners in the manner specified in Section 10-817(1)(e). The applicant for a permit shall furnish to the Department of Licenses and Inspections, on a form to be prescribed by the Department, the following information:

(i) The name, address, date of birth, description and signature of the applicant;

(ii) The reason for desiring a permit; and,

(iii) Any other information considered necessary by the Department of Licenses and Inspections to adequately evaluate the application. The Department of Licenses and Inspections shall issue the permit to such applicant if it appears that the applicant has a proper reason to carry, use or install a radio receiver in the manner described in Section 10-817(1)(e), and that the applicant is a suitable person to be granted a permit.

(b) The Department of Licenses and Inspections is authorized to issue any regulations necessary to implement this permit procedure.

(5) Penalty:

(1) The penalty for violation of this Section shall be a fine of not less than one hundred (100) dollars and not more than three hundred (300) dollars, and/or imprisonment of not less than thirty (30) nor more than ninety (90) days.

ABOUT THE COVER

Hahnemann University Hospital's "MedEvac 2" helicopter is shown flying over South Broad Street near City Hall in Center City Philadelphia. Hahnemann's medical helicopter transport service operates in conjunction with Lehigh Valley Hospital Center's "MedEvac 1" helicopter in Salisbury Township, Pa. The joint MedEvac service shares a communications center at Lehigh Valley and uses 155.220 MHz for in-flight patient information and communications.

Your Notes